The Swamp of East Naples

THE SWAMP OF EAST NAPLES.
ENVIRONMENTAL HISTORY OF AN UNRULY SUBURB

Valerio Caruso

Translated by Sara Ferraioli

Copyright © Valerio Caruso
First published 2021 by
The White Horse Press, The Old Vicarage, Main Street, Winwick,
Cambridgeshire, UK

Set in 11 point Adobe Caslon Pro and Lucida Sans

All rights reserved. Except for the quotation of short passages for the purpose of criticism or review, no part of this book may be reprinted or reproduced or utilised in any form or by any electronic, mechanical or other means, including photocopying or recording, or in any information storage or retrieval system.

British Library Cataloguing in Publication Data
A catalogue record for this book is available from the British Library

ISBN 978-1-912186-21-1

Cover image: processed and edited by Stefania Bonura from a photo by the author

To Carletto, and to my grandfather

TABLE OF CONTENTS

List of illustrations	1
Introduction	5
Chapter 1. The Country and the City	10
1.1 Living and working in the swamp	10
1.2 Hygienist thought and urbanisation	17
1.3 An industrial suburb	22
1.4 The miracle of work and the industrial curse	29
Chapter 2. The Roots of Deindustrialisation	39
2.1 Defining 'deindustrialisation': a social, political and economic process	39
2.2 Environmental foundations of the economic decline	44
2.3 Sustainability and urban planning in the Seventies	52
2.4 Unsustainable activities and pollution	65
Chapter 3. Assessing the Risks	81
3.1 Between human disasters and responses	81
3.2 Reversing environmental change: ambitions and delusions	102
3.3 Hopes and obstacles for an urban ecosystem	110
Conclusions	118
Appendices	123
Bibliography	199
Archival Sources	202
Sitography	207
Index	267

LIST OF ILLUSTRATIONS

Figure 1.1 *Bird's eye view of the city of Naples. Alessandro Baratta. 1629. 'Pianta della città di Napoli'.* Source: Wikimedia Commons, https://commons.wikimedia.org/wiki/File:Alessandro_Baratta,_pianta_di_Napoli_1629.jpg

Figure 1.2 *Detail of East Naples (and the 'pons paludis'). Giovanni Carafa, Duca di Noja. 1775. 'Veduta scenografica a ponente della città di Napoli in Campagna Felice'.* Source: Wikimedia Commons, https://commons.wikimedia.org/wiki/File:Duca_di_Noja_-_Veduta_di_Napoli_est_(dettaglio).jpg

Figure 1.3 *A drawing of the Cirio glass factory and the coastal area in the Thirties.* Source: https://napoli.repubblica.it/cronaca/2016/12/15/news/il_miracolo_cirio_a_san_giovanni_a_teduccio-154157303/

Figure 1.4 *Cirio tin can found in Shellal (Egypt) in 2015.* Source: © OeAW-OeAI (www.oeai.at).

Figure 2.1 *An aerial view of the Pazzigno district in 1980. This picture exemplifies East Naples' urban disorder: amongst the overcrowded houses, there are several factories, a railway line and an elevated motorway (crossing the district on the background of the photo). At the top, there is a comment by local communists: 'aerial view of Pazzigno. A proper ghetto, indelible fault of the older ruling classes.'* Source: from the private collection of Vincenzo Morreale: Partito Comunista Italiano, Sezioni di San Giovanni a Teduccio. 1980. Dossier 1980. S. Giovanni a Teduccio: un quartiere che cambia. Napoli.

Figure 2.2 *1972 GDP, borders of the new industrial area (pink).* Source: Archivi di UrbaNa - Urbanistica Napoli, via www.comune.napoli.it

Figure 2.3 *Naples Business Centre. 2019.* Source: Wikimedia Commons by Antuang, https://commons.wikimedia.org/wiki/File:Centro_direzionale_di_Napoli.jpg, https://creativecommons.org/licenses/by-sa/4.0/deed.en

Figure 2.4 *Early Eighties: a public fountain in the Ponticelli district.* Source: 'Dossier Periferie' in the Archivio 'Casa della Città' in Archivi di UrbaNa – Urbanistica Napoli, via http://www.comune.napoli.it

Figure 2.5 *The daily routine of metalworkers in a small manufactory in San Giovanni a Teduccio, 1981–1982.* Source: 'Botteghe e artigiani' in the Archivio 'Casa della Città' in Archivi di UrbaNa – Urbanistica Napoli, via http://www.comune.napoli.it

Figure 2.6 *A small blacksmithing manufactory in San Giovanni a Teduccio, 1981–1982. Source: 'Botteghe e artigiani' in the Archivio 'Casa della Città' in Archivi di UrbaNa – Urbanistica Napoli, via http://www.comune.napoli.it*

Figure 3.1 *A picture taken in San Giovanni a Teduccio by the local communists. March 1980. Comment above: 'Vecchia Villa neighborhood. Some families have been relocated in roulottes after a building collapse. Those are the consequences of urban planning "choices" supported by the Democrazia Cristiana party, which led to the extreme degradation of buildings in the peripheral areas.' Source: from the private collection of Vincenzo Morreale: Partito Comunista Italiano, Sezioni di San Giovanni a Teduccio. 1980. Dossier 1980. S. Giovanni a Teduccio: un quartiere che cambia. Napoli.*

Figure 3.2 *Coverage of the Pollena riverbed, 1980. Comment by the local communists above: 'Pollena riverbed. After many struggles, thanks to our brave actions, we managed to force the Cassa per il Mezzogiorno to intervene, with the coverage of the Pollena riverbed. It is a significant victory towards a better quality of life in the eastern districts of Naples.' Source: from the private collection of Vincenzo Morreale: Partito Comunista Italiano, Sezioni di San Giovanni a Teduccio, 1980. Dossier 1980. S. Giovanni a Teduccio: un quartiere che cambia. Napoli.*

Figure 3.3 *Piazza Pacichelli, central hub in San Giovanni a Teduccio, after its renovation. Source: from the private collection of Vincenzo Morreale: Partito Comunista Italiano, Sezioni di San Giovanni a Teduccio. 1980. Dossier 1980. S. Giovanni a Teduccio: un quartiere che cambia. Napoli.*

Figure 3.4 *Degraded areas in the city of Naples in 1978. Most of them are clustered in the eastern districts of Poggioreale, Barra and San Giovanni. Source: Archivi di UrbaNa - Urbanistica Napoli, via www.comune.napoli.it*

Figure 3.5 *Pazzigno district in the early Eighties, immediately prior to the Suburban Plan redevelopment. Source: 'Dossier Periferie' in the Archivio 'Casa della Città' in Archivi di UrbaNa – Urbanistica Napoli, via http://www.comune.napoli.it*

Figure 3.6 *Temporary structures in the Nuova Villa district, early Eighties: a caravan and some shacks made with metal sheets can be seen in the picture. Source: 'Dossier Periferie' in the Archivio 'Casa della Città' in Archivi di UrbaNa – Urbanistica Napoli, via http://www.comune.napoli.it*

Figure 3.7 *PSER areas of intervention in east Naples: new buildings will occupy yellow areas; existing structures in the blue areas will be demolished, as these*

List of illustrations

areas will host new buildings and equipment; red areas concern renovation programs. Source: Archivi di UrbaNa – Urbanistica Napoli, via www.comune.napoli.it

Figure 3.8 *The double row of residences that forms the Taverna del Ferro neighbourhood. Schools and a public park have been located in its immediate proximity. The huge murals, portraying Maradona and a local boy, were painted by street artist Jorit Agoch between 2017 and 2018. Source: Comitato di lotta Ex Taverna Del Ferro (https://www.facebook.com/comitatoextavernadelferro).*

Figure 3.9 *Explosion of the Agip oil tanks. 21 December 1985. Source: private collection of Vincenzo Morreale; photographer unknown.*

Figure 3.10 *General Development Plan, Municipality of Naples 2004. An overview of the projects for the eastern area. The project for the new urban park (Parco del Sebeto) is shown in dark green. Source: Archivi di UrbaNa - Urbanistica Napoli, via www.commune.napoli.it*

Figure 3.11 *An overview of East Naples in 2017, showing a mixed urban fabric (factories, greenhouses, residences and cargo areas). Source: photograph by the author.*

Figure 3.12 *Former Corradini war factory. September 2018. Source: photograph by the author.*

INTRODUCTION

Starting at Naples Central Station and riding by train to the eastern area of the city, tourists or (more-or-less) casual observers can certainly drink in peculiar landscapes with their eyes, but these are rarely such as delight the aesthetic spirit. The tracks of the State Railway (Ferrovie dello Stato) tracks and the futuristic skyline of the Centro Direzionale of Naples soon give way to endless expanses of warehouses and containers marked mostly with the same logos that assail drivers or passers-by from the windows and shop signs of the Gianturco neighbourhoods and Poggioreale Industrial Area, the gateway to eastern Naples. Continuing along the railway track, the long wall of containers crumbles before the eyes, now drawn by the imposing skeleton of the Tobacco Factory (Manifattura Tabacchi). On the opposite side, the silhouettes of the tanks and buildings of the oil area are visible. The nocturnal image offered by the disused tobacco factory might well stimulate the fantasies of a horror film writer, captivated by these large and ghostly halls only occasionally illuminated by the reflection of the nearby university residences; in reality, a deep and more justified sense of terror be aroused by reflecting on both past disasters and the destructive potential still anchored to the bottom of the immense cesspool that was and is the oil area of east Naples. Carefully hidden from view, even today, the effects persist of a terrible explosion one morning in 1985 that, for a moment, seemed another earthquake, five years after the horrific 1980 earthquake in Irpinia, or perhaps a new awakening of Vesuvius. On the other hand, it is clear that the supposedly rational desire for profit has thrust a limitless powder keg into the urban fabric of East Naples, close to the residential blocks of San Giovanni, Ponticelli, Gianturco, Poggioreale and Barra, the main centres of the eastern area. Ignoring for a moment its destructive effects, in its utter vastness, the oil area may be viewed as a further and autonomous district of the eastern area, characterised not by the chaotic vitality of the surrounding area but by the immovable strategic needs of oil as a resource.

Proceeding along the railway line, we witness the gradual densification of public housing, both planned and spontaneous and unregulated, the latter on the degraded remains of assorted old factories. Towards the sea, only the most alert observer will see the crenelated silhouette of the extraordinary former Cirio canning plant, in the Vigliena area: an architectural masterpiece whose value has recently been recognised, not surprisingly, by the artists of the San Carlo Theatre, who have installed a scenography workshop there. Far less aesthetically-pleasing, however, are the two thermoelectric power plants opposite, whose relentless whistles signal the enduring activity of at least one or the other. Along the eastern shore of Naples, a mixed landscape dominates, made up mostly of housing, often integrated with disused factories, interspersed with manufacturing and artisan activities, small pockets of agricultural activity that have held out against the tide of urbanisation and large dilapidated industrial skeletons, too often condemned to eternal abandonment.

Upon reaching the San Giovanni-Barra stop, the immense profile of a former armament factory, the ex-Corradini factory, cannot fail to intrigue the passenger with its imposing architecture comprehensively invaded by weeds: the same destiny that befell the old mills, the tanneries, the canning factories scattered all over the San Giovanni a Teduccio district, or the heterogeneous, small enterprises, once productive, interspersed with barrack-like public housing barracks and greenhouses or horticultural areas in the Ponticelli and Barra districts. The last part of the journey is all close to the coastline, yet the sea remains invisible, occluded by residences and small, old coastal factories, some active and others converted to homes. This barrier between the neighbourhood and the sea extends to the dilapidated San Giovanni a Teduccio water purification plant, recently decommissioned, almost on the border with the municipality of Portici, the eastern limit of Naples. Immediately afterwards, you can enjoy a unique moment. Perhaps it is mere aesthetic contrast, but the sudden spectacle of the Gulf of Naples in its entirety, from Posillipo to Sorrento, manages to capture even the most hardened and addicted commuter with its nuances, not to mention the tourist, who may be enchanted by a sunrise, a zenith, a sunset or a moon reflected in the waters of the Gulf. It is only a very short stretch, a few hundred metres travelled by a train that paradoxically runs close to the seafront of San Giovanni a Teduccio, disturbing its quiet: therefore, this is nothing more than an optical illusion, as well as a snapshot of the chaotic, dysfunctional relationship between the natural and the built in east Naples. Finally, passing the chain of Vesuvian villas, once magnificent noble residences but today too often besmirched by concrete and steel, we reach the splendid National Railway Museum of Pietrarsa, the final destination of this short journey and a rare virtuous example of redevelopment.

If the spatial path into the eastern area of Naples follows the neat linear paths of the road and railway arteries, the historical trajectory of the suburban

Introduction

environment through the processes of urbanisation, industrialisation and deindustrialisation is much more bumpy and tortuous; and these processes are are anything but pre-determined or terminal. In this book, the discussion of territorial and environmental issues will focus on the structural characteristics of the ecological unsustainability of East Naples. Digging down the layers of historical sedimentation, one reaches a source as richly metaphorical as it is literal in its emergence from the volcanic soils of the eastern plain of Naples to generate a marshy ecosystem. The swamp has imposed its will on the ground from time immemorial and some glimpses of it are, very rarely, still identifiable. The marshes or *parule* of the modern age, in various ways protagonists of the first chapter of this work, represent the human attempt to rationalise and bend that chaotic ecosystem to the cycles of agriculture and to a particularly profitable agricultural model, organised into gardens and orchards. Later, the model of rationalisation of the territory that was promoted from the early contemporary age will be dominated by the industrial paradigm, accompanied and mixed with residential and infrastructural expansion, in compliance with certain, repeated urban choices and development models that have dominated the mentality of administrators, both local and national. From the mid-nineteenth century onwards, for over a century, eastern Naples has been an industrial suburb. In spite of a centuries-old heterogeneity in the use of space, the industrial dimension will persist and proliferate as long as advantageous territorial and economic conditions exist and as long as the presence of secondary production is socially hegemonic, ideologically enhanced and ecologically tolerated.

From the late 1960s, the area has been affected by a slow process of deindustrialisation, still in progress, accompanied by ongoing environmental degradation. What are the characteristics of this new phase? And, above all, are its processes interconnected? The choice to privilege the central period of local deindustrialisation derives from today's collective perception of the phenomenon, translated into critical terms: one of the specific objects of this research is to distinguish between the actual impact of deindustrialisation processes on the degraded nature of eastern Naples and the impacts of incidental events. Likewise, emphasis will be placed on entrepreneurial, institutional and urban planning choices, attempting to identify their respective levels of responsibility in defining local processes of environmental degradation. The crux is, therefore, an attempt to intertwine territorial problems with the socio-economic sphere, as two sides of the same coin: in other words, to research and connect the causes of economic decline and environmental degradation in a single systemic perspective. The research covers a chronological span that roughly coincides with the history of local industry and its decline, with some preliminary forays into the late modern period and some corresponding concluding hints towards current events. In the first part of the book, a brief description is offered of the geographical and historical characteristics of the East Naples area, running through the processes of urbanisation and industrialisation. The core of the study, in the second and third parts, is the causes of and dynamics triggered by deindustrialisation, relating environmental disputes and ecological risks affecting the eastern territory of Naples between the end of the 1960s and the end of the 1990s.

Methodologically, in addition to research specifically dedicated to the East Naples area, which will often be interrogated through the text, reference is made to the established trend of European and US urban environmental history and the increasingly rich field of deindustrialisation studies. Thus, an attempt will be made to give shape to a discourse that can be both economic and ecological, the basis of which is the interpretation of the numerous political, entrepreneurial and urban planning choices made for the area, without the arrogance of assigning blame or issuing judgment, but with the aim of understanding the historical sedimentation of the urbanisation processes affecting the suburbs east of Naples and assessing its environmental sustainability. These trajectories will also be useful moorings for some significant forays into the political world and into the imaginaries of local society, often observed and described through the eyes and words of protagonists. The oral testimonies collected and transcribed in full in the Appendices section will therefore offer multiple ideas and elements for reflection, which affect in various ways all the areas mentioned: beyond the aims of this book, the economic, social, political, daily, urbanistic and ecological framework sketched by the oral testimonies will undoubtedly support researchers and fascinate readers. The interviews will be inserted in an interpretive framework that includes primary and bibliographic sources, collected mainly in the Urban Planning Archives, in the municipal library 'Antonio Labriola' of San Giovanni a Teduccio, through the digital archives of some national newspapers, via local and national statistical services and studies and, last but not least, thanks to the invaluable support of all the people mentioned below.

I would like to thank Professors Gabriella Corona and Elisabetta Bini, for giving me the skills necessary to put into practice an eternal passion for the historical discipline and for their patience in identifying, indicating

Introduction

and correcting errors and naivety. I obviously take full responsibility for any errors that remain in the text. An unquantifiable recognition goes to Enzo Morreale, for his willingness to pass on his inexhaustible knowledge of the territory and for his stalwart ability to defend its integrity and dignity. Further special thanks to Giovanni Dispoto and Antonio Di Gennaro, for having stimulated, clarified and criticised crucial passages of this work and for having accompanied me in the discovery of the territory. A special mention goes to Professors Roberto Parisi and Roberta Garruccio, bedrock references of this research. I thank again and with great affection Antonio Fondacaro, Giovanni Moliterno and Nino Daniele, for their enthusiasm and for having placed their full trust in me, allowing me to record and analyse the most hidden experiences. Huge gratitude to the employees of the 'Antonio Labriola' Municipal Library of San Giovanni a Teduccio and of the archives of Officina UrbaNa di Fuorigrotta, for their availability, patience and extraordinary cordiality. Thoughts too to Nazareno Rescigno, Enrico De Prisco and all my closest colleagues, for their support and for sharing the path of study and research in the best way. With great affection I would like to dedicate more than a thought to all the lads and lasses of Maestri di Strada Onlus and Trerrote and thank them for the indescribable work they carry out every day in the eastern districts. Great esteem, affection and gratitude to Sara Ferraioli, for a translation process that was also critical analysis, shared experience and exchange of ideas. Finally, I would like to thank my family, my dearest friends and Lilly, for their patience and support in reading the text with me. I feel I share the authorship of this book with you and I hope that you can each find your own voice somewhere in these pages. That would give me the greatest satisfaction.

1.
THE COUNTRY AND THE CITY

1.1 Living and working in the swamp

The wetlands that extended east and north-east from the centre of the city of Naples were defined during the period of Spanish domination from 1503 to 1707 as *padule* or *parule* (marshes) (Muto 2009, p. 28). From ancient times, swamps and marshes characterised the coastal alluvial plain (Barca 2005, p. 35) that forms the eastern area of Naples, a vast flat area reaching from the city centre to the slopes of Vesuvius. These were large and alienating spaces for the observer more accustomed to the claustrophobic tunnels of a city physiologically forced between the hills and the sea. In defining the marshy nature of the area, the presence of the Bolla aqueduct compounded the peculiar pedological composition of the volcanic soil which prevented the dispersion of rainwater: the water of the Bolla flowed from the slopes of Monte Somma towards the city and through one of its branches flowed into the Sebeto stream, with which the entire hydrogeological basin of the eastern area of Naples was identified. In the modern age the Sebeto, which has now completely disappeared, flowed just outside the city walls, at the Ponte della Maddalena, called *pons paludis* (bridge of the marshes) (Simonetti 2003, p. 575).

Imagining the eastern area of Naples in early modern times as resembling the chaotic Stygian swamp of Dante would be a fallacy. Indeed, the marshes performed the critical task of supplying the voracious monster that was the capital of the Neapolitan kingdom with both winter and summer horticultural products. It should be borne in mind that, during the Spanish period, the population of the city of Naples increased from 150,000 inhabitants in the early sixteenth century to 400,000 in the mid-seventeenth century, a rare demographic explosion even for a European capital in the early modern period. The massive demand for food goods therefore made an agricultural transformation of the eastern wetlands necessary and profitable:[1] in fact, beyond spontaneous regulation through wells to capture the groundwater

---

[1] The vast plain of the Phlegraean Fields (Campi Flegrei), west of Naples already supplied the city with horticultural crops traditionally also present in the hilly area and plains around the city.

The Country and the City

at depth, the first reclamation works date back to the end of the fifteenth century and great impetus was given by the viceroy Pedro de Toledo in the middle of the sixteenth century (Muto 2009). The continuous drainage and reclamation needs stimulated the first form of local proto-industry, the water mills: scattered in the area since the ducal period (sixth to twelfth centuries), between the fifteenth and eighteenth centuries the mills located along the course of the Sebeto began to increase in number, reaching fourteen at the end of the seventeenth century and eighteen in the last quarter of the eighteenth century.[2] These numbers can be interpreted in conjunction with a radical change in the consumption and food practices of Neapolitans, from 'leaf-eater to macaroni-eater', according to Emilio Sereni's famous definition (Sereni 1958). The mills in the eastern area were mostly involved in grinding grain and draining stagnant water to gain arable land; handicraft production, such as dyes, ceramics and leathers, also played a marginal role. The balanced character of the agricultural landscape of the marshes, dominated by water but also composed of farms, mills and horticultural crops, can be discerned in the Baratta plan (1629), while, describing Naples at the beginning of the seventeenth century, Giulio Cesare Capaccio refers to the amount of profit generated by the sale of agricultural and horticultural products from the marshes to the city market, approximately 500,000 ducats per year (Muto 2009). The economic system of the eastern area was therefore totally dependent on the needs of the city centre, which in turn supplied the eastern rural areas with cheap manure (Tino 1993, pp. 80–83), in accordance with the more classic city-countryside metabolic cycle.

With the advent of the Bourbon dynasty and the accession to the throne of Charles of Bourbon (1734), the eastern area of Naples was able to further tighten its economic link with the centre and open up to wider trade, through three infrastructural interventions: first, a reconstruction of the coastal road (called 'Strada Reale') (Lucarella 1992, p. 123), which connected the eastern rural areas to the city markets; then, modernisation of the port of Naples, a traditional landing and embarkation point for local goods and artefacts; finally, the demolition of some sections of the southern walls, a sign of openness to the free circulation of products across the border between city and countryside. Furthermore, in 1738 the construction of a new royal residence began: the Royal Palace of Portici, located at the eastern end of the coastal

---

2   Carlo Celano in his *Notizie del bello* (lit. 'News of Beauty') (1692) and the Duke of Noja in his map of the city (1775) testify to this respectively.

road. Once completed, in 1742, the presence of the new palace influenced the strengthening of coastal infrastructure, but above all it attracted a large

Figure 1.1

Bird's eye view of the city of Naples. Alessandro Baratta. 1629. 'Pianta della città di Napoli'. Source: Wikimedia Commons, https://commons.wikimedia.org/wiki/File:Alessandro_Baratta,_pianta_di_Napoli_1629.jpg

The Country and the City

number of noble families to the area. The result was the flourishing, along the coast and in surrounding areas, of numerous Vesuvian villas, combining the functions of noble summer residence and small to medium-sized farm and, as such, shaping the local landscape. The increase in the number of noble villas guaranteed the small and ancient farmhouses and the local rural towns (Villa, Pazzigno, Sannicandro, Ponticelli, Barra, San Giovanni a Teduccio, Pietrabianca) numerous privileges and tax exemptions (Simonetti 2003, p. 576). The images reproduced below allow us to observe the evolution of the city between the seventeenth and eighteenth centuries: on the right side, we can identify the characteristics of the eastern area of Naples, halfway between peri-urban and rural functions. One immediately notices the persistence of the marshes in the interior, interspersed with cultivated fields, roads, small villages and Vesuvian villas. Some factories can also be seen in the eighteenth-century images, especially near the *pons paludis*.

Figure 1.2

Detail of East Naples (and the 'pons paludis'). Giovanni Carafa, Duca di Noja. 1775. 'Veduta scenografica a ponente della città di Napoli in Campagna Felice'. Source: Wikimedia Commons, https://commons.wikimedia.org/wiki/File:Duca_di_Noja_-_Veduta_di_Napoli_est_(dettaglio).jpg[3]

---

3   The topographic survey carried out by the Duke of Noja in 1775 is freely available in full on the website of the National Library of Naples, dl.bnnonline.it

Chapter 1

The first major manufacturing activities arose close to this border and along the coastal axis: the presence of *faenzere* (ceramic factories) dates back to the sixteenth and seventeenth centuries, along with ironworks in the Poggioreale district and silk spinning mills in the villages (*casali*, lit. 'farmhouse') of San Giovanni a Teduccio and Barra (Parisi 1998, pp. 31–42); but in 1791 the first real giant was born, the Granili. Also known as the 'Grain Warehouse' or 'Public Granaries', this immense structure was able to contain more than three hundred *tomoli* of wheat.[4] It added manufacturing to its granary function, with the presence of an arsenal and a rope factory. Necessitated by the consequences of the famine of 1764 and the need to revolutionise the system of feeding the city following demographic increase, the warehouse of the Granili both represented and contributed to generating the morphological, urban and socio-economic transformations of the eastern area in the late eighteenth century. The construction of the immense warehouse made the increased cultivation of wheat profitable, thereby stimulating reclamation works in the marshes and influencing the increase in the number of mills. Since 1778, thirteen years before the construction of the Granili, a plan had been drawn up for the hydraulic arrangement of the marshes surrounding the warehouse (Parisi 1998, p. 47). In addition, the intense traffic between the rural areas and the city centre now found an immediate outlet in granary's capacious halls. In essence, the entire production and distribution network of the local primary sector revolved around the Granili, in the eighteenth century and in the first decades of the nineteenth century (Simonetti 2003, p. 581),[5] while the agricultural landscape was partially transformed. During the nineteenth century, however, the state of the eastern area of Naples was destined to change with progressively more intense rhythms. Between 1825 and 1831, the 'financial wall' was erected, a new enclosure of the city limits of Naples that involved both western and eastern areas: here the city began to expand, on paper, following the course of a small river, the Rubeolo, a tributary of the Sebeto that crossed the western part of the ancient swamps

---

4 The *tomolo* was an ancient unit of measurement used both for distance and quantity, very widespread in some Italian regions during the modern and contemporary eras. A *tomolo* corresponded to about 43 kg.

5 In 1799, during the turbulent Neapolitan republican period, the Granili warehouse was used as a hospital by reactionary forces, who conquered it from the local Jacobins on 13 June. The warehouse was transformed into a barracks starting from the 1920s and then into a factory and railway workshop. It was demolished in 1953 as a result of extensive damage caused by Allied air raids (Parisi 1998, pp. 42–46).

The Country and the City

(Buccaro 1992, p. 325). A much more intense thrust of the city towards the east was, however, linked to the infrastructure works enacted during the reign of Ferdinand II (1830–1859). The Bourbon administration, headed by the Corps of Bridges and Roads, identified in the vast open spaces of the eastern area the perfect place for a new road and railway network facilitating access to the city. If the economic development of the centres to the east of Naples and in the Vesuvian area made it profitable to encourage trade flows, at the same time the physiological shortage of space in the centre made these transformations necessary: the ancient oriental country houses quickly became an entry point to the city centre and the infrastructural function was joined abruptly with those of agriculture and manufacturing. Thus, in 1839, there were two major road construction projects and the Naples-Castellamare railway line, the first railway line in Italy (Parisi 1998, p. 52), was created. The railway was intended mainly to connect the two royal residences but, progressively, it would help to facilitate trade flows towards the centre, as well as stimulating the birth of local industry along this coastal axis.

The strengthening of roads and railways was accompanied by intense reclamation work to integrate the new infrastructure into the local settlement and production structure. These are the essential precepts of the 'Considerations on the means to restore the proper value to the gifts that nature has largely granted to the Kingdom of the two Sicilies' (1832–33) by Carlo Afan De Rivera, general manager of the Bridges and Roads administration from 1824.[6] These precepts were only partially welcomed by the new engineer of Bridges and Roads in charge the marshes of the outskirts of Naples, Antonio Maiuri. Placed in 1855 at the head of a new body, the General Administration of Reclamation, in the following seven years Maiuri organised the reclamation works on the basis of the existing road grid to facilitate a further expansion of infrastructure, close to which to install new buildings (Vitale 1992, p. 328). In other words, the newly constructed large road axes acted as guidelines for a grid of new roads perpendicular to or parallel with the main roads. Around the new roads, raising, drying out and waterproofing of the land began, in order to make it fit for building. On the contrary, Afan De Rivera's intention was to seek to impose a bal-

---

6   His accurate knowledge of the territories of Southern Italy was reproduced in the aforementioned *Considerazioni* in which the Kingdom was subdivided and analysed through twelve river basins. In this way, Afan De Rivera developed an organic vision of the systems that connected mountainous and flat areas: this made intervention possible in the upstream waters to allow the reclamation of marshy areas downstream. (Afan De Rivera 1832–33, pp. 94–103).

anced model of 'orderly agriculture', a mixed spatial planning, consisting of cultivated plains and irrigation channels intertwined with settlements and infrastructure (Parisi 1998, pp. 49–50). The Bourbon administration chose, instead, the path of pure urbanisation: the approach taken by Antonio Maiuri would characterise the entire work of reclamation of the eastern marshes carried out over the next fifty years. In 1903 the area of the eastern marshes of Naples was finally removed from the list of malarial zones (Barca 2005, p. 34).[7] The price was obviously paid by the local agricultural sector, which was badly affected: of the circa 100 mills surveyed in the 1880s only half remained at the turn of the century.

In fact, the first processes of urbanisation and rehabilitation were accompanied by the powerful thrust of industrialisation, undoubtedly favoured by the new infrastructure system. Near the *pons paludis* the first metalworking factories were built, but the real giant of local production was the Real Opificio della Pietrarsa, a large steel and mechanical centre located on the eastern borders of the marshes. Built in 1842, the Opificio della Pietrarsa produced steel and cast iron and assembled locomotives and steam engines, as well as rolling stock and armaments (Simonetti 2003, p. 578). In the mid-nineteenth century, Pietrarsa established itself as the first factory in Italy with over a thousand employees. Although affected by the economic changes following the unification of Italy, Pietrarsa continued to thrive and became a workshop for the maintenance of locomotives. Around these large and small factories began to rise the first workers' houses: when, in the turbulent autumn of 1860, the city of Naples fell into the hands of Garibaldi's troops, the Hero of Two Worlds himself stressed the need to build new homes for local factory workers (Buccaro 1992, p. 328). At the same time, representatives of previous administrations recognised the possibility of rationalising the irregular and burgeoning local industrial activity through urban planning tools. A proposal was advanced by the architect, inspector of the Corps of Bridges and Roads, Luigi Giura, for the construction of a large district for 'unhealthy arts', a true industrial area in its own right in which to concentrate the nascent factories. However, the area covered by the Giura project, close to the eastern gate of the city centre, was instead assigned to the new Central Station of the city, terminal of new railway lines that headed out across the

---

7 However, the disappearance of the marshes did not lead to the sudden end of the irrigation vocation of the eastern area: in 1955 the gardens still employed about 8,000 people and supplied the city with 350,000 quintals of vegetables a year.

The Country and the City

eastern area (Parisi 1998, pp. 51–52). As a matter of fact, the Giura project and the further upgrading of infrastructure confirmed the eastern area's function as a point of access to the city. Even more significantly, the absence of urban-planning solutions to regulate the emergence of the industrial district condemned the area to growth without a precise plan of expansion, without distinguishing the spaces of production from those of residence. This early and spontaneous urban and industrial development of the post-unification period can be traced thanks to the cartographic support offered by the Map of the City of Naples (1872–1880) by Federico Schiavoni.[8] Near the aforementioned Central Station stood a silk factory and a gasometer, while the Poggioreale district housed numerous tanneries and factories (Parisi 1998, p. 74). However, the largest concentration of production plants may be traced along the axis of the Naples-Castellammare railway line: near the warehouse of the Granili there appeared a naval engine factory and some foundries; then, towards the southeast, there lay a madder factory, silk factories, tanneries and armament factories (Simonetti 2003, p. 579). Most of these plants had in common a relatively small size and initial capitalisation mostly by foreign or northern investors.

1.2 Hygienist thought and urbanisation

In a second half of the nineteenth century that represents the golden age of hygienist culture,[9] such a concentration of 'unhealthy arts' could not go unnoticed. From the 1860s, the Provincial Health Council began to control the local factories, requiring the restructuring or disposal of those considered most harmful to the health of citizens. Many Neapolitan factories were forced to close their doors. The situation in the eastern area was aggravated by the absence of a clear urban planning strategy capable of rebalancing the productive system with the first residential development. In addition, the

---

8   Given the quantity and the large dimensions of the tables, I refer to the section 'Tavole Schiavoni' in the digital archives of UrbaNa, in particular to tables 14, 19 and 20, freely available online at: https://www.comune.napoli.it/flex/cm/pages/ServeBLOB.php/L/IT/IDPagina/15157 Last accessed 18 Jun. 2021.

9   Among the milestones in the history of hygienist culture are the London Public Health Act of 1848, which required the construction of new sewerage systems and a significant expansion of drinking water supply. In Italy, the birth of the Italian Hygiene Society in 1879 and the success of hygienic practices led to important local interventions, such as the law on the restoration of Naples in 1885, while at the national level producing the Public Health Code of 1888 (Corona 2015, pp. 43–44).

severe cholera epidemic of 1884 forced the city administration to relieve the overcrowded working-class districts of the centre[10] and, at the same time, to address the issue of reordering the eastern area. These suggestions merged in the 1885 Plan for Restoration and Expansion of Naples: the Municipal Council identified in the eastern area land suitable for a new 'industrial district'. Manufacturing was allocated an area of about three and a half million square metres and workers' residences about one and a half million square metres. The hygienist spirit of the plan emerged above all in the design of a large urban park, but the government blocked the whole initiative at birth due to the huge cost (Parisi 1998, pp. 75–76). The Municipality of Naples instead entrusted the drafting of a new project to a special commission: in this new plan of 1887, the proposal of an urban park was abandoned, but its health-giving function would be performed by a navigable channel twenty metres wide, equipped with subways and mobile bridges, intended to cross the new industrial district, before flowing near the *pons paludis*. The canal would also support the reclamation works still in progress, allowing the outflow to the sea of stagnant water present in inland areas. In addition, it was planned to build on 40,000 square metres near the existing factories, to provide a total of eleven new residential blocks reserved for workers.[11] Perhaps excessively ambitious, this project was also rejected by the Ministry of the Interior due to lack of funds (Rossi 1992, pp. 332–34). Once the new Public Health Code was adopted in 1888, and the need to relocate factories and factories to isolated places away from residential complexes was imposed by law, a new commission produced a third plan, approved by the City Council in 1897. The 1897 project showed a new approach to the application of hygienic principles, as it divided the future industrial district into distinct areas depending on the degree of pollution produced: the area surrounding the Poggioreale district was to be destined for harmful industries, while the areas recently reclaimed from the marshes were for light industry (Parisi 1998, p. 77). This plan too was rejected by the Superior Council of Public Works. Between the nineteenth and twentieth centuries, the eastern area continued to be devoid of urban regulation, while the city's housing and productive needs forced a chaotic expansion. The coastal strip was hit by new port structures, piers, wharves, a dry dock that extended southeast in the direction of the Granili, and new factories, such as a cement factory

---

10 Popular districts which together contained 200,000 inhabitants (Barbagallo 2015, p. 7).
11 Art.38, L. 12/22/1888, n.5849 in the matter of protection of hygiene and public health.

The Country and the City

in the village of Pazzigno and a glassworks in San Giovanni a Teduccio.

In the same district, about 2,000 square metres of warehouses began to fill with the so-called 'red jewel', in a factory that had hitherto provided only the logistics base (Signorini 2016, p. 54) of the future Italian produce empire created by the agro-food company Cirio. Founded in 1856 by Francesco Cirio and establishing itself on the international market thanks to revolutionary new preserving techniques, as well as a privileged relationship with the state railways that guaranteed the exclusive use of refrigerated wagons, at the end of the nineteenth century, the Cirio canning industry consisted of three plants, a smaller one in Turin and two in Castellammare di Stabia, as well as the large logistic depot of San Giovanni a Teduccio, of strategic importance for its proximity to the port area of Naples. In 1888 a series of hasty investments caused a serious crisis in the company that led to the deposition of Francesco Cirio by the shareholders: the subsequent turnover at the top and reduction of company capital revolutionised investment priorities and the plan to build a new plant was discarded in favour of the conversion of the warehouse of San Giovanni to Teduccio to a production location. The factory was thus inaugurated in 1889 (Morreale 2015, pp.12–16), while its actual activities began three years later. The main product was canned peeled tomatoes, the red jewel so much requested by the English market, but at the time the volume of production was relatively modest (Signorini 2016, p. 95).

The Corradini factory at San Giovanni Teduccio was a great force in local steel production between the late nineteenth and the first half of the twentieth century. Fifty-four warehouses and buildings on an area of about seven hectares (19,000 square metres) still bear witness to the glory of about eighty years of activity, from 1872 to 1949, and offer a valuable and impressive object of industrial archaeology (Vitale 1992, p. 291), unfortunately marred by the very poor care it has received from the municipal administration. The current size of the Corradini complex reveals a story marked by unstoppable expansion, to be broken only by the worst of fortunes. Founded in 1872 with French capital by the industrialists Deluy and Granier, the original building of the future Corradini plant included some eighteenth and nineteenth-century sheds, small pre-existing textile factories. The factory then passed to Duke Carafa of Noja, who arranged for the production of copper, brass and other metals, employing more than 200 workers. In 1882 it was taken over by the Swiss Giuseppe Corradini who enlarged its size, to the detriment of the surrounding coastal marshes, and changed its production to armaments (Lucarella 1992, pp. 530–34).

Chapter 1

On the whole, however, at the beginning of the new century the Neapolitan industrial sector was still characterised by an extensive network of small and very small companies, mostly created with foreign or northern capital (Simonetti 2003, pp. 580–81). On the basis of national need, the Royal Commission for Industrial Growth defined as a priority an expansion in manufacturing focused on large industry and the concomitant expansion of infrastructure. At the same time, a radical customs and tariff reform was needed to stimulate the integration and concentration of large factories in a single 'industrial area', the geographical layout of which, however, was yet to be identified. Finally, it is necessary to consider the constant hygienic impulses, returned to the limelight by the National Exhibition of Hygiene organised in Naples between April and October of the year 1900 and stimulated by the success achieved in 1903, in the removal of the eastern marshes of Naples from the national list of malarial zones (Parisi 2001, p. 55). This result accorded with the intention of disembowelling and rehabilitating the historic centre as well, removing part of the population and most of the unhealthy manufacturing activities concentrated in the lower districts of the city (Barca 2005, p. 36). It should be noted, however, that the hygienic idea of 'healthy cities' was not at all at odds with industrialisation. In the handbook of health planning written by the engineer Antonio Pedrini in 1905, it was stated that the 'health' of a city could be measured through the control of unsanitary or dangerous factories: in monitoring harmfulness, only olfactory or tactile parameters such as smoke, odour, fire or contaminating gases had to be considered, alongside maintaining a high level of vigilance over working conditions. The prescribed solution was to isolate the factory in the immediate suburbs, essentially accepting the urban centrality of industrial production (Parisi 2001, p. 54). In the first years of the new century, therefore, problems related to 'health', state taxation, infrastructure networks and the character and geography of production merged to create a new design season for the industrial area of Naples.

The special law n.351 (1904) for the economic resurgence of the city of Naples was the result of these impulses and represented a fundamental watershed in Neapolitan economic history: the establishment of two industrial zones, western and eastern, would long characterise the productive destiny of the city. If the western area was to be dominated by the steelworks of the Bagnoli district, the eastern area was instead declared to meet the 'public utility of the works necessary for the creation of an area to be declared open … and intended for the construction of workers' social homes and industrial

The Country and the City

plants', or a free zone (subsequently delimited by a special project approved in 1906). The entire area was to cover an area of about three and a half million square metres, of which about two million were allocated to new industrial and residential buildings and to road and railway infrastructure, in addition to the one and a half million square metres already built. In other words, a doubling of the built-up area in the entire eastern zone was expected. Subsequently, the General Town Development Plan of 1910 and the Royal Decree of 1913 went to further expand the free zone to the east, also committing San Giovanni a Teduccio. These interventions definitively defined the morphology of the vast area between the city centre and San Giovanni, now defined as a city district, structuring the industrial area into a grid of large quadrangular plots traced from the main roads. Both the existing factories and new structures were located within these plots (Parisi 1998, pp. 77–81).

While redesigning the industrial district, the municipal administration also revolutionised the local energy sector, through the management of electricity supply. A new body, the Volturno Autonomous Authority, chose the area of Vigliena, on the coast of San Giovanni a Teduccio, to install a thermoelectric power plant, inaugurated in 1911, that could supply the new industrial free zone (Parisi 2001, p. 69). Undoubtedly, the innovations introduced in the customs duty system were what provided a real magnet for investors: the new industrial plants were to be considered 'free warehousing', 'out of the customs line', exempt from payment of export duty and subject to other tax reliefs.[12] The immediate result was the installation of 28 new factories, specialising in different productive sectors, for a total of 9,000 new workers (Simonetti 2003, p. 581). There was considerable expansion of production by existing large plants, such as the aforementioned Corradini Metallurgical Society, which in this era became the leader of the entire local industrial sector. It included a number of smaller steel plants and also opened a satellite plant, a tannery. New developmental impetus determined by the economic resurgence had a strong impact on Cirio in Naples. Electrification, mechanisation and new infrastructure (well exemplified by the Vigliena thermoelectric plant) quickly doubled the production rates of the San Giovanni a Teduccio plant (Signorini 2016, pp. 103–04), on its way to becoming the beating heart of the company.

At that moment, housing was still secondary but it was certainly stimu-

---

12   Artt.6-13, L. 7/8/1904, n.35 in the matter of 'Measures for the economic resurgence of the city of Naples'.

lated by the special law of 1904 and new prospects for speculation. A first stimulus was given by the newly-created Public Housing Administration (1903), which, in the first decades of the twentieth century, began to clog the industrial districts with residential districts, often poorly built and literally intertwined with productive activities. The residential occupation of spaces close to the factories, land assigned to infrastructure for industrial production or a future expansion of the facilities, is the basis of the persistent conflict over the use of space between productive and housing functions (Simonetti 2003, p. 583) that would continue to characterise the eastern area in the following decades. However, in the urban philosophy of the age of industrialisation and urban expansion the two functions did not contradict each other, but rather constituted a unique sign of faith in economic and hygienic progress. It is not by chance that the first popular districts, such as the 'Ferrovieri' or the 'Vittorio Emanuele III', or the best-known (thanks in large part to the novels of Elena Ferrante) 'Luzzatti', cemented over the old drainage channels, which gradually turned into sewer drains (Boat 2005, p. 34).

Ultimately, in the early twentieth century the eastern Neapolitan industrial area witnessed an impetuous expansion, triggered by the planning and tax relief offered by the law on economic revival of 1904. The peculiarity of this intervention is, according to Salvatore Adorno (Adorno 2017, pp. 112–13), manifested in its creation of a link between development and territorial dimensions, industrial and local policies. State intervention focused on customs and tax concessions, but at the same time promoted the economic growth of the individual territory. In the following decades, the forms of public intervention would be modelled along these lines, right up to the threshold of deindustrialisation. At the same time, the first major thrust of urban expansion caused the area to assume a clearly chaotic character. Hygienic needs, first and foremost the reclamation of the marshes, and economic processes, namely the enhancement of production, translated into an urban fabric shared by housing and industry. Taking into account this potentially fragile or explosive urban mix, the fascist regime and the great conflicts of the century intervened with destructive force.

1.3 An industrial suburb

In recent years, much has been written in Italy on the specific relationship between factory, environment and urban land, primarily thanks to the

The Country and the City

works of Simone Neri Serneri: in *Incorporare la Natura. Storie Ambientali del Novecento* (2005) he sketches out the historical relations between factory and territory in Italy, from the second industrial revolution to the interwar period. The discourse focuses on factors affecting positioning of industries in heterogeneous contexts all across the peninsula, all sharing the same unhealthy environment. Another common factor is the relocation of industrial centres into areas that were once rural and became urbanised with low inputs of land and work, especially in the early twentieth century. A key element is the establishment of large plants at the instigation of public authorities, to trigger a dynamic of territorial economic development and secure both political consensus and social control: in these terms, the unhealthy nature of large industries was subordinated to political and socio-economic needs. The subsequent ghettoisation of industrial activities in their own districts often led to the urbanisation of areas with a dominant industrial vocation within large and medium-sized Italian cities: in the early twentieth century this translated into an integration of residential areas of social housing and industrial areas, with serious consequences for health, hygiene and environmental degradation. In Northern Italian society, the need to separate the two functions became apparent from the interwar period, but real attempts to place industrial production outside the urban limits were only instigated from the 1930s. On the contrary, the innate disorder in the use and functions of spaces would continue to be one of the structural elements of the urban and industrial trajectory of Naples East. In the first decades of the twentieth century, its characteristics changed in a radical way.

The First World War facilitated an impressive burgeoning of the Neapolitan industrial sector. Government incentives and military commissions mainly favoured large metal and steel factories such as Corradini, but all the existing local factories saw expansion in employment and production, stimulated by industrial mobilisation to the war effort (1915–1918). For example, Corradini tripled its size, further expanding along the coastline of San Giovanni (Lucarella 1992, pp. 533–34): in the interwar period, at the height of its fortunes, the complex reached its current size, comprising thirteen different buildings. For other factories, the industrial growth brought about by the First World War, far from revolutionising local production methods, mostly consisted in an increase in the number of workers employed in existing plants. In rare cases, emerging industrial activities annexed smaller factories. Thus, for example, the trajectory of the Southern Cotton Manufactories (Manifatture Cotoniere Meridionali, MCM), at the time the largest company complex

Chapter 1

in the Italian cotton industry: nationalised in 1918 with the ousting of the old Swiss proprietor, MCM began to control the entire process of the textile chain in East Naples and incorporated some existing related activities. In the Poggioreale district, two cotton mills were annexed to MCM and the resulting complex covered an area of 150,000 square metres, employing about 3,000 workers (Parisi 1998, p. 111). If the increase in employment in the 1910s was simply determined by contingent needs, as more manpower was needed for the war effort, the resulting strengthening of industrial production resulted in profound structural changes in the eastern area during the interwar period. In the early 1920s, the industrial zone of East Naples almost doubled its actual and administrative size: under the control of the newly established Autonomous Authority of the Port, constituted to deal with the increase in industry and maritime traffic, the industrial free zone reached about five million square metres, thus doubling again and incorporating the industrial activities that had previously arisen in the San Giovanni district. Only the coastal strip between Vigliena and Pietrarsa remained outside the free zone. At the same time, the municipal administration developed a new General Development Plan in order to coordinate the expansion of the free zone and connect it to the expansion of the residential fabric of the new eastern districts of the city. In fact, in 1926 the autonomous municipalities of San Giovanni a Teduccio, Barra and Ponticelli and the surrounding ancient rural houses were annexed to the city of Naples. It was a crucial moment in local history, as testified by urban planner Giovanni Dispoto:

> The famous *casali* that surrounded Naples were autonomous municipalities with their own territorial identity. So much so that it was only in 1926 that there was an administrative and urban reform that led them to be permanently integrated with the city. This event was the premise for the transformation ... of these places into the indistinct suburbs that we know today (Recording n. 5).

The eastern zone was definitely subordinated to the economic interests of the centre, primarily through institutional power. A General Town Development Plan would be approved in 1939, but the management of the industrial zone passed in 1926 to the High Commissioner for the city and the province of Naples: an institution of clear fascist stamp, created three years after the rise of Blackshirts, designed to remove local authorities and eliminate the interference of private enterprise in the field of public works. The High Commissioner could actually decide on the sale of public land for the installation of new industrial plants and the construction of houses and working-class districts. As such, it inherited hygienic conceptions and

The Country and the City

updated them to the new Fordist principles, boasting of the social policies of the regime.

In this sense, the case of Snia Viscosa is exemplary: it was founded in Turin in 1917 as a shipping company and converted in 1920 to the production of synthetic textile fibres. In 1925, the San Giovanni a Teduccio plant was born. Its size and technology were superior. The company itself undertook the construction, close to the factory, of a modern residential district equipped with a clinic, a kindergarten and other social and recreational services (Simonetti 2003, p. 583). Many other factories that arose in the same period followed the same principles and brought with them new housing and urban solutions, reshaping neighbourhoods (Parisi 1998, p. 83 and 153–65). Since political control and social discipline were a priority for the fascist government, creating social and recreational services was a useful tool to achieve these ends. The High Commissioner also had jurisdiction over the extension of the free zone: a further extension of the boundaries of the industrial zone to the east was sanctioned by Royal Decree n.359 of 1926. The free zone now reached the districts of Barra and Ponticelli and to the south it encompassed the coastal area from Vigliena to Pietrarsa, covering a total of eight million square metres. The same decree required the new plants to be placed in a regular grid of pre-established rectangular lots (Parisi 1998, p. 155), often flanked by houses. On the quantitative level, the rise of residential construction from the 1920s makes impressive reading: by 1919 there were 723 residential buildings in the districts of Barra, Ponticelli and San Giovanni in Teduccio. In the following 25 years about 750 more would be built (Municipality of Naples 2011), in other words the number more than doubled. The production system also underwent radical changes, due to the post-war crisis in the mechanical and shipbuilding sectors and the parallel rise of the energy sector. In 1925, a new thermoelectric power station was built by the Southern Electricity Society (SME).[13] In the Vigliena area, this private plant competed with the public plant built in 1911, but at the same time attracted the investment needed to allow the creation of a new Cirio canning facility, completed in 1931 (Signorini 2016, p. 130). The interwar period was undoubtedly positive for Cirio, whose canned products reached the four corners of the world.

---

13 The SME, Società Meridionale di Elettricità was a company set up with private capital to develop an electrification plan for Campania and Southern Italy (Marotta, Iannello 2006, p. 4).

Chapter 1

Figure 1.3

A drawing of the Cirio glass factory and the coastal area in the Thirties. Source: https://napoli.repubblica.it/cronaca/2016/12/15/news/il_miracolo_cirio_a_san_giovanni_a_teduccio-154157303/

Figure 1.4

Cirio tin can found in Shellal (Egypt) in 2015. Source: © OeAW-OeAI (www.oeai.at).

The Country and the City

'The decisive turning point in terms of urban planning' (Parisi 2001, p. 69) of the 1920s was, however, the establishment of the petrochemical hub, strongly desired and touted by the regime. It should first be noted that the presence of a production complex made up of oil infrastructure, refineries and industries specialising in the processing of petroleum products immediately extirpated any chance of planning; instead new priorities were imposed, resulting from the strategic importance of the oil resource. As a result, a substantial part of East Naples began to be handed over to absolute control by external interests, creating an area of extra-territorial management, under no formal jurisdiction and exempt from any official planning obligation, invisible for obvious military reasons in the cartographic restitution of the territory, in short, 'a void far from reassuring' (Barca 2005, p. 36). The area became a cesspool of disorder with which any rationalisation effort, past and future, would have to reckon. In 1926 the great Agip refinery was founded, 50,000 square metres in area, and ten years later that of Socony Mobil,[14] covering 130,000 square metres, both close to the districts of Barra, San Giovanni and Gianturco. Other small companies specialising in petrochemical derivatives were built near the refinery or connected to the Vigliena pier, where the tankers landed (Parisi 1998, pp. 154–56). Finally, pre-existing oil derivatives processing plants, such as the aforementioned Snia Viscosa, completed the production chain and the framework of the first petrochemical hub of Naples East (Parisi 2001, p. 70).

Overall, the years of the regime (the 1920s and 1930s) represent a fundamental watershed in local urban history. The former rural centres of the eastern area were definitively incorporated into the city limits and submitted to a jurisdiction, that of the High Commissioner, which indisputably decided their productive destiny. However, the rise of the oil industry and the strengthening of heavy industry did not negate the residential function, which indeed proliferated because of the demand for workers' housing and the new social policies of the regime, in addition to the constant demographic pressure of the centre. It must be considered, however, how these developments took place outside of a systemic urban plan, which would be conceived only at the end of the 1930s.

In fact, 1939 saw the approval of a new town plan drawn up at the instigation

---

14 Audiovisual evidence collected by the Istituto Luce of the inauguration of the Mobil refinery in Naples in 1937 is available online, https://www.youtube.com/watch?v=3oKbMoWy40o Last accessed 6 Apr. 2020.

Chapter 1

of the engineer Giuseppe Cenzato.[15] The project, conceived by the architect and urban planner Luigi Piccinato, was based on the idea of transforming the industrial area into a liminal area with the eastern suburbs, a sort of 'gateway' to the city itself. In practice, this meant significantly reducing the area of the free zone to the advantage of a new, immense business district and new houses. The huge area between the Poggioreale district and the city of Portici would thus have been reserved for the new commercial district, also equipped with an urban park; the western part of Naples would have instead borne the brunt of residential construction (Parisi 1998, pp. 85–86). The overall result would have been a halving of the industrial area and probably the premature relocation of many of the newly established plants. However, the devastation caused by the war and the new reconstruction imperative brought new priorities to the fore, as will be seen shortly, and would severely limit the application of urban planning regulations.

On the eve of the Second World War, the eastern part of Naples was almost completely saturated by 230 industrial plants, with a total of 21,000 employees. Surrounded by chimneys, pylons, roads and railway tracks, the concrete of the residential complexes became anonymous and increasingly crowded: between the beginning of the twentieth century and the end of the 1930s, the population of the eastern area more than doubled, as a result of a long process of transfer from the overflowing popular districts of the historic centre. The major demographic leap took place in the 1920s and 1930s, a crucial phase in local history, as we have seen. By 1921, the population of the eastern area amounted to 46,586 inhabitants, more than doubling by 1936 when residents numbered 102,131 (Simonetti 2003, p. 585). In defining the mentality of the new residents, however, it should be stressed that the close proximity between new workers' homes and modern workplaces in the free zone was not seen as a disadvantage or a sacrifice, but was perceived as a form of economic and social wellbeing (Parisi 2001, p. 73). This was a consequence of the flight from the overcrowded and miserable old town but also a sign of unconditional adherence to the industrial climate of the time and, simultaneously, a symptom of indifference or ignorance about the damage caused, to the environment and health, by smoke, soot, dust, metals, hydrocarbons and anything else polluting the soil, air and water.

The calamities of the 1940s are more evident. Naples was the Italian

---

15 SME leader, Cavaliere del Lavoro, president of the Industrial Union and the Polytechnic Foundation (Cardillo 2006, p. 62).

The Country and the City

city that suffered the largest number of bombings by the Allied side. The obvious strategic importance of the eastern industrial zone made it the first target of the Allied ordinance from 1941, but 1943 was undoubtedly the worst year: in April the coastal strip was knocked out by American B-17s, with significant damage to thermal power plants, coastal fuel depots, and to Corradini and Cirio di Vigliena (Morreale 2015, p. 18). The immense war factory Corradini did not manage to recover from the devastation caused by the bombing: in 1949 the factory would be definitively closed and its torn ruins still haunt the San Giovanni district. It was then the turn of the inland area, where the Cirio cannery was severely damaged, while the Snia Viscosa and the Mobil refinery were completely razed to the ground. Needless to say, the interwoven residential fabric around the factories was not spared (Simonetti 2003, p. 584). Having removed the spectre of the bombings with the armistice of 8 September 1943, East Naples had to deal with the retreating Nazis, between 18 and 30 September, who were particularly fierce towards the last factories still standing, in addition to looting the Cirio plant in Vigliena (Morreale 2015, n. 27). The state of the entire city in 1944 was therefore disastrous and further aggravated by conditions in its industrial area: the factories needed for reconstruction were essentially paralysed, as was local infrastructure. Therefore, an immediate commitment to strategic sectors and a reasoned urban planning was desperately needed to prepare the ground for the civil and productive recovery of the entire city. This had to occur primarily through a reconversion of industrial activities.

1.4 The miracle of work and the industrial curse

In the eastern area of Naples, the demobilisation of the war industry was felt through the closure of numerous factories, including the Corradini metalworking factory, which was decommissioned in 1949, as already mentioned. The causes of the lost pre-eminence of the Neapolitan and southern engineering sector were anticipated by a Conference on the problems of the South, organised in December 1944: fascist industrial protectionism and war needs had artificially inflated the weight of the southern metalworking sector, which now proved to be 'anti-economic'. 'Healthy industries should therefore be stimulated and, in particular, those linked to the magnificent products that our land has always given and will still be able to give' (D'Antonio 1990, pp. 1193–94). This was taken up by the Regional Commission for

Chapter 1

Industrial Reconstruction in 1945: the canning sector and the processing of agricultural products became priorities to meet the population's needs, as did other essential sectors, such as the building and basic materials industries, needed for the reconstruction.

In practice, at the local level, the measures adopted forty years earlier during the establishment of the industrial area were now repeated, by granting resources and tax concessions to companies active in sectors considered fundamental to the post-war recovery (Parisi 2017, pp. 24–26). In fact, the decline of Corradini was counterposed by the rapid reconstruction of and new centrality assumed by the agro-food company Cirio. The spearhead of East Naples' business expansion, at the end of the 1940s, Cirio extended in the dairy sector and took over the central dairy of Naples (Signorini 2016, pp. 136–38). The daily milk supply reached not only Neapolitan citizens, but also the American soldiers of the new NATO base, from 1952 onwards. As a company still deeply connected to foreign markets, Cirio was in fact ahead of its time, anticipating the process of internationalisation and penetration by foreign capital that, as will soon be seen, would revolutionise Italian industry in the 1960s. It was not by chance that tax concessions and large loans from American and Canadian banks allowed Cirio to rebuild its fortunes following the damage caused by the war, at a time when Naples became Italy's second city (to Milan) in terms of corporate turnover.

From the point of view of urban planning, the immediate post-war period briefly saw the futuristic and volatile General Development Plan of 1946: the plan provided for the transformation of destroyed and abandoned factories into residential areas, so it prohibited the installation of new factories. The eastern area would have been radically decongested, because new factories would have been located in satellite zones. However, the plan, often wonderfully innovative (as in the idea of peppering the coast of San Giovanni a Teduccio with skyscrapers), was first scaled-down, then procrastinated over for six years, then definitively abandoned by the new municipal council, dominated by the monarchists. At the instigation of the monarchist mayor (from 1952 to 1957 and again in 1961) Achille Lauro, a new Town Development Plan was put in place in 1955, confirming the cumbersome industrial presence to the east of the city and, indeed, anticipating further expansion. This plan, adopted by the Municipality of Naples in 1958, was never implemented (Parisi 2017, pp. 24–26). The most likely reason, in historiography, is that given by Vezio de Lucia: the urban anomalies of the immediate post-war period were the result of 'blackmail of the emergency',

The Country and the City

namely a series of exceptional reconstruction plans set above national urban law, which would therefore obstruct even municipal Town Development Plans (De Lucia 2006, p. 5).

The chronic hesitancy of town planning regulations did not help to solve explosive local contradictions, which received new lifeblood from the demographic boom: in the early 1950s the population of the eastern area grew continuously, reaching 125,000 inhabitants, divided into just over 20,000 residents in Ponticelli and between 30–35,000 residents in each of Barra district, Poggioreale and San Giovanni a Teduccio (Simonetti 2003, p. 585). Demographic increase brought with it new residential realities, while the old popular districts were expanded. Between 1946 and 1960 more than 1,300 residential buildings were built in the eastern districts:[16] if we take into account the fact that before 1946 there were only about 2,000 houses, we realise the power of the construction sector in the fifteen years in question (Municipality of Naples 2011). However, this is not exceptional for the Neapolitan context. The eastern zone was perfectly in line with Naples' processes of indiscriminate expansion that went on until the early 1970s, led by a constantly growing building industry and fuelled by the liberal policies of the mayor Achille Lauro.[17]

Secondly, the years from the second half of the 1950s to the early 1960s witnessed vast industrial growth in the eastern zone. In the years of the 'Italian economic miracle',[18] the expansion of the regional secondary sector was not able to keep pace with the national average but was nevertheless remarkable[19] and in this it was driven by the role played by its situation within the Neapolitan province, with its higher rate of industrialisation (D'Antonio 1990, pp. 1190–92). Therefore, if the province of Naples led the regional

---

16   In the above-mentioned censuses, reference is made to the districts of Barra, Ponticelli, San Giovanni a Teduccio, Poggioreale and Gianturco-Industrial Zone.

17   On this very broad theme, I can only refer to the texts of Vezio De Lucia and Gabriella Corona, such as *Se questa è una città* (2006) and *I Ragazzi del Piano* (2007). An essential film reference on building speculation in Naples in the 1950s and 1960s is *Le mani sulla città* (1963) by Francesco Rosi.

18   For Italian economic historians, the 'miracle' originates in the decision to liberalise trade, through first lowering tariffs in 1950 and especially with the accession to the Czech Republic, in 1951; and with the entry into the European Common Market, in 1958. In statistical surveys, starting from 1950, the accelerated industrialisation of Italy began, with its core in the period 1958–1964, or immediately after the formation of the European Economic Community in 1957 (Amatori, Bigazzi, Giannetti, Secreto 1999).

19   On the basis of the data contained in the 1951 and 1961 Industrial Censuses, the number of employees in the industrial sector in Campania increased by 21.8% compared to 26.9% nationally (D'Antonio 1990, pp. 1195–96).

Chapter 1

industrial boom, then East Naples led the municipal industrial boom in the 1950s. By 1961, eighty per cent of Neapolitan industrial workers were concentrated, or at least went to work, in the eastern area, where local factories had increased by ten per cent, and employees by 27 per cent compared to the previous decade (Simonetti 2003, p. 586). These data also reveal the extent of the recent concentration of new production plants: the mechanical sector, with the new Fiat and Alfa Romeo plants, recovered a first-rate role, flanked by the food sector, with Cirio in the lead. Then there emerged the tobacco industry, thanks to the newly founded Manifattura Tabacchi (1956) and its immense plant in the Gianturco district. The furniture and wood sector was also on the rise, with the creation in 1958 of the Feltrinelli Foundation in the same district. Other prominent sectors were textiles, with the Snia Viscosa rebuilt in 1948 and the recovery of MCM, and the petrochemical sector, relaunched by MobilOil, which had, since 1947, taken over and recovered the former assets of SoconyMobil (Parisi 1998, pp. 165–66 and 175). Here I briefly sketch only the major firms, which had an effect on subsequent dynamics. In absolute terms, the 1950s saw the birth of as many as 132 new plants, for a total of 9,000 new employees (Parisi 2017, p. 36).

Considering this double demographic and industrial swelling, the lack of control by effective state planning greatly affected these features of innate environmental disorder in the eastern area. This led to a process of saturation of urban spaces in the eastern zone, shared by production and residence. These structural problems became the subject of a new type of state intervention policy, feverishly at work in the three decades from reconstruction to the early 1960s. The post-war forms of intervention could boast an endogenous genealogy and exogenous references in the present: the endogenous model was offered by the technocracy of the turn of the century, which had produced the special law for Naples of 1904, of which some elements of the new ruling class were heirs; the exogenous model was instead that of territorial development, pioneered by the American Tennessee Valley Authority (1933), developed by the British Special Areas Development and Improvement Act (1934) for high-unemployment areas, and updated by the *Plan de modernisation et de Equippement* (1954–1957) of Etienne Hirsch in France, according to which planning could extend to a wider range of public investment areas, including school and hospital facilities, research and professional rehabilitation of the workforce. For Naples and Southern Italy, the experience of the Svimez (Association for the Development of

The Country and the City

Industry in the South)[20] opened this new path of interventionist models from its establishment in 1946. Therefore, as Salvatore Adorno emphasises, the 'industrialist breakthrough on a territorial basis that characterised policies from the 1950s' had its roots 'in the best national technocratic tradition', but at the same time kept pace with the present, evolving thanks to 'the most advanced Euro-Atlantic reflection on overcoming economic and territorial imbalances' (Adorno 2017, pp. 112–13).

In the Neapolitan case, the prospects of state intervention, according to Roberto Parisi, involve constant contrast between two different models of urban and industrial development, put forward by interest groups and intellectuals active in institutions and new associations. The progenitor of the first model was the IRI,[21] often supported by the union and municipal forces, actively attempting to maintain basic industry, primarily steel (the steel hub of West Naples) and oil (the oil hub of East Naples) within the municipal boundaries of the city of Naples. The second model, on the other hand, had its roots in the above-mentioned proposals of the 1946 Plan by Luigi Cosenza: decentralising large-scale industry on different territorial levels – namely inter-municipal, provincial and regional – and decongesting traditional industrial areas were ideas that arose in the early twentieth century. The first strand is evidently heir to the project of the nineteenth century; the second aims instead at industrial decentralisation (Parisi 2017, pp. 22–27). The question of the industrialisation of Naples and Campania was initially dealt with between 1947 and 1948 in the so-called *documento Svimez* in which they proposed three plausible alternatives: the first was to constitute 'Ente Zone Industriali' (an organisation made for industrial areas) to man-

---

20 The South was among the main socio-economic issues of Italy in the 1950s: since the 1930s, public entrepreneurship has been involved in the debate on the development of the south through industrial investment, but the birth of Svimez in 1946 and later of Casmez in 1950 allowed diversion of a large number of public investments to the South and the designing of new infrastructural interventions (Amatori, Bigazzi, Giannetti, Secreto 1999).

21 The culmination of the intertwining of the Italian state and enterprise, as well as the most lasting innovation of the fascist regime, was the Institute for Industrial Reconstruction, founded in 1933 following the effects of the crisis of 1929. The size of the debts contracted by banks in the post-war period made necessary, according to Franco Amatori, the state intervention that freed banks from their company holdings, avoiding the companies' nationalisation and with the state assuming direct responsibility under a 'super-Public holding' company, IRI. Within IRI there were, therefore, sectoral holding companies (limited companies with a partial private component) and, at the lower level, individual companies. In fact, the state was transformed into an industrial entrepreneur and placed at the head of Italian capitalism for the next thirty years. (Amateurs, Bigazzi, Giannetti, Secret 1999).

age new works, especially infrastructural, affecting east Naples. The area was thus reconfirmed in its industrial role for decades to come. In essence, the measures of 1904 were repeated. The second option was to stimulate a new industrial hub in the north, towards Rome, while the third was to encourage the establishment of new factories to the south, halfway between Naples and the city of Salerno. At the beginning of the 1950s, Svimez directed its interests towards this third aspect, which would have greatly reduced the presence of factories in areas of earlier industrialisation, such as East Naples, redistributing productive activities across the regional context.

However, in 1952, a counter-proposal was advanced by the Ministry of the Treasury, which wiped out all alternatives. The result was a new special law, which guaranteed the newly elected mayor Achille Lauro an extraordinary budget of 35 billion lire for the realisation of public works on the city's soil. In fact, it confirmed the validity of the project launched half a century earlier, focused on the two industrial areas to the east and west of the city (Parisi 2017, pp. 28–30). In the 1950s, however, funding, planning and execution of new works, factories and, above all, infrastructure[22] would be provided, designed and built with the support of the Cassa per il Mezzogiorno (Casmez), a new entity for the realisation of extraordinary works of public interest in southern Italy, established in 1950. For example, in the eastern area, the establishment of the Cassa per il Mezzogiorno enabled the funds provided by the Marshall Plan to be used effectively, particularly in the project for a new thermoelectric power station in Vigliena, which was carried out in 1953 and replaced the old one (Simonetti 2003, p. 585).

The second phase of Casmez's life, from the middle of the 1950s to the middle of the 1960s, was even more characterised by the pre-eminence attributed to the industrialisation of the South. Law Segni n.634 of 7/29/1957 introduced new criteria for the industrial development of Southern Italy, in the form of the definition of development hubs. The territorial management of the hubs was entrusted to Consortia for the Areas of Industrial Development (Aree di Sviluppo Industriale, ASI) and to Nuclei of Industrialisation (NI), newly instituted administrative agencies. The law aimed to install new industries in strategically prepared locations, in order to place them amidst appropriate infrastructure. Therefore, the Cassa per il Mezzogiorno would finance and create industrial districts equipped with all the infrastructure needed to successfully host industrial investments, according to the standards

---

22 Articles 4,5 and 9 L. 4/9/1953 n. 297 in the matter of 'Measures in favour of the city of Naples'.

The Country and the City

of the time. The financial foundation of the programme was the financing and facilities offered by Casmez, which could galvanise private enterprises or new urban settlements, depending on territorial needs (Adorno 2017, pp. 113–14). Overall planning was based on industrial presence. Local activities in other productive sectors (agricultural, commercial, tourism, urban) had to be functionally integrated with industrial development, in the belief that manufacturing production was the real driver of general economic growth.

In the Neapolitan case, the bureaucratic process for the establishment of the ASI Consortium began at the beginning of 1962, as did an integrated 'Town Development Plan for the new Industrial Development Area of the Province of Naples' (Parisi 2017, p. 35). The Plan aimed at the infrastructure development of the regional hinterland as a prerequisite for the progressive transfer thereto of all the industrial activities present on the entire Neapolitan coast. It was, therefore, a radical development of the Svimez projects of previous decades. The western and eastern industrial areas' overpopulation and disorder, resulting from proximity to residential areas, were finally recognised. However, as in the case of the 'Svimez' document, in conjunction with the bureaucratic process for the approval of the ASI Plan, a counter-proposal was put forward for a new special law for Naples, jokingly called the 'Forty-seventh'. The document, signed by Achille Lauro, was approved on 27 January 1962, and exceptionally guaranteed to the City of Naples the tax concessions and benefits for agricultural and industrial development provided by the Segni Law,[23] otherwise limited by the latter to municipalities below 200,000 inhabitants. In essence, the City of Naples was able, by purely political means, to obtain the tax benefits provided by Casmez for new infrastructure and new industrial activities, without having to change its spatial planning. The new special law was probably mainly aimed at healing the municipal deficit accumulated by Lauro's councils (Parisi 2017, pp. 36–37), but the ASI Plan was progressively distorted by an endless sequence of variants, each one evidently aimed at satisfying patronage (or clientelism) and corruption dynamics (Simonetti 2003, p. 586).

By the mid-1960s, the policy of extraordinary public interventions had therefore consolidated and produced new channels for the territorial redistribution of public resources (D'Antonio 1990, p. 1197). The price to pay would be development without autonomy, following the lessons of the sociologist Carlo Trigilia, or inability to activate endogenous development; while, for

---

23 Articles 17, 18 and 19 L. n.634 of 7/29/1957 on measures for the Mezzogiorno.

Chapter 1

Gabriella Corona, the 'culture of extraordinariness' established in the years in question would become the originating factor in local governments' avoidance of responsibility and, above all, the gap between decision-making centres and subordinated localities, at the mercy of legitimate or illegal interests (Corona 2015, pp. 79–80). In the specific case of East Naples, the maximum potential of this twofold process of deprivation of economic power and removal of responsibility from the local level would be revealed in the following decades, but from the second half of the 1960s some characteristics were already recognisable. The starting point lies in the increased penetration by capital of external origin, that is, foreign or State-owned: the former was mainly aimed at the creation, expansion and control of medium-sized plants (from 100–500 employees), the latter mostly at large factories (more than 500 employees). The real magnet for external investment was of course offered by the ordinary and extraordinary facilities and financing just described, but other general factors certainly contributed to the same end, such as the increased schooling and specialisation of the labour force, the improvement of infrastructure and communication routes and the increased internationalisation of trade, but also labour costs, which remained relatively low.

In the eastern zone, the process of penetration by foreign private capital was evident in the arrival at Ponticelli of the 'Industrie Riunite Elettrodomestici', then Ignis, then, under the aegis of the Dutch, Philips (Simonetti 2003, p. 586); and especially in the expansion of the working capacity of the American MobilOil, in the early 1970s: here as many as 600,000 square metres were occupied by the depots and tanks of the company, which made it the largest oil company in Naples. In addition to the large factory, small businesses arose for the production and distribution of liquid gases or the processing of petroleum derivatives (Parisi 1998, p. 156). The specific dynamics related to this company will be explored in more depth in the next chapter. This confirmed the strategic priority of the oil and petrochemical sector, also accentuated by the rising energy transition to oil and relative mechanisation of Italian society in the 1960s and 1970s (Corona 2015, pp. 63–64). But it was also confirmed by the process of local disempowerment, or the extra-territoriality of private capital just described. We can obviously also identify positive aspects of internationalisation: an example is offered by SAGRAF, a graphic, lithographic and printing company in San Giovanni a Teduccio, which in 1968 employed more than 200 workers and technicians, an absolutely remarkable number for the sector. Here, in 1968, fifteen-year-old Vincenzo Morreale arrived as an apprentice. From his words,

The Country and the City

SAGRAF emerges as an established reality in the field of local, national and international publishing: documents were printed for local administrative bodies, textbooks and school manuals were reproduced and often used by higher-level actors, such as the United Nations or the FAO, printing scientific texts in Chinese, or in Arabic, in short, 'all languages of the world'. Morreale also remembers, however, the working conditions, schedules and salary of the early years, 'not very exciting': more than twelve hours a day in close contact with harmful fumes, in exchange for a *guaglione* wage, that is, the wage of a young apprentice (Recording n. 1).

As for state-owned companies, a leading role was played in the eastern area of Naples by the new Southern Financial Society (or Financial SME, formerly 'Società Meridionale di Elettricità'), in which public and private capital coexisted. The sectors preferred by this financial company were food and large commercial distribution: Cirio in San Giovanni a Teduccio was, therefore, a delicious mouthful. The financial company managed to carve out a role as a minority shareholder from the early 1960s, but, after 1966, became progressively more aggressive, raking Cirio shares from the smaller shareholders to obtain a majority of the company in 1970 (Signorini 2016, pp. 163–64). Nevertheless, SME and Cirio were initially able to live together, as the SME limited itself to pure financial participation, leaving to private individuals the functions of control and management of the enterprises. The company situation would change during the 1960s, as will be seen in the next chapter, with the progressive integration of the SME into the IRI, making Cirio one of its many pawns on the financial chessboard at national level (Morreale 2015, p. 21).

These various types of 'external' capital therefore had two consequences: the first, essential, is the leaching of power from local economic systems: industry is increasingly dependent on external and uncontrollable decision-making centres at local level. The decision-making centres of local economic power begin to alienate themselves from the locality itself, to become extra-territorial. The other side of the coin of this specific process, namely the avoidance of responsibility by private companies with respect to the environmental limits of the territory, would not delay in manifesting itself. The second consequence, on the other hand, concerns State-owned companies: large plants, old and new, now increasingly took their place in wider-ranging national economic strategies and were therefore being taken away from the local level, thanks to The Ministry of State Participations and public bodies such as IRI. To summarise, the most obvious socio-economic process, on the threshold of

Chapter 1

the 1970s, is the progressive loss of a local foundation: in these terms, the industrial resource of East Naples became a kind of 'curse',[24] a reserve for external agents to plunder on occasion. The development prospects of the territory were no longer a priority of private companies, while the public appeared more interested in broad-based strategies, with an eye to political consensus. During the 1970s, these processes would add themselves to the territorial problems in determining the historical course of the deindustrialisation of East Naples.

---

24 This indirectly refers to the theories of the 'resource curse' by Michael Ross and the 'paradox of plenty' by Terry Lynn Karl (respectively, *The Oil Curse. How Petroleum Wealth Shapes the Development of Nations* (2012) and *The Paradox of Plenty: Oil Booms and Petro-States* (1997)) on the political and economic fate of oil-producing states: the idea of a source of profit alien to the territory to which it belongs because it is subject to external interests and undisputed.

2.
THE ROOTS OF DEINDUSTRIALISATION.

2.1 Defining 'deindustrialisation': a social, political and economic process

1973 was certainly a significant year in the economic history of the twentieth century: it was 'the beginning of the end of the golden age' (Frascani 2012, pp. 163–64) for countries that developed after the Second World War. Traditionally, the responsibility for triggering the crisis has been assigned to the OPEC countries, for their decision to artificially inflate the price of crude oil as a deterrent to Western pro-Israeli policies and in reaction to the monopoly of the oil majors. From the financial point of view, the death sentence of the *gold standard* (1971) had already put the Bretton Woods system in crisis, unmooring the global monetary system from the solid grip of the gold conversion. The steady rise in the price of oil triggered a global inflationary process and a seemingly irreversible energy crisis in the short term. It was a Great Divide, a structural division capable of causing radical consequences for the economy, politics, culture, human relations. On the mental level, the progressive increase in inflation, the public deficit and unemployment presented developed societies with a general picture of economic malaise, which translated into a negative judgment of the social and technological limits of Fordism and the political and economic limits of Keynesian thought. On the material level, however, the continuous increase in the speed and freedom of movement of capital generated competition mechanisms that increasingly extended to the supra-local scale, primarily through industrial investment in developing countries (Vergallo 2011, pp. 38–40). The geographical location and relocation of manufacturing in emerging countries, with cheap labour and relatively looser government controls, offered a way out of the crisis, in terms of productive reorganisation, for companies that could afford it. Many others, however, responded to the crisis by closing factories on a regional and national scale, with sharp cuts to the workforce, with fragmentation and outsourcing of investments, or with closure. On this basis, deindustrialisation began in the 1970s, understood as a contraction of the industrial contribution to the economic system, as regarded both employment and the value of manufacturing (Corona 2016, p. 9). At the same time, the collective certainties generated by the industrial system begin to crumble under the blows of relocations, cuts and divestments.

Overall, the impact on the global North was violent. The US manufacturing core was among the first victims of these processes: The Manufacturing Belt became a Rust Belt. Even on the Old Continent, traditional production areas were hit by the same industrial crisis. The Ruhr, the North-East of France, Asturias, the North-West of Italy, the Midlands and the North of England all went through this crucial phase (Corona 2016, pp. 9–11).

As far as scientific analysis goes, the first studies on deindustrialisation emerged in the Anglo-Saxon countries in conjunction with the phenomena themselves. Given the topicality of the matter at hand, historiographical studies would have to wait until the mid-1990s; in the 1970s and 1980s, the debate on deindustrialisation and post-industrial societies was instead the prerogative of economists, sociologists or political activists. The first analyses derived, basically, from the triple nature of the social, political and economic causes and consequences that preceded and followed the retreat of the industry. A milestone in deindustrialisation studies, an essential reference point in this research, was *The Deindustrialization of America* (1982), by economists Barry Bluestone and Bennett Harrison. The subtitle reads *Plant Closings, Community Abandonment, and the Dismantling of Basic Industry* and the text itself opens with a definition of the process that is also a forceful complaint: deindustrialisation is a broad systematic process of divesting the basic productive capacity of a nation and, in the American case, the underlying factor of high unemployment rates, stagnation and lack of competitiveness on international markets. At its basis there is no physiological problem but managers' lack of will to invest in national industry. In other words, deindustrialisation is neither a fatal accident nor a myth but stems from very specific investment choices and strategies. The great success and significance of *The Deindustrialization of America* is in its dedication to the movement of individuals and organisations resisting the economic destruction of their communities. More generally, its criticism of Reagan's deregulation policies guarantees the book's position in the national public debate. At the same time, the original theoretical approach combining a quantitative basis with general analyses made it the founding text of deindustrialisation studies (Garruccio 2016, pp. 39–40).

In the following decades, deindustrialisation studies focused on the analysis of specific cases, at local, regional or national level. This development

The Roots of Deindustrialisation

is linked to contemporary scenes of abandoned former industrial areas and the great complexity assumed by the phenomenon itself: the US stagnation ended, opening the door to a new phase of growth related to an increase in productivity driven by technology (Vergallo 2011, pp. 64–65). The new service-based economy also supports manufacturing in many areas of the world; but it is an equally new secondary industry and equally dependent on technology. Fewer and fewer workers were required, while cracks in the system of protection and unionisation became devastating collapses. Perhaps these negative evolutions made the structural characteristics of the previous phase identifiable and analysable to historical research, which since the mid-1990s has valued the results achieved by deindustrialisation studies. The first historiographical approach to contemporary deindustrialisation derived from the heterogeneous approaches of previous studies but initially applied these to a series of specific cases. These studies often had an anthropological flavour and focused on the consequences for urban social contexts. It was impossible not to start from the *Rust Belt*: Kathryn Marie Dudley, from the University of Chicago, wrote one of the first local ethnographic studies, with her *The End of the Line. Lost Jobs, New Lives in Postindustrial America* (1994), on the decommissioning of a major Chrysler plant in a city in Wisconsin. What is offered here is not an analysis of the causes, referred to external economic powers, but a dramatic reading of the process of deindustrialisation as it affected the life of a community. Daily life, income, wellbeing, social status and the very interpretation of the world are shown to have been revolutionised: the place where one lives and even the image of oneself loses value. Following this thread, the theme of urban decline develops in a long and lively series of studies dedicated to the impact of closures on local realities, with the focus restricted to the level of the city or neighbourhood. Often, the social consequences are intertwined with other issues, such as ethnic differences or environmental damage. The methods adopted by these researchers, relying on the testimonies of former workers and their families, giving voice to their convictions, should be emphasised because of their relevance to the present research. The focus is restricted to a specific location, to a single factory or to experiences shared by the same production sector, often accompanied by photographic evidence. Ultimately, the authors themselves convey on paper their closeness – physical, sentimental or cultural – to the cases analysed (Garruccio 2016, pp. 46–47).

These general developments and the opening of the new millennium brought new attention to and awareness of deindustrialisation in the historiographical discourse. In 2002, the *International Review of Social History* dedicated a special issue to deindustrialisation. It was the first history journal to focus on the economic, social and cultural aspects of deindustrialisation. According to the two guest editors, Marcel van der Linden and Bert Altena, the issue had to fit into the new climate of historical awareness that had emerged in recent years with regard to the social consequences of industrial decline, unemployment, impoverishment and migration. However, account had also to be taken of the impact of the process on the old forms of policy-making, as well as the emergence of anti-government attitudes in the former industrial communities. The other milestone of this new phase of deindustrialisation historiography was a 2003 collection of essays, which opened in absolute continuity with the past of deindustrialisation studies: the preface to *Beyond the Ruins. The Cultural Meanings of Deindustrialization* is by Barry Bluestone, co-author of the fundamental *The Deindustrialization of America*. Bluestone opens his essay with a quantitative review of the 'cataclysmic' (Vergallo 2011, p. 91) consequences of the waves of deindustrialisation on the labour market and on the living conditions of Americans. From a more general perspective, the editors of the collection adopt a long-term vision of deindustrialisation processes, with the intent to 'widen the scope of discussion beyond the plant shutdowns, the immediate employment policy, the tales of victimization, the swell of industrial nostalgia ... to shift the conversation away from the body count of job losses to interrogate the cultural meaning of deindustrialization in the aftermath of mill and factory closings' (Garruccio 2016, p. 48). The long-term perspective resonates with the authors' conviction that the industrial era is still current and in the process of transformation, just another phase in a cyclical history of capitalism made up of investments and divestments: in these terms, deindustrialisation is reduced to a temporal discontinuity, an interregnum critique that determines the nature of the social system, like previous industrialisation processes. It is, in short, the other side of the same coin (Vergallo 2011, p. 93).

As for the Italian academic context, the emergence of deindustrialisation studies has yet to be traced in current historiography. A significant step in this direction was the conference promoted by Istat (*Istituto Nazionale di Statistica*, National Institute of Statistics) and the University of Rome La Sapienza, held on 25–26 November 2016, on 'Italian society and major economic crises (1929–2016)'. In particular, the contribution by Professor Luciano Segreto of the University of Florence on 'Deindustrialisation in Italy: between conceptual vagueness and consensual instrumentalisation of

The Roots of Deindustrialisation

the debate' allows us to retrace some phases of the academic debate. What we can say with certainty is that it is a still young historiography characterised by heterogeneous methods and approaches, such as work history, sociology, urban history, industrial archaeology and, of course, economic history. It is necessary to mention here, therefore, the historiographical works on which a good part of the current synthetic narration is based, on deindustrialisation and studies related to it: *Una nuova era? 'Deindustrializzazione' e nuovi assetti produttivi nel mondo (1945–2005)*, by Luigi Vergallo (2011), offers an in-depth and varied view of the long-term processes of deindustrialisation and the relocation of industry, thanks to its analytical rationalisation of the heterogeneous literature and the historical research dedicated to it, retraced in the previous pages. Broad quantitative support derives from economic data and qualitative analysis of social transformations, both at international level and in relation to the specific cases of individual states. The very long perspective of *Le crisi economiche in Italia* (2012), from the nineteenth century to the present, by Paolo Frascani dedicates some chapters to the structural factors underlying the crisis of the 1970s in the international and national context, and to the causes and consequences of the processes of deindustrialisation and overcoming of Fordism in Italy. Finally, the 2016 special issue of *Meridiana, Rivista di Storia e Scienze Sociali* on deindustrialised areas, offers a general overview of deindustrialisation processes in international, national and local contexts, thanks to an essay by Gabriella Corona, 'Volti e risvolti della deindustrializzazione: alcuni interrogativi sulla contemporaneità'; and an in-depth analysis of the trajectory of historical and other studies on deindustrialisation, offered by Roberta Garruccio in 'Chiedi alla ruggine. Studi e storiografia della deindustrializzazione'. The issue presents extensive analysis of some fundamental European experiences, such as in the Ruhr and the French North-East, but the is mainly aimed at individual specific cases across a peninsula in crisis.

It should be noted that the economic crisis of the 1970s manifested itself relatively late in Italy, compared to the rest of the global North. Initially, it affected the main industrial hubs established in the decades of the economic miracle. Overall and in the long term, the process of deindustrialisation resulted in the transition to small and medium-sized local units or tertiary activities, as opposed to the large factories that had dominated Italian manufacturing in the 1950s and 1960s. Hence, many economic experts preferred the label 'productive restructuring' to the much more negative 'deindustrialisation', but, either way, it was seismic for the entire national industrial system, begin-

Chapter 2

ning in the processes of modernisation, rationalisation of labour and state interventionism characteristic of the economic miracle and gathering force after the oil crisis of the 1970s (Corona 2016, pp. 14–15). The individual industrial contexts of the peninsula were overwhelmed by the impact of the general crisis, by cuts in public resources, the flight of private capital, the increase in unemployment, the crumbling of collective certainties. During the 1970s, the industrial area of Naples East was no exception, and the national and international economic recession found a solid foothold in the chaotic conditions of this urban area.

2.2 Environmental foundations of the economic decline

Towards the end of the 1970s, tensions rose every day in the factories. By now, those working at full capacity could be counted on the fingers of the hands. Not a week went by without a small or medium-sized company closing its doors, putting workers on redundancy leave, thinking of demobilising production to relocate it elsewhere. Despite the mechanisms of state protection, even the largest companies, often dominated by the public sector or with a share of public capital, had to face the crisis through cuts, lockouts or relocation strategies. At the end of the decade, on 26 October 1979, the daily newspaper of the Italian Communist Party, *l'Unità*, offered an extraordinary analysis of the industrial mortality of the eastern zone of Naples, reproduced in full below:

> In the 'industrial triangle' between the districts of S. Giovanni a Teduccio, Barra and Ponticelli ... there is the largest concentration of manufacturing industries in Naples: 36% of which account for 46.87% of workers and an area equal to 50.4% of the total city, with an employee index per hectare equal to 65.5. But the eastern zone also has the record of the highest 'industrial mortality': 81.6% of the areas [are] occupied by bankrupt companies that have suspended their activity. And here is the 'x-ray' of the major crisis points. SNIA VISCOSA: chemical company, manufactures synthetic fibres; from July the 'rayon' department is closed: 600 workers in redundancy pay. Concerns also for the second main product, 'wistel'. INTERFAN: chemical company linked to the SNIA group; failed in the summer of 78, 140 employees dismissed. VETROMECCANICA: it has been stopped for five years, following the bankruptcy of the private entrepreneur; 120 workers in redundancy waiting for [state] intervention. It produces special glass. DECOPON: for this company we also expect the intervention [of the state]. Meanwhile, for five years, 280 workers have been on redundancy. ICM: chemical industry taken over and then liquidated by a large national group. 40 workers dismissed. RIVETTI [footwear and clothing Ndr]: after three years of paralysis should resume activity in March ... 30 employees. MOBIL OIL: employs

The Roots of Deindustrialisation

about a thousand. In the immediate future, it has no productive or employment problems. In 1993 the concession for the refinery will expire; a possible relocation is being discussed; it is a polluting company. CIRIO: food company of the SME-IRI group; employs 1,100 people. Following an agreement with the unions, it will be transferred to a new factory in the hinterland ... CMN: mechanical engineering company with 100 employees on redundancy; the entire carpentry sector is in crisis. WOOD COMPANIES (sawmills and furniture factories): Bifulco, 92 employees on unemployment benefit for two years; Di Pace, closed, dismissed 45 employees; L.I., 20 out of 26 workers on unemployment benefit; Romana, reduced its workforce from 30 to 12 units; De Conciliis, 100 workers on social security (*l'Unità*, 26 October 1979).

Bearing in mind the extraordinary vitality of the industrial area of Naples East in the previous decade, one wonders how it was possible to reach such a situation in a relatively short time. The then municipal councillor Nino Daniele advanced an analysis of the local and city crisis that was both remarkably synthetic and systemic. Inevitably, his discourse referred to changes in the productive structure and the 'curse' launched on the Neapolitan industry by external capital:

> The past years confirm a further process of crisis in the productive base of the city, an ever-weaker beating of the already feeble pulse of the city economic organism and the accentuation of its tertiarisation, its dependence on and subordination to the outside ... On the social level, the crisis mixes traditional economic profiles and social figures; the illusion is to be found in a subordinated economic system and in the presence of great factories in the middle of nowhere ('cathedrals in the desert'), unconnected with infrastructure, other activities and the social fabric. (Daniele, 10 November 1979).

Similarly, a few years later (1984) the anonymous researcher Censis (Center for Social Investment Studies) emphasised:

> The structural characteristics of dependence of the [Neapolitan] productive apparatus are manifested, among other things, by the lack of autonomy of local management groups in the companies and their strong reliance on public contracts. This guarantees a certain level of production, but mitigates the commercial aggressiveness of companies and accentuates trends of *political* engagement with the market (Censis 1984, p. 39)

From the purely economic point of view, it can be said that many industrial divestment trajectories in East Naples in the 1970s were actually triggered by the largely external nature of capital and the lack of local decision-making processes: the case of Snia-Viscosa di San Giovanni a Teduccio, an integral part of a national group active in the chemical and textile sector, is exemplary. In the 1960s, this giant synthetic fibre maker boasted more than a thousand employees, a galaxy of small and medium-sized companies connected to the mother industry, technologically advanced machinery

(Spadoni 2007, p. 4), a set of services dedicated to its employees and an extremely favourable location for any expansion of the factory: not surprisingly, in 1974 the company sent an application to CIPE (Interministerial Economic Planning Committee) to expand its existing plants, both in terms of employment and production, and quickly obtained approval.[1] Even in the early 1970s, therefore, the company enjoyed excellent health: the crisis would come soon after the middle of the decade, both because of reckless investment choices by the new owners, the semi-private group Montedison, and market competition from emerging countries in the synthetic fibres sector (*l'Unità*, 12 June 1979). In the red to the tune of eighty billion lire, the company slashed the workforce of its factories engaged in the production of synthetic fibres, now unprofitable and therefore deemed secondary. Far from an accident, or a necessary consequence of the crisis, the demise of the Snia di San Giovanni in Teduccio was the result of specific business decisions: during 1979, the company prepared a financial restructuring plan at a national level, the main focus of which was cutting the production of synthetic fibres. Public institutions, in the person of the Under-Secretary of State for Industry, fully endorsed the programme, deeming it necessary to ensure a significant 'increase in productivity' in other sectors (Chamber of Deputies, 23 September 1980).[2] Proving the lack of obstacles to decisions made outside the territory, the arc of decline of the Snia Viscosa factory of San Giovanni in Teduccio was extraordinarily abrupt: Between March 1979 and March 1980 the factory was progressively dismantled, department by department, until its closure (*l'Unità*, 18 March 1980).

This dynamic, the sacrifice of a plant considered secondary in the strategies of a company of national calibre, redcurs in the trajectories of decline of industrial activities in East Naples and is a structural symptom of the so-called 'decision-making acephaly'. In other contexts, however, the external origin of capital and the lack of a link between locations and decision-making centres of industry are intertwined with factors of a territorial nature in determining the course of decommissioning of an industrial activity. The reference case is that of one of the largest and most prestigious companies in the area, Cirio in

---

1   'The CIPE states ... that the projects referred to in the premises do not diverge from the national economic planning guidelines, in relation to the level of congestion of the areas of planned location of the facilities'. CIPE digital archives. CIPE resolution on request for expansion of the Snia Viscosa plant, 20 Sept. 1974.

2   Chamber of Deputies Digital Archives. Acts, XII Permanent Commission, 23 Sept. 1980.

The Roots of Deindustrialisation

San Giovanni in Teduccio, with its two factories (canning and glassmaking). The city food sector was among the most affected by the recessions of the 1970s, as shown by the data of the Istat industrial census of 1981: 41 fewer local units over the past decade, and about 3,000 workers laid off (Vitale 1992). The situation of the entire food sector, and especially of the tomato industry, became critical due to foreign competition and the progressive financial disengagement of the public sector. As mentioned at the end of the previous chapter, the transition to the SME-Financial System resulted in a very weak link between management and territory: if national investment strategies or the need for financial recovery so required, there was absolutely nothing, not even the force of unions, that could limit, restrain or counter cuts, forced mobility and marginalisation. In these terms, the critical phase of the Cirio dispute was between 1978 and 1979. In the summer of 1978, the first signs of financial disengagement by SME-Financial emerged in a meeting between it and the Cirio management: no production programme was drawn up, nor were any investments planned for the plants of San Giovanni a Teduccio; indeed the keywords of the meeting were 'mobility' and 'relocation' (*l'Unità*, 18 July 1978). Significantly, the position of the management, in these months, justifying the plans for decommissioning and delocalisation, focused on a factor repeatedly invoked: the saturation of space due to congestion between housing, industrial and infrastructural functions, whose origin has been described in previous pages and whose developments will be followed in the pages to come. 'The area' was said to be 'too congested for the traffic of a large company' (*l'Unità*, 25 February 1979). In addition to the logistical difficulties, Cirio claimed to need 80,000 square metres for its largest plant, the canning factory, not to be stifled, and to allow future expansion and restructuring; this represented 12,000 more square metres than were available in San Giovanni a Teduccio (*l'Unità*, 5 February 1979).

At first, the management chose to close the smaller factory, the glassworks, an act that provoked the immediate and fierce reaction of the entire district of San Giovanni a Teduccio (*l'Unità*, 25 October 1978), in solidarity with one of its loved ones. Failing to reach a compromise with the company and the increasingly intransigent SME, the unions threatened a general strike of all food companies with state involvement in Campania; this took place on 11 September 1978 in San Giovanni a Teduccio (*l'Unità*, 11 September 1978). The company and the SME responded with a sort of strategic retreat, letting the force of the autumn mobilisation weaken before moving on to a counterattack in the early days of 1979. Today, Antonio Fondacaro, then a young activist in the Communist Party, proudly remembers this period of constant struggles and repeated occupations: 'the occupation of Cirio was beautiful because a solidarity network of all the factories in the industrial area was created to support the families of the workers and we of the party stayed there night and day' (Recording n. 2).

Meanwhile, the company and the SME planned their own moves by raising the stakes but, at the same time, trying to neutralise trade union opposition with an offer difficult to reject. In the spring of 1979, the agreement was reached: the San Giovanni a Teduccio factory was sacrificed on the altar of employment and corporate development of the entire region, with the approval of the unions, the Communist Party and also the daily *l'Unità*, which in previous months had been particularly critical of the company. The compromise signed on 13 April 1979 between the unions and the SME, after about a year and a half of struggles was as follows: the SME 'promised to assume a central and propulsive role in the agro-industrial sector in the South, by the coordination and development of its activities in the various sectors' (*l'Unità*, 21 April 1979) and immediately demonstrated its good intentions by investing, for the next three years, fifty billion lire in the Cirio group of the Campania region (*l'Unità*, 14 April 1979). This represented a genuine restructuring on a regional scale, which also included new and upgraded plants. The price to be paid, however, was the relocation of the San Giovanni a Teduccio cannery to a municipality in the Neapolitan hinterland (Caivano), guaranteeing total protection of employment levels and without granting the land left behind to speculative building, indeed agreeing its use with the Municipality. The glassworks, on the other hand, was to be replaced by a production unit specialising in the mechanical engineering sector. 'The struggle of the workers of Cirio seems to have ended positively' summarised *l'Unità*, 'despite the abandonment of that old and collapsing factory' (*l'Unità*, 21 April 1979), in other words the San Giovanni plant, to be replaced with a state of the art plant in the hinterland. In the end, the stakes in the battle were too high and the Cirio establishments were sacrificed for a perceived superior good.

The story of the decommissioning of Cirio sheds a lot of light on the encounter between economic and environmental factors (territorial saturation and logistical problems). The motives of the management and the outcome of the dispute, the relocation,[3] can, however, be read as part of a process of a

---

3   The delocalisation processes confirm that the industrial decline of East Naples was connected not only to the demands of pure market dynamics and to the financial forces acting above the

The Roots of Deindustrialisation

historically environmental nature: in the general context of crisis, local deindustrialisation can be pushed by local environmental limitations. In 1982, the Cesan (Business Studies Center 'Giuseppe Cenzato'), published a study on *The Industrial Characteristics of the Eastern Area of Naples* (Simonetti 2003, pp. 589–90), dealing with the decade that had just passed. Three essential points were highlighted, the first of which concerned the rate of opening of new plants. Between 1971 and 1981 the 'birth rate' compensated for only seventy per cent of 'mortality', the latter serving as quantitative evidence of the phenomena of relocation, cessation or reduction of local production at the artisanal scale. In other words, the number of new industrial activities could not compensate for the old, decommissioned plants. The second process highlighted by Cesan concerned the beginning of the larger industrial crisis, in the process of relocation or restructuring: some of the cases mentioned refer to well-known established businesses, such as Cirio and Snia Viscosa. This was scale of industry that had been incapable of regenerating itself in the form of new local businesses in recent years. In addition, the surveys carried out by Cesan of a sample of forty large former industrial buildings of at least 1,000 square metres in size, testify to the failure, by 1982, to reuse about half the abandoned spaces. In other words, the emphasis in large-scale local industry was on cuts and relocation processes, a model which failed to attract new investment comparable to the existing, and there was insufficient growth in smaller-scale industry to cover losses. The old production hubs, meanwhile, were simply left to themselves. The third point, closely linked to the others, was that the space of production had to contend with the space of housing and the emerging space of services and commerce. This condition of persistent congestion and environmental disorder could not act as a stimulus for any new investment, but instead accelerated the multiple episodes of decommissioning, especially if connected to that lack of local decision-making processes inscribed in the industrial history of the eastern area.

In these terms, if the congestion of spaces could be considered a contingent problem for well-established factories, like Cirio, it could also be a

---

territories, but also to the specific local dimension. In other words, the continuous relocations to the provincial and regional hinterland, which intensified from the period under consideration (Frascani 2017), confirm the lack of competitiveness of the eastern territory of Naples with respect to new industrial investments. Instead, investments were made beyond the municipal boundaries, creating new hubs in the north and north-east of Naples. By 1991 these two areas together already housed 36% of the total workforce involved in provincial manufacturing (Municipality of Naples 1999, pp. 93–96).

Chapter 2

basic structural element from the point of view of the competitiveness of the territory: from the perspective of investors, during the 1970s the bustling territory of Naples East showed less prospect of generating profit and began to present obvious logistical problems due to chaotic urban expansion. Urban limits and ecological risks exacerbated the situation, as will be seen shortly. The low industrial birth rate, the first of Cesan's points, reflects exactly this process – the limited ability to attract new investment. In addition, the crisis in large-scale industrial activities (second point) was also induced by the same local and logistical problems, given the increasingly overcrowded territorial context. In such a context, local manufacturing giants were slowly suffocated and forced to close, relocate or wage constant war with the territory. It seems apparent that, given the slow pace of decommissioning processes, these large production spaces were destined to become brownfields, further increasing environmental dysfunction for still-active businesses and repelling investment prospects, generating a vicious circle.

On the quantitative level, thanks to Istat (National Institute of Statistics) data it is possible to draw a slow parabola of decline in local industry between the end of the 1970s and the 1990s. In 1981, local manufacturing units numbered 1,095 and still occupied 38.1% of the total workforce of the eastern area (Simonetti 2003, tab. 6). Nonetheless, local industry had already lost about 3,000 workers compared to the previous decade, and would lose another 5,000 in the following decade. In individual eastern districts, the decline in employment in the manufacturing sector between 1971 and 1991 is undeniable: in the Barra district, it fell from 54.8 employees in 100 residents to 37.3 employees; for Poggioreale, from 48.7 to 29.2 employees; for Gianturco-Zona Industriale, from 41.7 to 26.9 employees; for Ponticelli from 43.4 to 31.5 employees; for San Giovanni, from 52.1 to 36 employees (Simonetti 2003, tab. 4). The overall employment rate for the eastern area stood at 32.06% in 1981 but the figure for unemployment, 41.75%, was already worrying (Censis 1984, p. 50), a figure destined to rise over the decade to more than 52% (Municipality of Naples 1996, pp. 50–51). In the meantime, local manufacturing units in the eastern area fell in number from 1,095 in 1981 to 922 in 1991. On the whole, the course of the industrial decline of East Naples was anything but sudden, as would be attributable to a sudden extra-local economic shock, able to overwhelm the entire productive fabric. In 1991, the local secondary sector, although strongly downsized and in constant stagnation, still retained 18% of those employed in the entire province of Naples (Municipality of Naples 1999, p. 96). Hence, to understand economic decline as a long-term process, it is

The Roots of Deindustrialisation

necessary to trace the historical elements at the basis of the territory's 'loss of competitiveness': elements that simultaneously contributed to the deterioration of the environmental conditions of the urban landscape.

The following pages will attempt, in summary, to seek the environmental foundation of the economic decline of East Naples in historical processes of urban saturation and environmental disorder leading to urban dysfunctionality. This is the underlying character of a space that nature created as marshes and that man has transformed into a new form of 'swamp', a metaphor for a territory irreducible to any final rationalisation. This territory was also historically hostile towards external investments, such that, for about three quarters of a century, external investments in East Naples were facilitated by governmental financing, infrastructural planning and relief programmes.

Figure 2.1

An aerial view of the Pazzigno district in 1980. This picture exemplifies East Naples' urban disorder: amongst the overcrowded houses, there are several factories, a railway line and an elevated motorway (crossing the district on the background of the photo). At the top, there is a comment by local communists: 'aerial view of Pazzigno. A proper ghetto, indelible fault of the older ruling classes.' Source: from the private collection of Vincenzo Morreale: Partito Comunista Italiano, Sezioni di San Giovanni a Teduccio. 1980. Dossier 1980. S. Giovanni a Teduccio: un quartiere che cambia. Napoli.

From the 1970s, such investments occurred in an economic context of deep crisis and in an irreversibly disordered, overpopulated and undisciplined urban environment. These elements of environmental disorder have their roots in the entire local history of the twentieth century and, by the end of the 1970s the scale and nature of the phenomenon had become practically irreversible. The external elements (the structural factors that cascaded 'from above') have been exposed in the previous pages but they can be summarised again: negative economic conditions and alienation of the decision-making centres of large industry. The main internal factor behind deindustrialisation, on the other hand, was the area's loss of competitiveness, its inability to attract new industrial investment. This last point is mainly related to the chaotic expansion of the periphery, whose historical developments we should now sketch out.

2.3 Sustainability and urban planning in the 1970s

> It is evident that between the 1970s and 1990s, when a new urban era began in Naples, many things changed: the abandonment of existing productive activities, a new environmental culture, the prevalence of disorderly urban growth and land consumption. This disorder has many faces: hydraulic, environmental, urban in the strict sense (Recording n. 5).

As highlighted by urban planner Giovanni Dispoto, from the 1970s, along with radical economic change, the city of Naples entered a new phase of its urban and ecological history. New knowledge and legal and urban planning instruments arose to address urban environmental problems, health emergencies and environmental risks. To understand the characteristics of this new phase of city history, it is necessary to begin with urban planning. In terms of economic promotion, this phase of urban planning history, which roughly comprises the 1960s to mid-1970s, is characterised by the emphasis placed on the development of tertiary activities, seen as the natural superseding of the industrial model. At the same time, it is affected by the issues of public housing, urban services and facilities, due to the strong popular opinion in favour of improving housing conditions (Corona 2007, p. 4, pp. 28–29). The turning point for the city of Naples was 1972, the year of approval of the new General Development Plan, developed over more than two years and in force until 1999. The Plan took as its priority objective the achievement of a demographic balance between the relatively depopulated inland areas of the

The Roots of Deindustrialisation

region and the highly populated coastal zone. The material and economic basis of such a project of demographic engineering can be seen in the assignment to the city of Naples of a predominantly tertiary and directive role: an ambitious project of urban renewal that mainly concerned the transformation of the eastern area. The area, in addition to hosting the Nuovo Centro Direzionale (New Business Centre) close to the Poggioreale district, envisaged as the new core of the city's tertiary sector, exemplifies on a micro scale the general objectives of the planners. The plan's objective was to redistribute residential weight between the districts and to accommodate part of the population of the city centre, while trying to confine industry or permanently replace it with the tertiary sector and trade (Comune di Napoli 1999, pp.102–03).

In practice, large areas were assigned to district administrative centres, coinciding with the historical cores of the eastern districts. New shared spaces and green areas were also planned but a substantial part of the area was reserved for the expansion of social housing. The use of land was projected as follows: fifty per cent for housing, thirty per cent for facilities and services and twenty per cent for streets and squares (Municipality of Naples 1972, p.13). To understand the choices of the Plan, as regarded the provision of new housing, it is necessary to compare with the existing situation. As noted in the previous chapter, the period between 1946–1960 was marked by extraordinary activity in residential construction, with over 1,300 more homes built in the eastern districts: the following decade, the 1960s, saw the construction of another 1,200 houses in the eastern area, and a further 1,050 were to be built in the 1970s (Municipality of Naples, 2011).[4] The vast majority of the houses, about 700 in the 1960s and as many in the 1970s, were built in the Ponticelli district. Most were intended for the working class, both native and moving from the most crowded districts of the city centre. The new housing estates were mainly built on the last stretches of marshes and farmland. This is a significant and controversial element of the planning choices in this decade, also as regards the 1972 Plan, which chose to convert

---

4   Bearing in mind that the population resident in the eastern area remained near stable for the entire decade, rising from 156,825 inhabitants to 159,578 inhabitants, the improvement of housing conditions is extremely partial, another side of the coin of residential expansion. In the eastern area, the number of inhabitants decreased from 1.66 per room to 1.25, and the number of rooms perf house increased from 2.74 to 3.33. In quantifying the phenomenon of residential congestion, and the actual need for new housing, the figure for unused building stock, at 6.07% in 1971 and at 4.60% in 1981, is secondary but not negligible (Municipality of Naples, 1996, p. 54). Finally, it is necessary to take into account the unregulated construction, obviously difficult to quantify but a constant scourge in the collective perception of citizenship.

Chapter 2

agricultural areas to construction needs, thus avoiding further saturation of the old industrial districts but in fact confirming a development model that depended on the dissipative use of land as a resource.[5] The last glimpses of the ancient swamps began, therefore, to be irretrievably obscured by scaffolding.

After Ponticelli, Barra was the district most affected by the residential expansion, with about 560 new homes built between the 1960s and 1970s. In addition to the construction of some popular districts and new building yards close to the perimeter of the oil area, in terms of the urban layout of the eastern districts, the construction of the Via delle Repubbliche Marinare was important: this imposing new artery, unusually broad for the district, ran from the highway junction to the municipal borders of San Giorgio a Cremano. The new road was in fact intended to relieve traffic between the centre of Naples and the eastern suburbs, then lighten the load of the parallel Corso San Giovanni, the main coastal artery (Parisi 1998, p. 151). It is not by chance that the street is usually defined as the 'Residential': it would be progressively taken up by building sites. On the urban level, the new road also served to connect the housing units of the three main districts of the eastern area (Barra, Ponticelli and San Giovanni) to each other, and also to involve some smaller villages (Pazzigno, Casale and Sannicandro). With this intervention, it can be said that the eastern area assumed the appearance of a single, indistinct suburb: it is difficult today for the citizen to identify the clear boundaries between the individual neighbourhoods. The effects of another major infrastructural intervention of the decade were diametrically opposed, in terms of the urban heritage of the eastern area: the construction of the east-west ring road of Naples. Built from 1972, and adopted by the 1972 GDP, the fast-flowing road surrounds the entire perimeter of the metropolitan area and functions to facilitate movement between the centre and the vast outlying areas of the city. However, its bridges and flyovers definitively separate the eastern area from the centre of Naples, preventing connection with the centre over vast areas. In other words, it breaks the semi-peripheral ring and central-suburban continuity is ruptured (Municipality

---

5   During the decade 1971–80, a comparison between the building expansion of Ponticelli (701 new homes) with that in districts with the oldest industrial vocation, namely Poggioreale (82 new homes), San Giovanni a Teduccio (23 new homes) and Gianturco-Industrial Zone (3 new homes) (Municipality of Naples, 2011) significantly highlights the long-term choice to redistribute the demographic weight into that neighbourhood, the last agricultural redoubt of the eastern area. Conversely, the state of territorial saturation of neighbourhoods historically more engaged in industrial activity also emerges.

The Roots of Deindustrialisation

of Naples 2000, pp. 30–31). As a whole, the infrastructural choices of the seventies can therefore be defined, at best, as ambiguous in their results for East Naples:

> This area has, over time, been characterised by a relationship with the wider territory of the metropolitan area through the development of a delusional infrastructural network: railways, highways, interchanges, viaducts, oil pipelines, etc., which 'cross' the area, in fact not serving it and even 'jumping over' it. Therefore, this territory was defined by infrastructure indifferent to the identity and historical distinctions that exist between [the eastern districts]. From this point of view, the territory was unified, but in a vision that overall confirmed its characteristics as an industrial periphery (Recording n. 5).

It should be stressed that a priority aspect in the planning of the early 1970s, interconnected both with the choices of urban infrastructure and the location of housing, was to facilitate the relocation of local industrial activity. As we saw in the previous chapter, from the second half of the nineteenth century the local administration was unable to delimit an industrial area proper, rationalised with dedicated infrastructure and separation from the nearby residences. The result, through long historical sedimentation, was the development of a chaotic industrial area, in which the productive and logistical needs of the largest and minor factories overlapped with the daily life of increasingly densely populated districts. By way of example, in the case of the heavy industry located along the coast of the San Giovanni a Teduccio district, the engineer Ugo Grippo, the future secretary of the Christian Democrat Party (Democrazia Cristiana) in Naples, in 1971 commented:

> The heavy industries located along the coastal arc, in immediate continuity with the Neapolitan centre [pose] constraints to spatial planning ... which, depending on the economic and social cost, affect development, [in the form of] a double pollution of the urban landscape and marine waters, [in addition to causing] functional and formal rupture to the urban structure and dysfunctional connections (Grippo 1971, p. 61).

Reserving for the next section the issue of coastal pollution, the perceived need to rationalise the industrial structure of East Naples, reorganising it in relation to the urban fabric and infrastructural networks of the area, should be emphasised. These issues are addressed by Article 18 of the implementation rules of the new GDP. The new industrial areas would be dealt with through detailed execution plans aimed at respecting the maximum ratios between space intended for production sites and public space intended for collective activities, public parks or parking lots. Therefore, it was expected that heavy and harmful industries would be moved in order to open up space for public facilities 'amounting to not less than thirty per cent of the eastern area' (Municipality of Naples 1972, p. 20). These activities would be concentrated in the new eastern 'Industrial Zone' proper, in fact a new district geographically located in a relatively small space and away from the neighbourhood residential areas, but close to the port, the railway tracks and new infrastructure, roads and motorways, in order to facilitate industry's logistical needs (Municipality of Naples 1999, p. 103). In this area, the presence of residential houses would be forbidden, with the exception of custodians and factory management personnel: manufacturing and construction companies, and a whole complex of auxiliary activities, both secondary and tertiary, were to be concentrated there, opposite the port of Naples (Municipality of Naples 1972, pp. 15–16).

Although part of a general instrument that was quite ambiguous in terms of environmental choices for the suburbs, it can be said that Article 18 of the implementation rules of the 1972 GDP closes, at least in terms of the of principles behind its intervention, an important historical phase for East Naples. On paper, the proximity of manufacturing and residential units was no longer feasible, neither sustainable nor acceptable. In theory, heavy industries and polluting activities were to be separated from the urban fabric and concentrated in specific places or delocalised to different parts of the region. In all plans, however, there is a profound gap between aspiration and actual implementation. Even as regards choices for industrial activities, the results of the 1972 Plan were ambiguous. In practice, bureaucratic complications and political obstacles led to a failure to define and approve the implementation plans, as witnessed by urban planner Giovanni Dispoto:

> The main limitation of the 1972 GDP was to postpone its deployment to the 29 areas into which the whole territory was divided, intended to be subject to as many executive urban plans (these are now deemed 'effective plans'). This never happened, because it was up to the Public Administration to provide them. Therefore, only some initiatives that had already been decided, such as the Business Centre, went ahead. Let's say that there has been no development of the contents of the 1972 plan (Recording n. 5).

It is necessary, then, to trace the specific dynamics and the balance of power that affected the progress of the intended projects. On the one hand, only a few heavy and polluting productive activities were relocated or separated from the urban fabric: others, like the immense oil area, continued and still continue to occupy the territory of East Naples, generating significant problems. This tortuous path will be outlined in detail in the next paragraph. Another key moment, offering significant background as to the *modus operandi*

The Roots of Deindustrialisation

Figure 2.2

1972 GDP, borders of the new industrial area (white). Source: Archivi di UrbaNa - Urbanistica Napoli, via www.comune.napoli.it

Chapter 2

Figure 2.3

Naples Business Centre. 2019. Source: Wikimedia Commons by Antuang, https://commons.wikimedia.org/wiki/File:Centro_direzionale_di_Napoli.jpg,https://creativecommons.org/licenses/by-sa/4.0/deed.en

of the local public administrations of the time relative to urban projects, can be traced in the aforementioned case of the new Business Centre. Pivotal to the entire urban plan elaborated between the late 1960s and the early 1970s, and a revolutionary intervention for the East Naples, the Business Centre project was, however, also an exemplary case of wasteful use of land resources in the name of political and economic profit. Francesco Erbani writes:

> The Business Centre flaunts itself, to anyone who arrives in Naples by train, with its mirrored glass skyscrapers of fantastical geometry. It is a kind of disguise, an optical illusion that baffles the visitor, causing him to think that a piece of Chicago has moved to the foot of Vesuvius (Erbani 1998, p. 106).

The theoretical foundations of the new project were outlined in a report of 1965, in which it was argued that 'alongside the existing commercial and industrial developments, alongside those of the port, of the heads of the major motorway nodes, the development of tertiary activities must be at the

The Roots of Deindustrialisation

forefront, directional, touristic', to make sure that 'Naples [comes] to assume the logical physiognomy of a centre with mainly tertiary functions, as is logical in a system so large and at a higher economic level' (Municipality of Naples 1967).[6] The general objective, subsequently taken up by the Plan approved in 1972, was to complete the economic development of the city through a new boost to services. Thus, the project drawn up from 1967 by the real estate company Mededil,[7] and approved in December 1971 (Municipality of Naples 1999, p. 138), extended geographically over a wide area of about 110 hectares located between the Central Station of Naples and the Poggioreale district. This was a formerly marshy area, reclaimed and occupied by some large industrial activities and the public slaughterhouse of Poggioreale. Skyscrapers were to soar out of this land, intended to accommodate public and private offices and city courts, flanked by new houses (fifteen per cent of the total area) and commercial activities (Municipality of Naples 1999, pp. 103–04, p. 138). In addition to facilitating the tertiary processes of the city, the new management centre would have a further function: it was, at the time, a priority to decongest the old administrative centre and the ancient lawcourts situated in the historic centre of Naples, now saturated and unsuitable for the needs of a metropolis in continuous expansion. Superficially, the demand for new structures made the urgency palpable, as in these words pronounced by the urban planning bureau on the project in 1967: 'it is necessary, in short, to begin today, without waiting for the GDP with its provisions to determine the provisions of land use' (Municipality of Naples, 1967). This expression of haste manifests a cynical way of looking at urban planning: the priority, here, is to anticipate long planning times to facilitate individual projects by relying on political support. In this specific case, the entire municipal council agreed with the strategy, or almost all of it.

As futuristic and necessary as the project may have seemed, in the immediate future a voice from the chorus resounded forcefully in the corridors of power – that of Antonio Iannello. Architect, provincial secretary of the

---

6   Municipality of Naples, *Resolution of proposal on the location of the new Palace of Justice and for a variant of town planning concerning the overall area concerned with the explanatory report of the Assessor avv. Alberto Servidio [Deliberation by the Municipal Council on the location of the new Palace of Justice and for a modification of the General Urban Plan, concerning the entire area, with an Illustrated report by Councilor law. Alberto Servidio]*, 1967. Urbana Archives (herein. UrbArc), Iannello Collection (herein Ianco), 225/a.

7   Società edilizia mediterranea Spa, formed in 1963. In the second half of the 1970s, IRI (the Italian State) took over up to 99% of its shares (Cardillo 2006, p. 39).

Chapter 2

Republican Party from 1965 to 1968, tireless political activist and environmentalist, he collaborated with WWF, *Italia Nostra*[8] (of whose Neopolitan section he was President from 1973 to 1985, Regional President from 1976 and Secretary-General from 1985 to 1990), the Legal Committee on Ecological Defence and many other institutions: over the course of forty years of battling, Antonio Iannello gave national resonance to the great issues of the city of Naples and Southern Italy, from land speculation to illegal building, from pollution to the relationship between city and industry. Iannello died on 2 May 1998, leaving a rich legacy to Italian environmentalism, one of whose founding fathers he is accounted (Erbani 1998, pp. 105–11); and a rich archive of documentation accumulated and catalogued during his frenetic campaigning, today preserved in the Iannello archival collection, located in the Naples Archives of Urban Planning. Here may be found numerous articles and documents, concerning, among other issues, the public discussion and the project for the new Executive Centre, between the end of the 1960s and the early 1970s. On this issue, Iannello's position was inflexible:

> The history of the Business Centre… is emblematic of a distorted way of evaluating the development of the city … Two souls face each other. The soul of profit and slave of waste, wedded to the realisation of the new for its own sake, on the one hand; and, on the other, a new development model based on the conservation and utilisation of existing resources (Iannello 1974).[9]

In addition to serving as secretary of the Republican Party, in these years Iannello was invited by Michele Martuscelli, General Director of Urban Planning, to participate in sessions of the Superior Council for Public Works and verification investigations on the ground for the spatial planning of the new GDP, which would be approved in 1972, and in which there were hopes of including too the project drawn up by Mededil for the Executive Centre. In the halls of a municipal council obsessed with the immediate approval of the project there was a 'very different … attitude' from 'the republican exponents (the arch. Ianniello [*sic*] and prof. De Luca), which instead required that all discussion on the Business Centre return to the starting point, so as to be considered within the framework of the restructuring of the entire urban area'

---

[8] Among the first associations openly aimed at the protection of the environment in Italy, founded in 1955 (Corona 2015, pp. 80–85).

[9] Based on an undated typescript entitled *The New Business Center of the City of Naples and the New Court*, signed by Antonio Iannello, as secretary of the Ecological Defense Legal Committee. On the basis of this and the references cited in the text, it can be said that the drafting of the text was certainly later than 1974. UrbArc, IanCo, 125/o.

The Roots of Deindustrialisation

(*La Cronaca di Napoli*, 21 July 1967).[10] The position of the two republican exponents was based on fear of endorsing a purely speculative operation. Professor Giulio De Luca, one of the editors of the new GDP and Professor of Architecture (teaching colleague of Iannello) at the University of Naples 'Federico II' (Erbani 1998, p. 105), was against the location of the Business Centre close to the Poggioreale district, a choice that would exacerbate the congestion of the city and would, in fact, sentence to death the industrial activities of the neighbourhood. In other words, the Business Centre would have produced large profits only for real estate companies able to speculate on the surplus value accruing to the surrounding land, companies, not surprisingly, according to De Luca, owned by the consortium that had drawn up the project, Mededil (De Luca, 1967).[11]

The Business Centre project was seen as purely speculative by the Communist Party as well. For the Neapolitan communists, the priority was to protect the flagship of East Naples engineering, concentrated in the spaces adjacent to the perimeter of the project. The virtuous conditions of these activities were underlined repeatedly, both in terms of production and in terms of controlling polluting emissions. Yet, with the approval of the project, large manufacturing companies such as Aerfer would have been literally obliterated by the new office structures; others, such as Mecfond, would have lost their leading role in the local economic system. Other non-metalworking manufacturing companies in the area, such as MCM textiles, were to be razed to make room for skyscrapers. About 900 workers, mostly women, were suddenly forced into relocation or layoffs, immediately after the approval of a project that entailed the disposal of the 100,000 square metres[12] (*l'Unità*, 2 July 1972) occupied by a plant active since the 1920s. Alongside these obvious problems, the local communists also emphasised the possible worsening of road, logistical and housing conditions in the area following the realisation of a project ready to 'commit from 300 to 500 billion [lire] for a purely speculative operation, to produce five to seven million cubic metres of tertiary building destined to frighteningly aggravate the congestion of the

---

10   *La Cronaca di Napoli*, 'The council has to decide on the business centre', 21 July 1967. UrbArc, IanCo, 145 / f.

11   Letter from prof. Giulio De Luca to the director of *La Voce Regionale*, 1967. UrbArc, IanCo, 12 / a.

12   According to *l'Unità*, only male workers (170 out of about 900) obtained the guarantee of immediate reoccupation (at Alfa Sud in Pomigliano). The women, on the other hand, were laid off for a year and a half and then had to go through a 'qualification course' specifically for 'female skilled workers' before being relocated to a company in Pozzuoli.

city and to increase urban real estate income' (*l'Unità*, 30 October 1973).

How to block a project of these proportions? For Antonio Iannello, it was necessary to reveal the strictly speculative aspects, eliminating from consideration the elements universally deemed necessary, such as the construction of a new Palace of Justice. Indeed, it was Iannello's deep conviction the latter was a sort of 'smokescreen ... respectable facade of an ignoble building speculation': if the diversion – the construction of the court – was stopped, the rest of the project would collapse too, losing the political consensus necessary for approval. Three years after the approval of the project, Iannello postulated a renovation of the ancient seat of the court of Naples, Castel Capuano, and the reconversion of the adjacent buildings to create a sort of 'judicial citadel' within the historic centre of the city. In this way, on the one hand, a substantial part of the historic centre could be redeveloped and, on the other:

> [There would be] no lack of positive effects from an economic and social point of view too. In fact, the area where the Business Centre is to be built would maintain its natural destination for settlements of non-polluting manufacturing industries ... So ... the 500 billion envisaged for the Business Centre could be used to create stable jobs (Iannello 1974).

In spite of the opposition, the project continued to make progress. A variant of the Business Centre was adopted in December 1971, a few months before the approval of the new GDP, which allowed for its full implementation. Finally, the Superior Council of Public Works approved the project, though imposing as a necessary condition the halving of building volume.[13] In fact, on this occasion a thirty-year-old Iannello gave up his academic career in Architecture due to 'deep differences' with Professor Giulio De Luca, who was among the members of the Commission for the Regulatory Plan and the signatories in favour of the variant (Erbani 1998, p. 105). It was a substantial victory for the local political class which, in the opinion of the urban planner Attilio Belli, needed to quickly give signals of efficiency and effectiveness (Corona 2007, p. 63) and thus had an underlying political motivation for both the choice of settlement and the speed of the approval process for the Business Centre project. The pharaonic project would be completed only in 1995, attracting much criticism in the meantime. The variant plan still in force for the business centre was proposed in 1982 and approved in 1983,

---

13 *Note n.2 on the Business Center addressed to Director Martuscelli*, signed by Antonio Iannello, undated. UrbArc, IanCo, 169/e.

The Roots of Deindustrialisation

after the project was entrusted to the Japanese architect Kenzo Tange who revolutionised the original structure, inserting a central green axis and three pairs of buildings. At the same time, the percentage of residential construction was increased, from fifteen to thirty per cent of the total (Municipality of Naples 1999, p. 104). Yet, despite the continuous variations and changes to the initial project, it should be added that it was deliberately decided to place the most important administrative and commercial centre of the city of Naples in an area not only heavily congested with a mixture of residences, businesses and infrastructure but still so swampy that every day it is necessary to use massive mechanical drainage pumps (Chamber of Deputies, 23 September 1993).[14] This risk factor is apparently ignored by the tens of thousands of workers and residents.

Overall, it can be said that the urban planning phase of the early 1970s had contrasting effects on the territory of east Naples. The great push for housing and major infrastructure deprived the area of the few remaining vacant places and last redoubts of bogs: in the following decades, urban planning would see the error of its ways and try desperately to carve a green belt through the interior of the eastern area, to break the concrete and tarmac chain of social housing and streets. At the same time, bearing in mind that housing was a priority in those years, the planned provision of urban services and green areas remained, for the time being, a mirage. Awaiting a new boost in urban planning, which would take place at the end of the decade, the eastern suburbs knew only the greyness of cement and industrial fumes. The polluting factories, in fact, far from abandoning the urban fabric to retreat into the new zone granted them, often remained at the mercy of economic tribulations or found a way to negotiate their permanence in situ, as will be seen shortly. Certainly, the most important town planning instrument launched since the war failed to prepare the ground for a new expansion of local manufacturing: in spite of the inspiring principles of Article 18 – indeed a watershed as regards the proximity of productive activities and residences – bureaucratic uncertainties, political priorities and the balance of power between companies and institutions severely limited the rationalisation of the local industrial system. Having missed this opportunity, the effects of the economic crisis would make the profit prospects in the eastern area of Naples increasingly barren, rapidly arriving at the picture of stagnation outlined by the Cesan in 1981. Moreover,

---

14 Parliamentary question 4/17991 presented by deputy Giuseppe Gambale, 23 Sept. 1993, Digital Archives of the Italian Chamber of Deputies.

Chapter 2

Figure 2.4

Early 1980s: a public fountain in the Ponticelli district. Source: 'Dossier Periferie' in the Archivio 'Casa della Città' in Archivi di UrbaNa – Urbanistica Napoli, via http://www.comune.napoli.it

the ineffectiveness of the long-term strategic decisions of local governments is well summarised by a project, that of the Business Centre, aimed entirely at ensuring profits and consolidating political certainties in the immediate term, perhaps in the name of the dogma of tertiarisation, which was universally ascendant at the time. All this, however, was orchestrated without considering the limits and needs of the territory and the pre-existing economic system, thus ignoring the parameters of sustainability. If one accepts a definition of 'sustainability' as a defence and enhancement of an 'ecological network' comprising both natural biodiversity and the distinguishing characteristics of human society (from culture to modes of production) (Belli 2001, p. 76) it can, in short, be said that the urban expansion of East Naples in the period approaching deindustrialisation was 'unsustainable' and that the urban planning of the time could not reverse this fate. In the years immediately following, the contradictions hidden both in the character of the territory and in the limits of urban planning applications would manifest gradually until they, quite literally, exploded.

The Roots of Deindustrialisation

2.4 Unsustainable activities and pollution

Between the end of the 1960s and the 1970s, the Italian landscape was affected by environmental protection issues. The extraordinary rapidity of the industrialisation and urbanisation processes of the post-war decades had a radical impact on the eco-systemic balance of Italian territories. At the same time, changes in Italian consumption behaviour also affected the resilience of ecosystems, especially urban ones, suddenly flooded with cars, waste and polluting emissions. Atmosphere, water and soils were subjected to continuous attacks, to counteract which the first environmental associations arose: in addition to the aforementioned *Italia Nostra*, founded in 1955, 1970 saw the creation of the National Federation pro nature, followed in 1975 by the Italian Environment Fund and, in 1977, by the *Amici della Terra* (Friends of the Earth) association. In the meantime, the Ministry of the Environment was created as an autonomous institutional body in 1974, having previously been one with the Ministry of Cultural Heritage (Corona 2015, pp. 80–85, 98). At the heart of these associations' struggle was the fundamental objective of countering the paradigm of unlimited growth inherent in a development model centred on industrial production and consumer goods: a purely dissipative model from the point of view of natural and human resources. Although somewhat late in the day, compared to other countries in the north of the world, Italian public institutions also began to address the problems associated with various forms of industrial and urban pollution. National studies and reports, such as *Project 80*, which in 1971 subjected national economic planning to respect for natural resources and urban limits; or the 1973 *Report on the Environmental Situation of the Country*, which recognised the polluting impact of industrial activity and building expansion in the most densely populated areas of the country, paved the way for a new season of reform, which would culminate in the late 1980s and 1990s (Corona 2015, pp. 70–71). At the same time, though with different responsibilities and well-defined objectives, the trade unions, citizens' committees and companies themselves started to make claims and to bargain among themselves on the matters of pollution and the fight against pollution. According to Gabriella Corona, cooperation between institutions and social actors is fundamental, in order to measure the global impact of pollution on local environments and societies, through the lenses of both emotional perception and scientific knowledge of the phenomenon. In fact, in these years, the matter of pollution started to appear in surveys, research and reports, put out by local associations,

Chapter 2

research centres or the very same companies that were accused of polluting the environment. These companies had to be very careful in their reports, if they wanted to hide or reveal only the minimum of the damage caused by their factories to the health of those inhabiting the local environment. The main protagonists were the great hubs of Italian industrial development such as Gela, Syracuse, Manfredonia, Taranto, Brindisi, Bagnoli, Porto Torres, Porto Marghera-Mestre (Adorno, Serneri 2009, pp. 20-24).

The city of Naples, one of the main industrial hubs of southern Italy, inevitably ended up under investigation: among the first studies on the industrial pollution of the city, we should mention a 1971 study (which will be explored further in the coming pages) by the Zoological Station of Naples on the effects of hydrocarbon pollution on the biological state of the Gulf, and a study published in 1975 by the Institute of Hygiene of the University of Naples, on atmospheric pollution rates recorded in the two industrial areas. The eastern industrial zone was described as having a high index of dust pollution, with monthly average values equal to ten tons per square kilometre (Institute of Hygiene, 1975). With regard to citizenship, in the early 1970s the ecological awareness of the Neapolitans was burgeoning. East Naples was no exception. In San Giovanni a Teduccio, on 11 June 1972, a protest was held, which *l'Unità* reported. This event is a particularly significant testimony to the perception, perhaps still unripe but already shared, of hygienic and environmental issues. The reason for the event was to be found in the failure to cover over a stretch of a stream into which waste from local industrial production was habitually discharged. For two hours on a sunny summer day, as many as 300 demonstrators blocked Corso San Giovanni (then, as today, a crucial junction of traffic flows from the city centre to the east), demanding immediate intervention by the authorities. Inflamed by the anger and the summer heat, these men and women decided to set fire to the dozens of tyres and piles of household goods piled up on the street corners, to the point that firefighters had to come to the rescue (*l'Unità*, 2 June 1972). A year later, in another summer article dated 5 July 1973, the polluted state of the coast, besmirched by industrial waste from small and large businesses, was confirmed. Nonetheless, the author stressed the paradoxical constant presence of numerous bathers (*l'Unità*, 5 July 1973). This paradox is still alive today.

During 1973, however, the general perception of Neapolitan citizens on ecological issues was destined to undergo a radical surge, due to a cholera epidemic which caused fifteen deaths and about 120 confirmed cases between August and October of that year. The epidemic caused enormous

The Roots of Deindustrialisation

concern in the city, but above all surprise: it was not thought that such a disease could spread in an urban context with a modern sanitation and health system. Yet, if the immediate cause was the widespread consumption of raw shellfish, freshly caught from a sea often polluted by sewage and industrial discharge, the hygienic-sanitary conditions of the city of Naples were more generally precarious[15] (Treccani, 2020). Significantly, in September 1973 *l'Unità* reported, under the headline 'Poor health (in addition to mussels) causing the infection':

> We find the answer in our continuous complaints and in the constant action of the PCI and the workers to gain new health infrastructure for the citizens. The problem is called unhealthy houses (240,000 people live in Naples alone), it is called sewers, purification plants, incineration plants, efficient sanitation services, health facilities that guarantee prevention; it is still called occupation, fighting malnutrition, overcrowding, underdevelopment (*l'Unità*, 4 September 1973).

Fierce public debates and local and national reflections on causes and solutions quickly followed, but neighbourhood councils, popular struggles and other forms of bottom-up discussion also spread, helping to increase general interest in the prevention of hygiene risks in all social strata of the city. Protests demanding the covering of open-air discharges in the eastern area seemed almost daily (*l'Unità*, 17 September 1973) and the solutions proposed from below were also noteworthy: the Casa del Popolo (People's House) in Ponticelli, managed by Communist Party militants, was in fact transformed into the first vaccination centre in the city (Treccani, 2020). Overall, it can be said that in that autumn of 1973 the city came to terms with its own urban past: the deregulation of sewers, the glaring deficiencies in the water and sewage systems, the illegal landfills, the overcrowding and the expansion of deregulated construction all contributed to worsen the city's health conditions (Corona 2007, p. 4). Obviously, in industrial areas of the city, such as the eastern suburbs, the impact of emissions produced by factories compounded these issues.

Among the smaller but most widespread polluting activities in the eastern area were leatherworks, tanneries and all other activities related to the tanning process, such as woodworking or metalworking to make tools necessary for tanning. This represented a fabric of 'small businesses, but very consistent' (Recording n. 4), among the oldest manufacturing activities in the area. The

---

15. An incredible testimony of East Naples' declining hygienic, as well as social and economic, conditions at the end of the 1960s can be found in a short, mostly silent documentary (1966) by Luigi di Gianni: https://www.youtube.com/watch?v=Uls5Bkzr6rA&ab_channel=LuigiDiGianni Last accessed 18 June 2021.

Figure 2.5

The daily routine of metalworkers in a small manufactory in San Giovanni a Teduccio, 1981–1982. Source: 'Botteghe e artigiani' in the Archivio 'Casa della Città' in Archivi di UrbaNa – Urbanistica Napoli, via http://www.comune.napoli.it

Figure 2.6

A small blacksmithing manufactory in San Giovanni a Teduccio, 1981–1982. Source: 'Botteghe e artigiani' in the Archivio 'Casa della Città' in Archivi di UrbaNa – Urbanistica Napoli, via http://www.comune.napoli.it

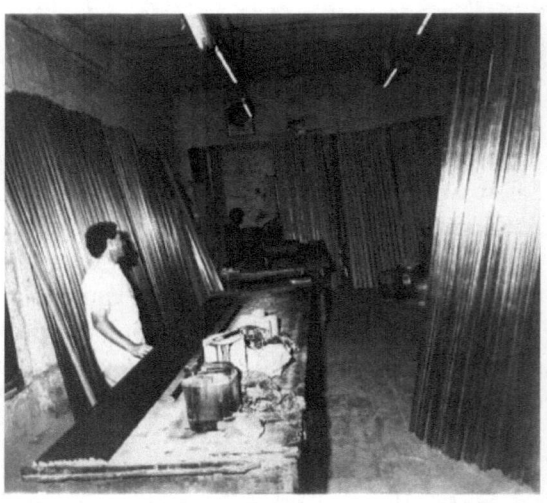

daily routine inside the tanneries was extremely intricate, including centrifuging, scraping, drying[16] and processing hides, but highly harmful to the health of the workers and equally polluting. 'I know the dye, the tannin they used and all this stuff here ... the meat that remained attached to the hides ... it all

---

16 For details on leather processing and the production of supplies for tanneries, I refer to the testimony of Giovanni Moliterno in Interview n.3 of the annex.

The Roots of Deindustrialisation

ended up in the sea' (Recording n. 3), recalls Giovanni Moliterno, who worked for about forty years in a small factory making equipment for tanneries. The discharges of hexavalent chromium, among the most toxic substances deriving from tanning plants, were mixed with other discharges, creating 'a compost, made of sewage, of leather and then of who knows what more' that gave the water a colour now grey, now 'milky white, more or less, even if faded', and exuding a peculiar stench (Recording n. 3). In the second half of the 1970s, this local craft industry, often characterised by forms of home-working akin to 'the English textile manufactories of the Industrial Revolution' (Recording n. 4), was crushed by increased external competition. In addition to the advance of the Chinese and Maghrebi markets, the Italian tanning sector was restructured in these years and the production concentrated in large hubs, such as that at Solofra in the hinterland of Campania (Recording n. 3), specially designed to accommodate forms of highly polluting activity. In terms of national legislation, moreover, in 1976 law n.319 (Merli law) on the pollution of waters was passed: it was the first legislative instrument in Italy dealing with the protection of water and it stipulated that all discharges must be subject to institutional authorisation, regardless of use or destination. In the following years, with the commissioning of public purifiers, the water purity would gain an additional protection mechanism (Corona 2015, p. 71). As evidence of the effectiveness of these tools, and the impact of the other factors described, in an interview with some workers in the Barra district, the communist newspaper *l'Unità* summarised the crisis in small tanning businesses as the loss of about 3,000 jobs in the three-year period 1975–1977 alone (*l'Unità*, 16 December 1977).

Obviously, the priority of local communists was the defence of jobs, especially during a period of crisis and especially in a party stronghold such as the eastern area of Naples, where there were between 2–3,000 members (Recording n. 4) and voting percentages between 35 and fifty per cent. Yet, faced with conditions of degradation and increasingly oppressive and widespread pollution phenomena, even the Neapolitan communists began to give priority to ecological problems. In the years that followed the communist victory at the municipal election of 1975, the new council led by the mayor Maurizio Valenzi started ongoing dialogues with local sections of the party, in order to understand and deal with environmental issues alongside labour and social issues, with particular regard to peripheral areas of the city. On one of these occasions, Nino Daniele, then secretary of the San Giovanni Teduccio section of the party, briefly explained the critical economic situation of the eastern area, marked by 'the slow and progressive dismantling of the

Chapter 2

productive apparatus, [by] the dripping away of small and medium-sized companies ... [from] the forced shift from industrial to service economy' (*l'Unità* 15 January 1977). In the immediate future, the first result of these processes was observable in the 'abandonment, the degradation, the squalor typical of the peripheral areas of the city ... and in a series of abandoned, underused and even disused productive locations (large industrial settlements, a whole series of small industries, port)', to which was added 'the absurd situation in which the neighbourhoods find themselves: absolute lack of civil structures, schools, sports equipment, services' (*l'Unità* 15 January 1977). This latter issue, which, like the state of urban services during the 1973 cholera epidemic, confirmed the shortcomings of the 1972 GDP, soon became a priority for the municipal administration and would lead to the development of the Periphery Plan, to be discussed in the following pages. More heated, problematic and immediate for the Communists, however, was the issue of the relocation of polluting factories: a matter that often pitted labour and environmental priorities against each other.

> In the industrial area there are many polluting companies: for these a presumption of permanent presence in the area must be studied very carefully. In any case, any resolution cannot ignore the interests of the workers. Take the emblematic case of Mobil Oil (*l'Unità* 15 January 1977).

The historical trajectory of East Naples Mobil Oil in the 1970s is significant due to the contrast between economic and environmental needs, and is also a nodal point in the ecological history of the area and the city. Since the 1920s, the inland areas of East Naples had been occupied by the entire supply chain of oil and petrochemical activities. The black gold was refined here and the fuel deposited in tank farms, then to be distributed through pipelines and tankers, in accordance with local, city, regional and even supra-regional needs (Recording n. 2). In the early 1970s, oil activities covered an area equal to fifteen per cent of the eastern industrial area identified by the 1972 GDP. In this context, the US multinational occupied a leading role, owning the largest refinery in terms of dimensions and output (630,000 square metres in area, with three crude oil distillation units of 7.4 million tons per year), as well as numerous auxiliary plants including a dedicated thermoelectric power plant and a 342-unit tank farm with a capacity of over a million cubic metres (MobilOil Italy, 1971).[17] Yet, from April 1968 the Italian MobilOil management was committed to putting

---

17   *Letter from MobilOil Italy to Michele Martuscelli*, 17 Feb. 1971. UrbArc, IanCo, 45/b.

The Roots of Deindustrialisation

pressure on the authorities, at every level, to obtain permission for a substantial expansion of the tank fleet and go from a capacity of one million to ten million tons per year (MobilOil Italy, 1969).[18] After a few months, the local institutions responsible for economic promotion communicated to the Ministry of Industry their sincere approval of and assent to the Mobil expansion project, as virtuous architect of a 'real development hub for the petrochemical industry of the region': a 'further expansion', it was argued, would not raise 'problems and perplexities' not even 'in relation to the fact that this expansion is taking place in an already heavily congested area' (Crpe Campania, 1968).[19]

In fact, if the localisation of these activities in the first half of the century had not had the slightest regard for the surrounding urban fabric, overlapping civil infrastructures and nearby residences, it is also true that the urban expansion of the second half of the century had done nothing but accentuate the chaotic proximity of spaces for the production, storage and distribution of oil, on the one hand, and the quotidian spaces of the Barra, Gianturco, San Giovanni and Ponticelli districts, on the other. All this should have changed with the new General Development Plan that had been in the pipeline since 1970 (approved in 1972, as mentioned). During that year, Mobil, galvanised by recent success, went so far as to ask for authorisation to expand the refinery, as well as the tank park (MobilOil Italy 1969). However, authorisation to proceed with the project depended on the decision of local territorial planning offices, and explicitly requested by the Ministry of Public Works, which had to consider the provisions of the General Development Plan on site. The answer was, of course, no:

> The oil refining plant, whose expansion is required, is located in the eastern area of the municipal area of Naples, covered by the town planning legislation in force for industrial settlements. This area, as is well known, has found itself – due to disorderly increase in building – in an unacceptably intimate contiguity with residential settlements, with serious consequences too for the very functionality of the productive areas (Regional Superintendency, 1970).[20]

No expansion was possible: on the contrary, 'the refining plant of the Italian MobilOil Society [has] such characteristics that it cannot remain in

---

18 Letter from MobilOil Italy to the Ministries of Industry and Trade, Merchant Navy and Finances, 28 July 1969. UrbArc, IanCo 99/b.

19 Letter from the Regional Comittee for the Economic Development of the Campania region to the Ministry of Industry, Trade and Craftmanship, 4 Apr. 1968. UrbArc, IanCo, 39/b.

20 Note from the Regional Superintendency for the Public Works to the Ministry of Public Works, 23 Dec. 1970. UrbArc, IanCo, 99/c.

its current location, as it is, practically inserted in the urban fabric of Naples' (Regional Superintendency, 1970). The GDP actually advanced the possibility of relocating the oil hub to an alternative point on the regional coast: the main objective, as mentioned, was once again to decongest the Neapolitan urban scene and, in doing so, free it from the 'problem of pollution ... deriving from the activity of some industries' (Regional Superintendency, 1970).

Evidently deflated and taken aback by the institutional reaction, at the beginning of 1971 Mobil tried a different path to gain authorisation for the much-needed expansion. The company management forwarded to the Director General of Urban Planning, Michele Martuscelli, a study on protection from the various forms of pollution produced by its refinery, published a few months earlier in the *Inquinamento* magazine. The author of the essay was the engineer Carlo Funel, deputy director of the Mobil refinery in Naples. After briefly describing the long history of the plant and having outlined its impressive dimensions and equipment, Funel tackled the issue of atmospheric pollution produced by the plant: everything was under control, according to the engineer, thanks to the 'low percentage of sulphur in the fuels used' and above all thanks to 'the prevailing winds' (MobilOil Italy, 1971). Neither, with regard to water pollution was there any need to worry, given that the company had in the pipeline the creation of drainage trenches to prevent the infiltration of hydrocarbons into aquifers, disposal systems for refrigeration water and for ballast water from oil tankers, networks of drainage channels and many other measures (MobilOil Italy, 1971). A few months later, however, the 'ecological' line adopted by the company suffered a severe blow, with the publication of the aforementioned study by the Zoological Station of Naples, dated 6 April 1971, on the state of water pollution by hydrocarbons in the Gulf. The biological state of the Gulf of Naples was described in terms of an unhealthy meeting of a whitish patina from the steel hub of west Naples and the black oily patina resulting from oil discharges from the port and the eastern area. As regarded the dangers of hydrocarbon water pollution, the Station's report did not limit itself to highlighting, on a technical level, how the spread of benzopyrene had harmful consequences for marine flora and fauna: it also developed an analysis aimed at briefly demonstrating how a possible expansion of refining activities would bring with it a further expansion of the tank fleet and a greater number of oil tankers in the port. The logical culmination of this vicious circle was, in these years, clearly visible in the eyes of the world due to the resonance assumed by the *Torrey Canyon* disaster,

The Roots of Deindustrialisation

the case of a BP super tanker that sank off Cornwall in 1967 (Zoological Station of Naples, 1971).[21]

In addition to playing up the ecological legitimacy of its plans, Mobil also adopted more unscrupulous strategies to put pressure on local and national institutions. In March 1971, the local situation must have caused some irritation in the upper echelons of the company. Not only had the refinery expansion project not yet been approved but news had come that the new General Development Plan in the pipeline intended to transform a substantial part (150,000 square metres) of the newly expanded tank park into public spaces, for activities, public green spaces or parking. The idea of losing even the new storage spaces was unbearable, so the company decided to counterattack with a coup, the first in a long series. After having described the situation to local and national authorities 'perhaps in too much detail', the company threatened to relocate most of its own oil tanks to another Italian location (MobilOil Italy, 1971),[22] implying a gradual disengagement from Naples. This threat was far from vain and actually had the desired effect of causing panic high up in national institutions. For the Ministry of Industry and IRI, at the head of the Italian economic system, the priorities were obvious:

> For the oil distribution and production system, it is essential that the Neapolitan area has an adequate refinery, refining capacity and distribution system. We must also find a solution that guarantees the continuance of this activity in the Neapolitan area. I believe that, given the levels of consumption in the Neapolitan area ... the risk of losing the refinery may not exist ... If we were to verify that there is no possibility of conciliation, that the risks for the economic structure ... are serious ... we should meet again to resolve the matter with a different kind of solution (High Council for Public Works, 1971).[23]

In other words, while viewing favourably a possible conciliation between the needs of the company and the urban and ecological needs of the area, the strategic importance of the Mobil hub made it an absolute priority for the proper performance of the local production system. In addition to the city and regional energy needs,[24] it had to be borne in mind that the number of

---

21 *Letter from prof. Carrada, director of the Zoological Station of Naples, to the High Council for Public Works*, 17 Apr. 1971. UrbArc, IanCo, 99/b.

22 *Letter from MobilOil to the Urban Planning Board and the Superintendency for Public Works*, 1 Mar. 1971. UrbArc, IanCo, 45/b.

23 The opinion was expressed by Giovanni Landriscina, general manager for the implementation of the Iri Economic Planning. *High Council for Public Works extraordinary meeting report*, 10 May 1971. UrbArc, IanCo, 99 / c.

24 These needs were abundantly satisfied, according to *Italia Nostra*, to the point that most of the refined oil was destined for exports. *Italia Nostra* press release, 18 July 1971. UrbArc, IanCo, 99 / d.

Chapter 2

Neapolitan companies alone with working and commercial relations with the refinery was 'about fifty, among which were ten civil construction companies ... seventeen metalworking companies ... five electromechanical companies ... twelve painting, cleaning, thermal insulation firms and... six firms with significant business relations'(Grippo 1971, p. 64). Such a circulation of wealth could not be questioned, so the Minister of Industry, Silvio Gava, personally urged the General Urban Planning Directorate to make its definitive resolution on Mobil's request for expansion known 'urgently'. (Ministry of Industry, 1971).[25] The use of this kind pressure was unbearable for environmental associations such as *Italia Nostra*, which said 'we [are][once again witnessing politics on a case-by-case basis as a fall-back to the lack of a binding economic planning and urban planning, both nationally and regionally' (*Italia Nostra*, 1971). Yet, in spite of all the power play going on, the position of the General Urban Planning Directorate was immovable: 'this Administration cannot fail to confirm its point of view ... according to which, for obvious reasons of an urban, hygienic and environmental nature the restructuring and expansion of the current Mobil refinery, located in the old industrial area of Naples, as proposed by the Company, cannot be considered admissible'. The necessary energy supply could be secured by relocation to 'another area that is able to accommodate the new plants of the refinery ... within the Campania region' (Urban Planning Board, 1971).[26] In practice, completely turning the Mobil threat on its head, the proposal entailed not only a different location for the Mobil refinery but, as regarded the related industries and the network of dependent companies, a first step towards the delocalisation of the entire oil area and a substantial part of the industrial activity of East Naples. The stakes were obviously much higher than the expansion of a single company but, between 1971 and 1972, the territorial planning bodies diligently tried to identify the most suitable area to accommodate oil activities, finally tracing this to a place near the mouth of the Volturno river, to the north of Naples. On 4 April 1972, the regional administration signed off the transfer of the refinery from Naples (Iannello, 1972).[27]

Nonetheless, in mid-1973 the relocation was still entirely on paper. In-

---

25 *Phonogram by the Ministry of Industry and Trade to the Ministry for Public Works*, 14 June 1971. UrbArc, IanCo, 99/c.

26 *Letter from the Urban Planning Board to the Ministry of Budget and Planning*, 24 July 1971. UrbArc, Iannello collection, 99/c.

27 *Typescript by Antonio Iannello on the Mobil refineries' delocalisation*, 11 Jan. 1972. UrbArc, IanCo, 91/h.

The Roots of Deindustrialisation

evitably, problems had arisen regarding the construction of infrastructure capable of connecting the Volturno area to the port of Naples, the main logistical hub for petroleum products, and to the rest of the region (High Council for Public Works, 1973).[28] Furthermore, evidently alarmed by the delays, the Neapolitan section of *Italia Nostra*, in those years directed by Antonio Iannello, strongly denounced 'the inertia of the competent public administrations', raising 'the suspicion' that the entire relocation operation could be 'postponed indefinitely' (*Italia Nostra*, 1973).[29] From the point of view of central institutions, however, the priority in this transition phase was to give a sign of stability to local oil companies, to prevent a definitive flight of capital that could have brought the entire regional industrial system to its knees. Thus, while studies and preliminary works for the relocation project were still in progress, the Ministry of Industry decided to act decisively: the old concession to operate the Mobil refinery expired at the beginning of 1973 and the Ministry extended its terms for another twenty years. However, this was not an about-face on the relocation projects, given that permission for the much-debated on-site expansion of the plant was absolutely not granted; rather, it was a solution perceived (or advertised) as temporary, pending progress of the project signed-off in April of the previous year (MobilOil Works Councils, 1975).[30] That progress was minimal, such that in October 1975 the situation was still unchanged. That month, however, something unusual happened:

> The SAGRAF was only tens of metres from the refinery. I won't tell you about the alarms I've heard over the course of my working life. Every now and then the sirens could be heard. I remember one in particular, where there was a fume leak and many of my colleagues fainted or got sick. *Je rimanett'allerta* ['I endured it without problems'] in such circumstances. It is an occurrence that has always accompanied and accompanies production (Recording n. 2).

As testified by Vincenzo Morreale, in a congested context such as that of the East Naples Industrial Zone, toxic fumes must have often been on the agenda in those years. However, those of October 1975 must have been exceptionally harmful and frequent if the District Court of Barra was forced to open an investigation after repeated complaints by workers suffering from

---

28 Note by the High Council for Public Works concerning the relocation of the refinery of Naples, 17 July 1973. UrbArc, IanCo, 99/b.

29 *Italia Nostra*, Naples branch, press release, 16 Nov. 1973. UrbArc, IanCo, 119/s.

30 *Letter from MobilOil Works Councils to MobilOil management, to the regional administration and to the Municipality of Naples*, 31 Oct. 1975. UrbArc, IanCo, 45/b.

Chapter 2

sudden illness. Initially, the magistrate sent judicial notices to the directors of Mobil, Snia and other factories on site, showing the difficulty in determining liability of this sort in an area literally saturated with polluting plants. At the same time, the scientific expertise was entrusted to the Faculty of Industrial Chemistry of the University of Naples. The reaction of Mobil management was, however, revealing. In the previous months, the company had allocated substantial capital, seven billion lire, for the construction of water purification and air depollution plants (*l'Unità*, 10 October 1975).[31] This capital and these projects were anything but progressing, indeed were temporarily blocked. In October 1975, however, the right opportunity arose to make the investment payoff: the necessary anti-pollution equipment would be installed, in fact, 'on the condition that the planned relocation of the company would not be implemented at least for a certain number of years' (De Tilla, 19 October 1975).[32] This was a species of 'ecological blackmail', the costs of which would have been paid not only by the 1,500 workers at the plant but by about 200,000 people including inhabitants and workers of the eastern area. This was the harsh indictment of Maurizio de Tilla, a Neapolitan lawyer and environmental activist, in the pages of the daily newspaper *Il Roma*. De Tilla attached to the article the atmospheric readings conducted by the astrophysicists of the Capodichino Observatory, whose instruments were compromised by the fumes produced by the refinery; and the chemical analysis of pollutants in the water discharge from refinery processing carried out by the University of Naples. Nonetheless, Mobil's blackmail was effective.

'Nobody talks about relocation anymore', was the headline in the newspaper *La Voce di Napoli* (24 October 1975).[33] Indeed, a few weeks later the Regional Committee for Atmospheric Pollution granted Mobil authorisation to proceed with the allocation of the aforementioned seven billion, to the construction of an incinerator furnace for sludge and a water purification plant. *Italia Nostra* gave immediate warning, supported by the WWF and the Committee for the defence of the environment, as the solution adopted appeared partial, premature and, above all, as striking the death knell for any relocation project. The decision of the Committee, supported by studies

---

31 *l'Unità* editorial, 'Judicial communications for pollution cases', 10 Oct. 1975. UrbArc, IanCo, 45 / b.
32 M. De Tilla, 'The Mobil affair is getting more and more nebulous', *Il Roma*, 19 Oct. 1975. UrbArc IanCo, 99 / g.
33 *La Voce di Napoli* editorial, 'The blackmail of Mobil', 24 Oct. 1975. UrbArc, IanCo, 99 / g.

The Roots of Deindustrialisation

carried out at the provincial and municipal level, finally managed to guarantee Mobil a much-needed ecological legitimacy, the last step needed to definitively sink the relocation project. Not surprisingly, the solution to the long argument over the shifting of oil activities seemed to public opinion 'a responsible and competent decision that cuts short the speculations and controversies born out of ignorance of objective facts' (Grasso, 2 November 1975).[34] Mobil employees themselves showed their lack of confidence in relocation projects as a 'real alternative', capable of guaranteeing 'employment certainty for 1,500 jobs plus related employees': confidence in the permanence of activities on site was instead strengthened by apparently sudden 'realisation of effective environmental protection systems [which] can allow us to continue the discussion of Mobil's stay in Naples'.[35] Nonetheless, Mobil workers clearly expressed the requirement for further investment in anti-pollution measures, especially the urgent need to modernise older structures, such as the distillate treatment plants whose construction dated back to 1939. Through these interventions it would be possible, according to the workers, to give the local oil hub a positive role again, finally removing the spectre of delocalisation, overcoming those 'ambiguities still existing about the territorial structure of the eastern area, affirming the validity of the permanence of the existing industries in the place they currently occupy' (MobilOil Works Councils, 1975).[36]

In the following years, the company's priorities would prove themselves far from these principles. Undoubtedly thanks to the global effects of the oil crisis, Mobil's investment strategies in the second half of the 1970s clearly aimed at 'achieving reasonable profit margins': which, in other words, resulted in constant attempts to circumvent the failure of the plan to expand the refinery by means of individual requests for authorisation to build new plants (MobilOil Italy, 28 July 1976).[37] Obstructed again by environmental associations (World Wildlife Fund, 30 November 1976)[38] and by repre-

---

34 L. Grasso, 'Yes to the Mobil facility', *il Mattino*, 2 Nov. 1975. UrbArc, IanCo, 99 / g.

35 In spite of the touted urgency of the intervention, in April 1977 the wastewater treatment plants had not yet been completed. *Letter from the MobilOil Works Councils to the regional administration and the Municipality of Naples*, 22 Apr. 1977. UrbArc, IanCo, 45 / b.

36 *Letter from MobilOil Works Councils to MobilOil management, to the regional administration and to the Municipality of Naples*, 31 Oct. 1975. UrbArc, IanCo, 45/b.

37 *Letter from the MobilOil Italy management to the Ministry of Industry, Trade and Crafts*, 28 July 1976. UrbArc, IanCo, 45/b.

38 *Letter from the WWF to the Public Authorities*, 30 Nov. 1976. UrbArc, IanCo, 45/b.

sentatives of public institutions, who emphasised the possible worsening of pollution and congestion conditions in the area (MobilOil Italy, 4 March 1977),[39] the company resorted to all necessary means, threatening employment cuts (MobilOil Italy, 25 January 1977),[40] legal action, divestments (MobilOil Italy, 4 March 1977) and finally even the permanent closure of the refinery, in order to obtain the necessary authorisation for expansion projects. Mobil managers did not even want to hear the word 'expansion': for engineer Funel, director of the refinery, the company had to 'survive' through the general crisis. This was the ultimate rhetorical legitimisation. Through these manoeuvres and this type of rhetoric, the company was able to force political parties and local authorities, finally obtaining the much-needed permission, in July 1977. The only limitations imposed by local authorities were in confirming the terms of the concession, extended by twenty years in 1973, thus expiring in 1993, and in subjecting polluting plants to checks at five-year intervals (Troise, 5 July 1977).[41]

Nevertheless, the WWF did not give up, primarily thanks to the activism of de Tilla, according to whom the new expansion projects were 'actually criminal' if one considered the further introduction of toxic substances into the atmosphere 'in an already heavily polluted area', close to which new popular districts had been built or under construction (*il Mattino* 26 April 1977).[42] The consequences of the increased air toxicity would, in fact, be paid for by the inhabitants of the eastern area, especially in the new residential complex of Ponticelli (which 'started life as an unhealthy ghetto'), by the future employees of the new Business Centre, not far from the Mobil perimeter, and in already scarce and polluted city water resources, without taking into account the further submission of the entire infrastructural network (roads, ports and railways) to the needs of a single company. Far from being an emergency, continued De Tilla, these were the general realities of a company that, in 1977, exported about a third of the Naples' refinery output: 'its strengthening, therefore, is equivalent to inflicting on the city very heavy

---

39 *Letter from the MobilOil management to the Ministry of Public Accounts and Economic Planning*, 4 Mar. 1977. UrbArc, IanCo, 45/b.

40 *Letter from the MobilOil management to the president of the regional administration*, 25 Jan. 1977. UrbArc, Iannello collection, 45/b.

41 S. Troise, 'Mobil modernization approved, capital of former Merrell increased', *l'Unita*, 5 July 1977. UrbArc, IanCo, 99 / g.

42 'Mobil projects: why the World Fund for Nature is opposed', *il Mattino* editorial, 26 Apr. 1977. UrbArc, IanCo, 99 / g.

The Roots of Deindustrialisation

damage from which it derives no advantage', for the exclusive benefit of the 'poor oilmen' (De Tilla, 4 August 1977).[43]

A few days later, on 7 August 1977, the risks associated with the embeddedness of oil activities in the urban fabric of eastern Naples suddenly manifested themselves to the public. A liquid gas tank filled beyond the safety limit exploded in the perimeter of a small petrochemical factory adjacent to the MobilOil factories, injuring a worker. 'The whole city could have blown up', screamed *il Roma*'s headline, if the rapid intervention of the fire brigade had not prevented the spread of the flames through the oil area (Bruzzano, 8 August 1977).[44] Not surprisingly, the Mobil fire inspector stated:

> At any moment, the gas tanks could have exploded and then there would have been nothing more to be done: all the fire-fighting measures even at the Mobil refinery would have been useless. There would be chain explosions for a huge radius ... The entire district of San Giovanni a Teduccio could have been destroyed by a terrible explosion if the intervention of the fire brigade and the Mobil firefighting team had not been swift (*il Roma*, 8 August 1977).[45]

The presence of immense deposits of highly flammable material in the urban heart of the eastern suburbs would soon reveal itself for what it was: an immense powder keg, ready to explode. In a discourse on historically relevant dynamics, however, two aspects must be emphasised. In the first place, the story of MobilOil confirms the role played by the oil area in eastern Naples: an unmovable strategic priority, closely linked to economic needs and local political balance (and beyond), therefore a 'cursed resource' for the area, which was wholly subjected to external interests. Since the 1972 GDP, which, as we have seen, provided for the transformation of part of the Mobil concession into a green area and urban services, much needed in the area, the economic interests of the oil companies manifested their real power, by exploiting the 'military' condition of an area that was historically removed from public jurisdiction, because of its strategic importance for the local industrial system: in the following decades, Neapolitan urban planning would come back to deal with the 'cesspool', as will be seen. In the immediate future, the mechanism behind the failure to relocate oil activities during the 1970s, far from being unique in local or national history, can be traced

---

43   *Letter from Maurizio de Tilla, on behalf of the Wwf, to Antonio Iannello*, 4 Aug. 1977. UrbArc, IanCo, 91/h.

44   G. Bruzzano, 'Flames in a liquid gas depot. The whole city could have blown up', *il Roma*, 8 Aug. 1977. UrbArc, IanCo, 91 / g.

45   'Factory workers were the first to flee', *il Roma* editorial, 8 Aug.1977. UrbArc, IanCo, 91 / g.

Chapter 2

back to that 'blackmail of the emergency', identified by Vezio de Lucia in his analysis of urban planning anomalies in Italy during the post-war years. What is striking in the adoption of this mechanism by Mobil is the exploitation of the same slogans pervading the contemporary atmosphere of economic crisis (explicit in the word 'survival', as a socially acceptable alternative for 'enlargement'): the 'risk of deindustrialisation' is flanked, however, by 'ecological risk'. Mobil also exploited the emerging ecological discourse, now recognised as an undeniable source of legitimacy, bending it repeatedly to the interests of the company. This assumed legitimacy took advantage of the local context and the effects of the 1973 cholera outbreak on Neopolitans' levels of ecological and health awareness, in addition to national and international transformations. In this way, the company artfully constructed its 'emergencies'. Perhaps inevitably, these artificial 'emergencies' of economic interests soon gave way to actual ecological risks, long ignored and anchored to the contradictions of eastern Naples.

3.
ASSESSING THE RISKS.

3.1 Between human disasters and responses

'With the concept of "constructed" risk, we want to recall the need to go beyond the defence of nature, to acquire the awareness that it is above all necessary to defend oneself from the unforeseen effects of human action, that is, from the risks that we ourselves build with our own hands' (Belli 2001, p. 75). The events reconstructed in this section, the earthquake of 1980 and the explosion of Agip tanks in 1985, can be traced back to this specific meaning of risk: an anthropogenic risk, generated by human deficiencies. Whether it is an unexpected accident, an underestimated dynamic or trends ignored in the long or short term, even with the advancement of technology and scientific awareness, in these cases humans expose themselves to danger. If we want to categorise the nature of the 'risk', the second case, the explosion of 1985, is more direct: it is the result of the dynamics described in previous pages, which can be summarised as a more or less voluntary disregard for the obvious risk linked to the proximity of oil activities to the urban fabric, despite continuing contrary opinions. An equally constant attempt to legitimise this neglect emerges from its reconstruction in the name of 'strategic priorities', the 'risk of deindustrialisation', employment or a tailor-made ecological science. The explosion of Agip deposits in 1985 unfortunately dramatically unmasked this kind of rhetoric, suddenly revealing the actual characteristics of the risk associated with the oil area. The explosion was also a highly symbolic moment for local citizens: it offered a violent and indelible image of the economic, ecological and social decline of its community and environment. The first case, the earthquake, involves a more complex and systemic meaning of 'risk', built gradually, brick by brick, over the course of about a century of intensive land consumption, wild and deregulated urbanisation and deficiencies in the provision of urban services. For the eastern area, as for the entire city, the earthquake served as a watershed, amplifying and accelerating structural fragilities or producing new ones: the issues of territorial degradation, housing conditions, productive dynamics and social structure were none of them immune to the effects of the cataclysm. The earthquake, in other words, was a litmus test that allowed us to observe the structural fragility of Naples' urban environment, and its eastern periphery in particular. However, the earthquake was also the event that allowed a new urban planning phase to blossom.[1] Mindful of limits, obstacles and contradictions, the urban planners forged by the earthquake season would try to propose a different model of urban environment in the suburbs, attentive to the enhancement of urban environments and living conditions. This model would lead to the drafting of projects for the systemic redevelopment of the suburbs in the nineties. For East Naples, this new way of thinking about the urban environment can be traced back to the development of the Suburban Plan.

The victory of the Communist Party in the 1975 local elections brought new social and economic issues to the fore in the Neapolitan city context. The policies that had to emerge from the economic recession had to be based, for the PCI, on fighting parasitism and privileges, on resolving social and territorial inequalities and on reversing the ecological problems produced by the capitalist dogma of unlimited development. These themes were particularly appreciated by the new cohort of young Neapolitan urban planners, already inspired by the great mobilisations to develop housing and health services in the period of cholera. An idea of territory as a 'resource to be valued rather than consumed', no longer 'a place of waste and robbery', but a heritage 'to be converted productively', made its way into the minds of the new urban planners, and took shape in the preliminary study for the 'Framework Plan for Urban Services' (1976). The first step in this urban planning project was a precise assessment of building plots in the entire urban environment of Naples. The objective was to solve, once and for all, the problem of the shortage of amenities, services and green areas already quantified by the 1972 Plan as a deficit of 2,000 hectares over the whole city (Corona 2007, p. 40, p. 55). The preliminary studies conducted by *the boys* of the Urban Planning Office at the end of the 1970s also revealed intolerable conditions of urban degradation –

---

1   In *I Ragazzi del Piano. Napoli e le ragioni dell'ambientalismo urbano*, Gabriella Corona has sketched a wide historical overview of the last quarter of the Neapolitan twentieth century through the experiences, testimonies and work of the cohort of urban planners, sociologists and geographers active in town planning from the late 1970s to the 1990s. The image of the city that emerges from the oral testimonies of this group, the analysis of political and social paths and natural transformations suffered by the territory is fiercely critical of the generalisations and stereotyped representations that still oppress the image of Naples today, instead offering a historical perspective that, starting from virtuous planning, allows the identification of operational elements aimed at the environmental sustainability of the Neapolitan urban ecosystem.

Assessing the Risks

housing, social and economic – concentrated in the suburbs of Naples. The crowding and population density of suburban centres were found to be higher than the city centre. The situation was aggravated by the systematic shortage of equipment and services, including sanitation, as well as by the low incomes of families (Corona 2007, pp. 75–80). In this general picture, the eastern area leapt to the attention of urban planners for its complex and chaotic reality, made up of industrial agglomerations, social housing districts, rare pockets of surviving agriculture, Vesuvian villas, new building projects (Ring road, Business Centre, residential buildings) and some early abandoned areas. The citizens of East Naples themselves called loudly for new social spaces, green areas and cultural structures, in other words, more modern districts, able to 'elevate the quality of life', but also to grant the most essential services.

> A large part of the area lacked sub-services; some roads were without sewerage and the existing sewers were old and obsolete; many roads had no street lighting and some were even impassable; the districts [popular] were in a state of frightening degradation; the citizens did not know what a square metre of green space meant; finally the citizens of the [popular] districts had never known what it meant to have a tap for drinking water in the house as they had always used public fountains (Municipality of Naples 1988).

This is the memory of the state of degradation of the San Giovanni a Teduccio district at the end of the 1970s. The new communist council was preparing, then, to define a historic turning point, with a rehabilitation plan for twelve districts of the outskirts of the city. The 'First Plan for Urban Recovery' in Naples, as the Suburban Plan was institutionally called, was approved on 16 April 1980 (Vicinanza, 18 April 1980). Its starting point was in the so-called 'historic centres' of the suburbs:

> The innovative element ... was to concentrate on the redevelopment of urban features in areas of the periphery. However, in this area the 'periphery' ... also meant ancient villages of eighteenth-century and rural origin. Places inhabited without interruption from their foundation until today ... We must consider the difficulty of re-reading these places that have transformed over time into the suburbs we know today as a result of everything going on around them: from public and private building districts, to uses of all kinds (motorway junctions, warehouses, parking lots, shopping centres), illegal construction, etc. This urban disorder had ended up completely emptying these villages, these hamlets, of value, thus rendering them the periphery of the periphery. There were no more degraded places in the suburbs than these: poor, unhealthy, left to fend for themselves. In the photographs of the time, we see not only the deterioration of buildings but the miserable conditions in which these people lived. The original historical centres had dissolved due to neglect and decay; it is easy to think that such a reality should be 'healed' by demolishing everything, erasing all traces and starting again. Exactly the opposite of the principle affirmed with the Suburban Plan – namely

Chapter 3

```
Rione Vecchia Villa. Alcune famiglie alloggiate in roulottes per
il crollo di un fabbricato. Queste sono le conseguenze delle "scel-
te" urbanistiche della Democrazia Cristiana che hanno ridotto al
l'estremo degrado il patrimonio edilizio della periferia.
```

Figure 3.1

A picture taken in San Giovanni a Teduccio by the local communists. March 1980. Comment above: 'Vecchia Villa neighborhood. Some families have been relocated in roulottes after a building collapse. Those are the consequences of urban planning "choices" supported by the Democrazia Cristiana party, which led to the extreme degradation of buildings in the peripheral areas.' Source: from the private collection of Vincenzo Morreale: Partito Comunista Italiano, Sezioni di San Giovanni a Teduccio. 1980. Dossier 1980. S. Giovanni a Teduccio: un quartiere che cambia. Napoli.

> the recovery of what already existed ... We start from there, with the idea of restoring these areas, replacing where necessary,[2] but safeguarding the urban fabric, avoiding new buildings that are isolated and unrelated to the context (Recording n. 5).

---

2   On the legal level, the Plan for the Peripheries proposed an interesting experiment, trying to integrate the norms of the old law n. 167 of 1962 with the new objectives of the law 8/5/1978 n.457 in the matter of *Norms for the residential building*: the latter provided for public financing of the construction of new houses or of the rehabilitation of public buildings. The redevelopment of the existing housing stock was entrusted to private individuals, while the municipalities would play a coordinating role. The law was, however, considered inapplicable, in these terms, in Naples, due to the complex urban and socio-economic fabric, the lack of cooperation by private individuals with the public and the gravity of the housing issue in the suburbs. It was then integrated with the area plans outlined by Law 167, which favoured the acquisition by the municipality of areas where economic and social housing would be built (Corona 2007, p. 81).

Assessing the Risks

Alveo Pollena. Anni e anni di lotta dei cittadini e dei comunisti di Barra, Ponticelli e S. Giovanni, con azioni talvolta dure e clamorose, hanno imposto alla cassa per il Mezzoggiorno la copertura dell'Alveo Pollena. E' una vittoria significativa per una migliore qualità della vita nella zona orientale.

Figure 3.2

Coverage of the Pollena riverbed, 1980. Comment by the local communists above: 'Pollena riverbed. After many struggles, thanks to our brave actions, we managed to force the Cassa per il Mezzogiorno to intervene, with the coverage of the Pollena riverbed. It is a significant victory towards a better quality of life in the eastern districts of Naples.' Source: from the private collection of Vincenzo Morreale: Partito Comunista Italiano, Sezioni di San Giovanni a Teduccio, 1980. Dossier 1980. S. Giovanni a Teduccio: un quartiere che cambia. Napoli.

The historical centres of the eastern suburbs, from the early months of 1980, began to accommodate the first construction sites: it started with services (schools, areas for sport), essential equipment (renovations to the sewer system, water connections, covering drains), then moving on to the urban green (Italian Communist Party 1980, pp. 7–24). Overall, in the eastern area, the Suburban Plan involved about 600,000 square metres and over 9,000 residents directly involved in the new structures (Municipality of Naples 1980, p. 2), but its operational application coincided with the immense problems raised by the Irpinia earthquake. The cataclysm that struck Southern Italy between 23 and 24 November 1980 resulted in 280,000 displaced, about 9,000 injured and 2,914 dead. In the great southern metropolis, the uneven roads, the collapsed houses, the families without a roof were difficult to count and even more so to restore, rebuild and relocate. In Naples, in 1981, the army

Chapter 3

Figure 3.3

Piazza Pacichelli, central hub in San Giovanni a Teduccio, after its renovation. Source: from the private collection of Vincenzo Morreale: Partito Comunista Italiano, Sezioni di San Giovanni a Teduccio. 1980. Dossier 1980. S. Giovanni a Teduccio: un quartiere che cambia. Napoli.

of 'nomads of the earthquake' still amounted to about 170,000 displaced people who camped in the most disparate and desperate conditions, while there were 7,000 condemned buildings and 170 destroyed roads. A state of natural disaster was declared immediately, by the decree of 11/24/1980, and the appointment of an extraordinary commissioner was allowed. The most urgent issue was of course the immediate resolution of the housing emergency, to be achieved by extraordinary interventions such as the requisitioning of private accommodation, the conclusion of agreements with hotels and religious institutions and the preparation of container camps (Corona 2007, pp. 85–87).

In the eastern area, San Giovanni a Teduccio was the neighbourhood most affected by the earthquake with 531 families, 2,731 people, displaced and relocated to temporary structures, not counting those who took refuge with relatives and family members: twelve schools, two ships, 24 caravans, four areas provided with 138 containers and countless hotels and railway

Assessing the Risks

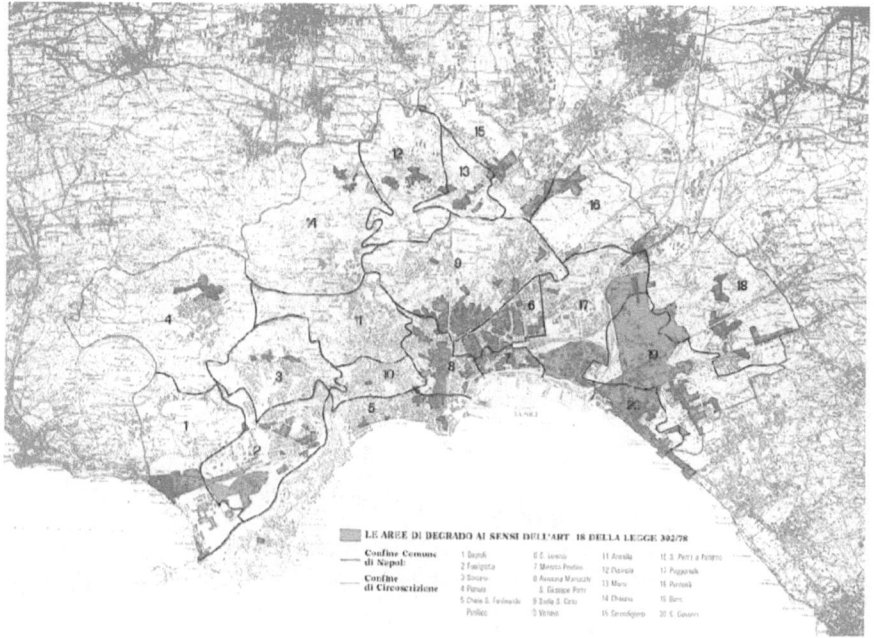

Figure 3.4

Degraded areas in the city of Naples in 1978. Most of them are clustered in the eastern districts of Poggioreale, Barra and San Giovanni. Source: Archivi di UrbaNa - Urbanistica Napoli, via www.comune.napoli.it

wagons comprised the extraordinary housing interventions for San Giovanni only. It was a 'chilling post-war scenario' (Municipality of Naples 1988, pp. 2–4) that would last for the next four years (Recording n. 5). As regards the Neapolitan suburbs in general, the extent and ambitions of the Suburban Plan would now face almost surreal obstacles, according to the experts themselves, without the availability of 'extraordinary reconstruction tools' (Corona 2007, pp. 64–65). Indeed, it could be argued that the emergency situation would surely have made ordinary planning tools obsolete, without the strong will of the administration to carry out those projects. The Suburban Plan, on the contrary, was not only confirmed but found the necessary financial support in the extraordinary intervention, namely Law 219 of 14 May 1981, on 'Organic measures for the reconstruction and development of the affected territories', of which Title VIII was dedicated to state intervention for build-

Chapter 3

Figure 3.5

Pazzigno district in the early Eighties, immediately prior to the Suburban Plan redevelopment. Source: 'Dossier Periferie' in the Archivio 'Casa della Città' in Archivi di UrbaNa – Urbanistica Napoli, via http://www.comune.napoli.it

Figure 3.6

Temporary structures in the Nuova Villa district, early Eighties: a caravan and some shacks made with metal sheets can be seen in the picture. Source: 'Dossier Periferie' in the Archivio 'Casa della Città' in Archivi di UrbaNa – Urbanistica Napoli, via http://www.comune.napoli.it

ing in Naples, called the 'Extraordinary Programme for Residential Building' (PSER). Thanks to the progressive allocation of huge public resources, which would reach 13.5 billion lire (D'Antonio 1990, p. 1216), the construction of over 20,000 dwellings and related urbanisation works in the metropolitan area of Naples, in derogation from the current town planning legislation[3] (i.e. the 1972 Plan), was intertwined with pre-existing instruments such as the Suburban Plan and the law 167 area plans. In the specific case of the eastern area, San Giovanni and Barra saw over 1,000 interventions but, thanks to the area plan of law 167, which included the construction of over

---

3   Law n. 219, 5/14/1981, on *Organic measures for the reconstruction and development of the affected territories*, art. 80.

Assessing the Risks

3,700 apartments, and the approximately 350 interventions envisaged by the Suburban Plan for its historic centre, the Ponticelli district was, in fact, the most affected area in the entire urban spectrum (Corona 2007, p. 95). In absolute figures, for the area of Ponticelli named after law 167, a commitment of 1,706,000 square metres of surface area was foreseen, equal to 3,760 new homes. In the historic centre of Ponticelli, the integral redevelopment involved an additional 134,150 square metres of area compared to the 52,544 square metres involved in recovery and renovation; 607 Ponticelli families were involved in the redevelopment interventions and 663 families in the recovery interventions. For San Giovanni and Barra, 5,600 square metres were planned for new building, equal to 36 new apartments, mostly included in the law 167 plans for three new popular districts (*Nuova Villa, Pazzigno* and *Taverna del Ferro*). The redevelopment of buildings was much more substantial, with 403,550 square metres of area involved and 1,571 families, in addition to the 123,440 square metres and 597 families of San Giovanni and Barra affected by the restoration of existing buildings (Dal Piaz 1982, pp. 18–19).

A colourful description, both of the work in progress for the PSER construction in the eastern area and of the dysfunctional and heterogeneous character of the territory, was offered in 1983 by the newspaper *la Repubblica*. The interviewee is Roberto Giannì, 'one of the relentless engines of the extraordinary programme':

> Architect Roberto Giannì describes the district of Taverna del Ferro, close to the district of San Giovanni a Teduccio, which extends along the coast to the south. We get there through a network of alleys, sudden widenings, patches of countryside, muddy areas, mountains of garbage, everywhere the leprosy of abandoned plastics, rags on the balconies, the old houses in pieces, the new houses all illegal, the chaos of typologies, the orgy of columns, of wrought iron, of the bright colours and the barracks of bins, the extreme ruin. Here, public green space does not exist, apart from that of small cemeteries ... And right here the architect Giannì, after showing the foundations for the blocks of houses that will soon begin to rise, stretches his arm outwards: 'here, from that side, a large tree-lined avenue will branch off and just to the right ... there we will create a park of ten hectares bordered by a long strip of amenities [editor's note: a parking lot, a sports field and the secondary school hub] and at the edge of the park there will be an artificial lake of about one hectare ...'. But is it all true or is the architect joking? (De Luca, 17 February 1983).

PSER's attention to school facilities, sports facilities, green areas, public areas and parking was very real, in fact, and resulted in the projection of 54,000 square metres for amenities for Ponticelli and 251,100 square metres for San Giovanni and Barra: the first quarter would thus have attained an

Chapter 3

average of twenty square meters of amenities per inhabitant, and 36 for the second (Dal Piaz 1982, p. 19). Ponticelli, on the other hand, received a park of fourteen hectares, in order to 'humanise both the ancient settlement and the lunar constructions of the 167' (De Luca, 17 February 1983). It was not a mere aesthetic or contingent choice, but the recognition of a structural deficiency in the territory of the eastern periphery. In the words of urban planner Giovanni Dispoto:

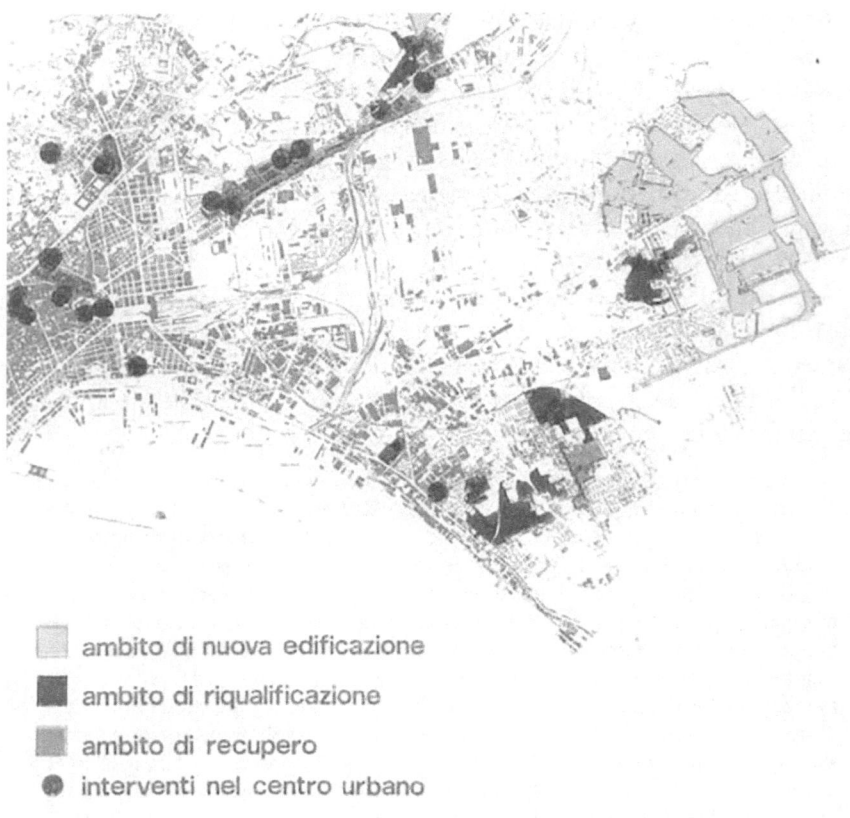

Figure 3.7

PSER areas of intervention in east Naples: new buildings will occupy light areas; existing structures in the dark areas will be demolished, as these areas will host new buildings and equipment; medium areas concern renovation programs. Source: Archivi di UrbaNa – Urbanistica Napoli, via www.comune.napoli.it

Assessing the Risks

> For the first time in our city's public planning history, all urban services (many new urban services, even for the outskirts of Naples that had previously lacked them all) had been put in place by the extraordinary programme. These services were needed, in order to satisfy the entire area's requirements. For once, even public green space was not neglected: indeed, public green and open space (courtyards, squares, streets), but more generally urban services in themselves were conceived as the foundation of the new public city system ... Each of the twelve neighbourhoods had a park of at least two or three hectares on average, not to mention the large parks built in Taverna del Ferro ... and Ponticelli, which were as large as fifteen hectares. After a long time, we can see that the interventions carried out have survived, some in the best, some in worse conditions, even in spite of poor maintenance (Recording n. 5).

In East Naples, as in other areas of the city, the programme, including residences, services and urban amenities, was completed over the course of the decade, immediately gaining enthusiastic praise but also attracting numerous criticisms. This is a complex issue which requires prior chronological situation. As highlighted by historian Piero Bevilacqua, in the years that followed, an image of the reconstruction in Naples spread throughout the city, building a narrative uniquely centred on the distorted use of public resources and on the dissemination of illegal activities. This collective image, for the historian Francesco Barbagallo, has a sure foundation in the report of the Parliamentary Commission of Inquiry into the implementation of interventions for the reconstruction and development of the territories hit by the earthquake, which recognised the existence of different phases in the reconstruction process (Corona 2007, p. XIII, p. 85): if the 'first reconstruction', marked by the aforementioned PSER interventions soon after the earthquake, was dominated by attention to recovery of the existing services, liveability and urban green areas in compliance with the needs of local populations, the 'second reconstruction' was the reign of business groups, planning amnesties and infrastructural interventions. First of all, Law 80 of 1984, passed by the new Christian Democrat-led council established in 1983, transferred the bulk of the extraordinary financing to infrastructural works, mostly road and motorway works (Corona 2007, p. 138). These interventions had 'little or nothing to do with the reconstruction' (De Lucia 2006, p. 164). Another fundamental difference, compared to the previous phase, has to do with public control, clearly loosened in this second phase. In fact, Law 80 granted to the Extraordinary Commissioner for Reconstruction the power to entrust the new works to private subjects who would gradually become immune to the verification of the technical office. In other words, companies began to act independently of the verification consortia, constantly proposing expensive,

Chapter 3

imaginative or unrealistic projects only to accumulate funding (Erbani 1998, p. 102): in this way a twisted system was launched, whereby building companies would start a project, to gain financial support from the State through the funds assigned to the Extraordinary Programme, only often to abandon the projects and pocket the funding. This system was not completely immune to Camorra infiltration, as demonstrated by a Bicameral Commission of inquiry (Cederna, 12 January 1990). On this substratum was then built the 1985 amnesty, a national law that essentially provided for a progressive remediation of building abuses committed by October 1983 (Corona 2007, pp. 104–05). Thus, the never-defunct religion of the 'emergency', 'worship of extraordinary procedures', whose ceremonies attracted a 'host of professionals, technicians and magistrates to the idolatry of cement' re-emerged forcefully (Erbani 1998, p. 102).

At the same time, as highlighted by Piero Bevilacqua, the stereotype of a reconstruction entirely marked by waste, corruption and clientelism has obscured the urban goods created by those who faced the emergency and designed urban redevelopment, inspired by those new urban values (sustainability, healthiness, greenery, beauty of the landscape) that emerged with conviction in the years of cholera (Corona 2007, p. XII–XIII). Quantitatively, in the entire metropolitan area, over 11,000 new homes were built and 34 new green lungs: the average size of residences grew from 1.78 rooms to 4.5, while the average endowment of green space per inhabitant went from a depressing 0.11 square metres to 1.91. In line with the contemporary British legislation on green belts and with the dogmas of the Garden city movement, even the Neapolitan urban environment gained awareness, according to Gabriella Corona, of new principles of protection of green belts, in the name of the wellbeing and health of citizens (Corona 2007, p. XV, pp. 100–04). Close to the interventions of the PSER, urban planner Antonio Cederna figuratively assigned the Neapolitan suburbs 'the reconstruction medal', both for the record speed of construction and the number of interventions carried out: in this context, the eastern districts were among the most virtuous, thanks to the restorations but above all to the new pedestrian paths, green areas, schools, sports fields. The new park of Taverna del Ferro (now named after the actor Massimo Troisi), in San Giovanni, with its gardens and a large artificial lake was hyperbolically defined as 'a piece of Scandinavia in the Neapolitan suburbs'.

> 'Is everything perfect?' the smart guy might ask at this point. Of course, there are some issues. Some productive activity that turns out to be incompatible with residences, a

Assessing the Risks

still unresolved distinction between public and private spaces ... some design flaws as in the large park we mentioned ... But these are marginal problems: what matters is that a grandiose urban, social and economic operation is being completed (Cederna, 20 May 1987).

Obviously, a project with such ambitions could not fail to present some contradictions, especially in the creation of new popular districts. An example of this is the case of the Taverna del Ferro district, in San Giovanni a Teduccio. Today defined daily as 'Bronx' both for its similarity in layout to the (much larger) New York district and for the strong perceived social exclusion of the inhabitants in a sort of 'ghetto', since its construction the district has not found a positive response from the population or the local ruling class. Since 1988 limitations have been found in its 'construction defects', in the 'industrialised construction techniques', in the 'negligence of those who built and those who had the task of supervising', i.e. the Municipality and the private management company to which the real estate assets of the PSER were entrusted, whose lack of maintenance has resulted in the current decayed state of the buildings and the deficiencies in essential services.[4] It is possible, however, that what underlies the social exclusion of the inhabitants of the Taverna del Ferro district is also of a 'cultural' nature, as testified by Nino Daniele, or lies in the choice to concentrate social housing interventions all in one location. This is a conviction that turns to self-criticism, because it is closely connected to the ideals of the time, in turn linked to the long struggle for the improvement of housing conditions that was discussed in the previous chapter:

> [It was] a cultural mistake for which I also feel responsibility. In the sense that we thought that giving a house was 'the way of emancipation', of redemption and so on. That was a mistake, because in the end we concentrated the margins all at the same point. We created a mechanism for reproducing marginality ... when you have assignment mechanisms whereby you put all 'poor people' in a single place ... both in the idea of social housing and in the assignment of those houses to the same social typology, you create a self-reproducing mechanism. It hasn't redeemed anything. (Recording n. 4).

---

4   In subsequent years, the malfunctioning of the sewerage networks and water connections is on the agenda in the new popular districts such as the 'Bronx' of San Giovanni and the '167' of Ponticelli. The districts are forced into degrading shifts that often reduce water availability to a few hours a day. In addition, the continuous faults in the pipes often make the water a real slime. The situation will become intolerable in the summer of 1990, when the 'water revolt' explodes, a protest led by overwhelming women conducted with the methods of revolt established since the years of cholera (roadblocks and fire of household goods and garbage) (Riccio, 1 June 1990).

Chapter 3

However, the reasons for the non-permeability of the 'Bronx' must also be traced to the assessed needs of the earthquake emergency and the structural shortcomings of collective services in the neighbourhood (Italian Communist Party 1988, p. 14). As regards these last two aspects, it should be specified that the housing estates making up the Taverna del Ferro district were concentrated very close together (as evident in Figure 3.8), creating a hermetically-sealed residential context. This was the result of a precise urban planning choice – to carve out as much space as possible for the surrounding services and amenities, to save 'in terms of time and also land to create the adjacent park of more than ten hectares', together with a school and sports centre, as witnessed by Giovanni Dispoto (Recording n. 5). This choice was also dictated by the geographical position of the district, on the border between the Barra and San Giovanni a Teduccio districts: the creation of a large urban park and school and sports facilities just there could, in short, allow both districts to take advantage of the new structures (Recording n. 5). Unfortunately, the new park also faced management problems, which would postpone its opening to 1994 and then complicate issues relating to its maintenance (Recording n. 3).

Figure 3.8

The double row of residences that forms the Taverna del Ferro neighbourhood. Schools and a public park have been located in its immediate proximity. The huge murals, portraying Maradona and a local boy, were painted by street artist Jorit Agoch between 2017 and 2018. Source: Comitato di lotta Ex Taverna Del Ferro (https://www.facebook.com/comitatoextavernadelferro)

Assessing the Risks

Praiseworthy for facing an extraordinary emergency with ordinary instruments and 'an extraordinary programme' that, given 'the inhuman condition of Naples ... is still a breath of fresh air' is the overall judgment of Vezio de Lucia, considering the cultural limitations and above all the new priorities affirmed by the 'second reconstruction' (De Lucia 2006, pp. 163–64). What the emergency, the short timescales, the cultural limits and the structural needs of Naples' peripheral territories preclude addressing immediately is the possibility of a restructuring of the economic system. In recent years, emphasis has been placed on the PSER's inability to build a 'network of new centralities' in the outskirts of Naples, or a new system of economic functions capable of attracting business entities and public investments. In other words, resolving the age-old question of the competitiveness of the peripheral territory with a decisive intervention and an innovative solution capable of integrating the environmental and economic development of the area: obviously, such a revolution could not be carried out with only 'standard equipment', but would require an overall rethinking of the urban fabric so as to guarantee the involvement of private individuals through attractive investment conditions (Gasparrini 2010, pp. 275–90). It should be specified that these issues would become the object of study of Neapolitan planners in the following years and, as will be seen, would form the core of the new interpretation of the territory of East Naples, in the projects of the 1990s. In the immediate future, however, we must consider the 'landowner' mentality of southern entrepreneurship in these years, certainly galvanised by the choices of the 'second reconstruction' and perhaps too attentive to the immediate gain guaranteed by building speculation (De Lucia 2006, pp. 163–64) to submit to the long timescales of systemic planning.

In the specific case of East Naples, moreover, a similar systemic rethinking of the territory would have had to deal with the increasingly intrusive spaces decommissioning and with that immense urban 'void' that had been established since the 1920s in the heart of the eastern area, the oil activities that remained firmly anchored to the territory following the failure of the relocation projects. In these years, the 1980s, the spaces surrounding the large oil concessions experienced the devastation of the earthquake as much as the construction sites of the restoration works and the new council housing. Slowly, the Ponticelli, San Giovanni, Gianturco and Barra districts returned to the normality of a daily life shared with the residual spaces of industrial production, including the refineries. In those days, crossing the eastern districts, it was hard not to notice a perennial flame, a sort of North

Chapter 3

Star for the inhabitants, which dominated the entire landscape from the top of the Mobil refining tower (Recording n. 3). Today, it is more difficult to identify the immense expanses of petrol tanks, hidden in full view by their anonymous form or by scaffolding, causeways, rows of containers or, more simply, by houses. A paradoxical normality, if one thinks of the events of December 1985.

On 21 December at around 5:00 a.m., an Agip tanker was completing its unloading of 20,000 tons of petrol into the tanks of the San Giovanni a Teduccio depot. A security guard was making his night patrol. There was an intense, too intense, smell of petrol. Out of the corner of his eye he saw the flames rising from one of the tanks but could do nothing else: the explosion was 'an incredible roar', a flight into the void. He managed to recover after a few seconds and all around him was an inferno. Everywhere flames, smoke, debris and screams (*Corriere della Sera*, 22 December 1985).[5] In the following hours the fire spread: the much-feared chain reaction materialised, now, before the terrified eyes of citizens, awakened with a start by a roar that rekindled recent memories of the earthquake or the most atavistic fears of an awakening of the volcano. Twenty-five tanks (Simonetti 2003, p. 593) were engulfed one after the other by the flames and provided additional fuel to the fire, despite the efforts of the Fire Brigade and Civil Protection.

The inferno spread rapidly, overcame the fences of the oil concessions, invaded the streets, engulfed homes. A vortex of flames broken by the occasional displacement of air by explosions: both consumed concrete and bricks, devastated glass, sent rubble flying in all directions. Thousands of people, often still in pyjamas, poured into the streets. Often those pyjamas and slippers would be all that survived of a life suddenly gone up in smoke (Foresta Martin, 22 December 1985).[6] Others did not even have this luck. Caught unprepared by the hellfire, some were forced to jump off their balconies (*l'Unità*, 22 December 1985)[7] while many, over 150, were seriously burned or injured by debris. Five people lost their lives (Cardillo 2006, p. 42). Many others were saved by the pure intervention of chance. The disaster broke out just about twenty minutes after the beginning of the morning work

---

5   'A worker: "I saw two comrades disappear in the flames"', *Corriere della Sera* editorial, 22 Dec. 1985. UrbArc, IanCo, 99 / g.

6   F. Foresta Martin, 'Naples enveloped by a volcano of fire', *il Corriere della Sera*, 22 Dec. 1985. UrbArc, IanCo, 99/g.

7   'After the roar, the walls collapsed', *l'Unità* editorial, 22 Dec. 1985. UrbArc, IanCo, 99/g.

Assessing the Risks

Figure 3.9

Explosion of the Agip oil tanks. 21 December 1985. Source: private collection of Vincenzo Morreale; photographer unknown.

shift in the warehouse, saving twenty workers. Even more extraordinarily, but further proof of the risks inherent in the environmental disorder of the area, a railway train passing close to the depot, transporting hundreds of commuters to the city centre, was hit by the shock force of the explosion but avoided derailment thanks to its very low speed, limited by works in progress on the line (*Corriere della Sera*, 22 December 1985).

Even today, it is difficult to establish the causes of the disaster. According to the security officers of the plant, a malicious motive can be excluded: a hypothetical attacker would not have had time to sabotage the instruments without being immediately identified (*l'Unità*, 22 December 1985). The hypothesis of an involuntary breach is more likely, linked to an external intervention, but without the specific intention of causing a fire. It seems that one of the gates of the plant was forced during the night: among the suspects were a group of smugglers known in the district for the cheap sale of gasoline. In short, a night theft from the tank, perhaps hastened by the arrival of security guards, then a daring escape and a spillage of petrol (Baglivo, 24 December 1985).[8] A spark would do the rest. Yet, in the following days doubts also arose about the condition of the plant: a few days before the disaster, a Civil Protection technician examined the security systems of the Agip depot and found the situation unsatisfactory. The oil ducts were uncovered, therefore easily damaged. If the contents had leaked, it could have invaded the entire plant, if the Civil Protection technician had not immediately ordered their covering (*La Stampa*, 24 December 1985).[9]

In any case, once the fire had broken out, it took a good 130 hours (*il Giorno*, 27 December 1985)[10] of struggle to contain and tame those flames almost inexhaustibly fuelled by the petrol in the tanks. Overall, the environmental impact of the disaster can be quantified as two tons of petrol and diesel fuel poured into the sewers that reach the sea through the small Pollena stream (Esposito, 2015), in six days obscured by a constant dark cloud; or forty billion lire of fuel gone up in smoke; not to mention the unspecified tens of billions worth of damage to the surrounding homes and shops (*La Stampa*, 24 December 1985). The most problematic dynamic to be addressed, however, was the relocation of displaced persons. Hundreds of families joined those

---

8   A. Baglivo, 'Another hypothesis: gasoline smugglers', *Corriere della Sera*, 24 Dec. 1985. UrbArc, IanCo, 99 / g.

9   'The city of the homeless', *La Stampa* editorial, 24 Dec. 1985. UrbArc, IanCo, 99 / g.

10 'Tank 16 extinguished, calm returns', *il Giorno* editorial, 27 Dec. 1985. UrbArc, IanCo, 99 / g.

Assessing the Risks

hit by the earthquake, who still crowded the temporary camps. With the fire still underway, one of these camps risked being engulfed by flames and was urgently evacuated (Corona 2007, pp. 100–01). In other cases, misfortune struck with a particular vengeance: about 600 citizens newly returned to their homes after the post-earthquake refurbishment work, were forced to abandon them again due to the devastation of the fire (*l'Unità*, 27 December 1985).[11] In the meantime, over 200 families were temporarily transferred to ships provided by the Prefecture (and already used during the earthquake emergency) or to the city's hotels (*La Stampa*, 24 December 1985), and were then relocated to none-too-hospitable social housing located in the hinterland (Recording n. 3).

Like the earthquake of 1980, the Agip depot fire of 1985 raised a profound awareness both in citizens and in the administration. This was an immediate consequence of media coverage of the event (the same goes for the earthquake, indeed), to the point that Roberto Parisi has defined it as one of the 'most evident media phenomena of the new season of deindustrialisation' in Naples (Parisi 2017, p. 47). Clearly, the national and local newspapers from which the story is being reconstructed here cannot fail to confirm this reading. Alongside the unfolding events, the pages of the newspapers also convey brief descriptions of the context, which conceal synthetic analyses of local problems. The accent is placed on economic decline, on social problems, on crime, but each of these short texts seems to start with the urban decay of the eastern districts of Naples, therefore from the lack of social services, the high population density, the building speculation, the mixing of spaces and the risks deriving from the proximity of production activities and homes.[12] 'This area has now become like a dirty tablecloth … and you know, if a tablecloth is white, be careful not to stain it, but if it is full of stains, everyone feels entitled to continue to smear it', is the homemade metaphor offered by *il Mattino* to challenge the 'urban crime' of the failure to relocate

---

11   'The fire has been tamed but the emergency begins for 2,300 displaced persons', *l'Unità* editorial, 27 Dec. 1985. UrbArc, IanCo, 99 / g.

12   This is the description of *l'Unità*: 'The explosion took place in the heart of the old industrial area of Naples, the traditional productive lung of the city … an area where industrial activities have progressively reduced in recent years … and where localised polluting and dangerous activities, fuel and fuel deposits still remain. This was all while residential settlements grew. The responsibilities of those who have allowed this degradation are great'. And below: 'Factories and houses, one close to the other. Two hundred thousand Neapolitans work and live there, imprisoned among the concrete snakes of the large motorway links, the asphyxiating chimneys of the chemical industry and the inviolable barrier of the port' (*l'Unità*, 22 Dec. 1985).

oil activities in previous years (Romano, 24 December 1985).[13] This choice had now revealed its most dramatic consequences. The pens of Antonio Iannello and Antonio Cederna are brutal in recalling the long battles of environmental associations against the permanent presence in the heart of the city of high-risk plants such as oil tanks. 'Ineptitude' and 'irresponsibility' have monopolised the ruling class and the public powers (Iannello, 21 December 1985)[14] and brought to birth that 'distorted, uncultivated territorial policy that has afflicted Italy for decades: made up of mockery of elementary rules of urban planning, of contempt for the needs of human life and for the environment that surrounds us' (Cederna, 23 December 1985).[15] Even the local communists, from the headquarters of the party and through *l'Unità*, recognise the 'need to overcome an industrial model that does not solve the relationship with the environment positively and in a balanced way and does not give guarantees on safety issues', hoping that the drama would promote 'a renewed programmatic and cultural awareness of the workers' movement itself' (*l'Unità*, 22 December 1985). This unanimous indictment of the localisation of risky activities could now translate into concrete action. In practice, with the fire still in progress, the mayor of Naples Carlo D'Amato, after comparing the oil tanks to 'bombs placed inside the city' (Corsi, 23 December 1985),[16] pronounced his sentence: 'What I see is terrible. It is a situation we cannot bear. Plants of this type cannot be hosted in the city; all must now be relocated' (Foresta Martin, 22 December 1985).

The Agip plant was irremediably compromised but, as mentioned, the real pivot of the East Naples oil area was the MobilOil concession, with its complex of refinery and storage activities, on whose permanence the entire local oil supply chain depended. In spite of the catastrophe of 1985, and proof of the strategic importance of the company, addressing the question of the permanence on-site of Mobil's activities would be postponed until the expiry of its concession (1993): in the meantime, an explosion would occur in the Mobil refinery in February 1987; a flue collapse in the same refinery in December 1990, which would cause the death of three workers (Faenza,

---

13   S. Romano, 'An urban crime', *il Mattino*, 24 Dec. 1985. UrbArc, IanCo, 99 / g.
14   *Typescript by Antonio Iannello concerning the 1985 Agip oil tanks fire*, 21 Dec. 1985. UrbArc, IanCo, 99/e.
15   A. Cederna, 'How the Bel Paese is destroyed', *La Repubblica*, 23 Dec. 1985. UrbArc, IanCo, 99 / g.
16   E. Corsi, 'All those refineries are bombs in the city', *La Repubblica*, 23 Dec. 1985. UrbArc, IanCo, 99 / g.

Assessing the Risks

22 December 1990); and a further fire in December 1992, with the death of two employees (Cardillo 2006, p. 42). In the wake of these accidents, the perception of the risk associated with these plants became widespread and unanimous. However, at the beginning of 1990, the Italian MobilOil was fully acquired by Kuwait Petroleum (Q8), including the East Naples plants and the surrounding reservoirs (Borriello, 21 March 1990): the vicissitudes of the national oil company of the small Arab country, in these years embroiled in the first Gulf War, slowed down the discussion on the disposal of the refinery by a few years. In any case, reinforced by the recurring incidents, eight years after the great explosion, the positions of the public opinion had not changed at all: during 1993 the new Party of Left Democrats (Partito dei Democratici di Sinistra) repeatedly imposed itself on the doubts of the company by mobilising citizenship through pickets at the gates of the plant, information campaigns, even the threat of a citizen referendum on the fate of the plants (*la Repubblica*, 25 August 1993). 'We have been talking about moving the refinery since 1972', states urban planner Alessandro dal Piaz:

> What is certain is that on that immense area, one and a half million square metres, a reclamation project such as never before carried out will have to happen; perhaps all the land will have to be renewed to a depth of ten metres. What is certain is that a refinery can no longer exist. The task of intervening is up to the Region, which has been standing still, as has the Province, for twenty years (Faenza, 14 January 1993).

Under these pressures and due to the media coverage affecting the site in question, in 1993 the regional body decided to act and, in agreement with the company, contracted a gradual reduction in production, now at an all-time low, by the refinery until it stopped completely. This was only a partial success, not followed by the reclamation of the perimeter of the refinery and, above all, not removing the tank park from the eastern area of Naples where, indeed, the tanks are still present and used for the storage and distribution of fuels, with an operating capacity of over one million tons of fuel and LPG (Iannello, Morreale 2006, pp. 16–17). In the 1999 variant of the Town Development Plan, the oil tank area was to provide new space for activities different from the past ones – sustainable, integrated with the residential fabric and natural areas. Yet the vast oil storage area is still there, holding out despite the decommissioning of the refinery and the visible damage to many tanks.

Chapter 3

3.2 Reversing environmental change: ambitions and delusions

In Italy, the period from the second half of the 1980s to the end of the 1990s coincides with that of maximum resonance of the environmentalist political discourse. This was a moment of widespread awareness of ecological risks, not least because of the affirmation of the nuclear question[17] linked to the 1986 Chernobyl disaster. On the legislative level, the start of this new phase can be traced back to the previous year and to the Galasso law of 8 August 1985, which made it possible to recognise and protect the environment as a public good in and of itself. The law extended its protection to the shores of seas, lakes, rivers and glaciers as well as volcanoes, mountain peaks and archaeological areas. Shortly thereafter, the autonomous Ministry of the Environment (separated from that of Cultural Heritage) was established with Law 349 of 8 July 1986 and introduced new regulations on the identification and remediation of areas at high risk of environmental crisis. In spite of strong criticism by building entrepreneurs, the season of political environmentalism would continue in the following decade (Corona 2015, pp. 98–99). As for the national urban planning situation, however, at the end of the 1980s we are still in full 'counter-reform', that is a period of reaction by the speculative building world to the successes of public planning in previous years, marked by a strong push towards urban deregulation. One of the key moments, in this sense, is 1985, with the aforementioned amnesty that would soon be followed not only by a new golden season of unauthorised building but, more generally, by a crisis about the role of urban planning itself (De Lucia 2006, pp. 167–89, p. 191). Brutally privatised or negotiated in the name of private profit and to the detriment of community needs, urban planning in Italian cities remained in the early 1990s at the mercy of speculative projects, *ad hoc* emergencies and extraordinary procedures (De Lucia 2006, pp. 197–99). Naples also witnesses a flashback to the neoliberal climate and seemed ready to succumb to a new wave of concrete. In 1993, however, the establishment of the new left-wing junta led by Antonio Bassolino allowed the reconstitution of the group of urban planners who had been active in the Communist administration of Maurizio Valenzi, *the boys* of

---

17   In 1987 the abrogative referendum on nuclear power took place, with an almost plebiscite victory for the yes camp (80%). The same year the Greens obtained their first parliamentary representation, with thirteen deputies and two senators (Corona 2015, p. 92).

Assessing the Risks

the Suburban Plan and the first phase of the PSER. Urban planning 'in the classical sense' was able to reassert itself, enriched by the new achievements of national political environmentalism and reinforced by a new 'aggressive' and systemic conception of sustainable planning (Corona 2007, p. 3, p. 143).

To try to escape 'the traditional practice of the double track of rule and derogation: the first to prohibit and the second to do' (Ceci 2016, p. 41) and restore urban legality, we rely, on a political level, on democratic participation by citizens and building a basis of popular consensus. On the technical level, on the other hand, it is necessary to develop systemic responses to an urban reality which, amidst economic crisis and stagnation, social problems, repeated disasters and speculative processes, is at the mercy of uncontrolled forces and interests. In 1994, these impulses found programmatic expression in the 'Urban planning addresses', later confirmed in the drafting (from 1995 to 1998) of the 'Variant of Safeguarding', both of these a manifesto for the urban policies of the Bassolino council. In clear continuity with the phase of the Suburban Plan, it affirms, in the first place, the need to centralise the conservation and redevelopment of historic centres in the hands of public agents (Ceci 2016, p. 41). Secondly, and in line with the ideals of the European Garden City Movement, the need to defend the integrity of the territory is confirmed by protecting the soil and providing green spaces and green belts. The most innovative and 'aggressive' element, however, is in the integration of environmental redevelopment interventions and the promotion of new forms of sustainable production (Corona 2007, p. 56), both secondary and tertiary, which replace abandoned activities or those in crisis and can coexist with the urban fabric.

The territorial framework of the eastern area in the early 1990s was far from this ideal model: East Naples was still one of the main spaces of industrial production, albeit in severe crisis, littered with abandoned relics and eternally contested by residential and infrastructural expansion. The process of deindustrialisation, far from being sudden and brutal, was rather subtle and gradual. Looking back, the twenty-year period between 1971 and 1991 brought in total a 33 per cent decline in manufacturing units. One in three factories was no longer active by the end of the period. At the end of the same period the death rate of industry exceeded the birth rate by 22 per cent (Municipality of Naples 1996, p. 69). A slow process of stagnation was thus unfolding, which progressively suffocated the old production spaces and, above all, prevented new industrial investment from arising, due to scarce prospects of profit and the increasingly declining competitiveness of the territory. Furthermore, the explosive events of the past decade (the earthquake, the Agip explosion) only accentuated structural problems and confirmed the image of a territory in decline. Now, thanks to the new awareness of city planning, the productive relaunch of East Naples became a desirable reality, to be intertwined with an environmental requalification of the urban fabric. In these terms, the interventions planned for the eastern area not only contained the most ambitious perspectives of Neapolitan planning of the 1990s but constituted one of its pillars. The role of East Naples in the economic revitalisation of the city was easy to state: it would host 'a new industrial development hub', which, according to mayor Bassolino, would be populated by 'light industry ... with a strong technological qualification' (Cambi, 4 August 1997). The Municipality of Naples therefore signed a memorandum of understanding in September 1997 for the establishment of an industrial promotion company called 'Napoli Est', with mixed public and private capital (*la Repubblica*, 2 September 1997), but relied above all on planning to prepare newly equipped areas, incubators aimed at accommodating the company's private capital.

This ambitious urban intervention took the form of a project of 'Proposed modification to the GDP for historic centre and eastern area', completed in 1996 and inserted, with some important changes, in the 'Variant to the GDP of Naples: historic centre, eastern and northern-western area' approved in 1999. Firstly, it was planned to relocate still operating heavy and/or polluting industries outside the municipal boundaries (in line with the aims established since the 1972 GDP) and place them into the existing ASI consortia in the Province of Naples (Municipality of Naples 1996, p. 94, p. 377). Following the relocation of these activities, the 'smart areas', would be prepared to accommodate new industrial investments following four fundamental principles. First of all, it would be necessary to implement environmental interventions aimed at solving the problem of territorial degradation, not only a reduction in pollution but a general improvement of the urban landscape through new equipment and infrastructure that could offer 'the image of a prestigious area'. Secondly, traditional start-up grants could be re-proposed as financial subsidies, updated according to new rental and leasing formulas. Thirdly, it would be necessary to free up space for logistical infrastructure, with the priority assigned to sea and rail transport, in order to reduce the weight of road transport. Fourthly, it would be possible to offer companies technical and technological services through integration with local research centres, and then commercial, financial and insurance, information and communica-

Assessing the Risks

tion services, thus integrating new industrial activities with the service sector (Municipality of Naples 1999, pp. 378–79). Ultimately, these 'smart areas' could offer a solution to the age-old question of the competitiveness of the territory, outlining 'an attractive and convenient direction for new investments' (Municipality of Naples 1999, p XII), in a sort of enhanced and updated revival conforming to new ecological dogmas of the special law of 1904. As further proof of the osmosis between economic and territorial factors in East Naples, the entire mechanism aimed at relaunching the area's production was based on the first of the listed principles, environmental requalification.

On the territorial level, the new planning pursued the simple objective of overturning the effects of the long historical sedimentation of the twentieth-century industrialisation and urbanisation processes, which had progressively relegated the eastern area to a 'border area' between the city and its hinterland, saturating it with infrastructure, factories, residential areas and tertiary services (such as the Business Centre, completed in 1995): now an attempt was being made to transform the 'suburbs into the city' (Municipality of Naples 1996, pp. 107–08), or to give back to area its continuity with the city landscape as a whole. To obtain this result, and in the meantime regain the environmental balance of the area, it was decided to restore integrity to the floodplain of the ancient river Sebeto, the hydrogeological basin that formed the ecological cornerstone of the urban plan,[18] through the construction of a large urban park (Sebeto Park) in the heart of the ancient marshes, the spaces occupied by oil depots. 'The keystone of all this was certainly the displacement of oil depots, the problematic nature of which had already been stigmatised in the plan of 1972' (Recording n. 5), Giovanni Dispoto confirms: the delocalisation of the oil area in its entirety (entailing reclamation of disused refineries, displacement of the tank park and disposal of the oil pipelines and the coastal terminal) was the 'fundamental condition of the redevelopment of the city and in particular of its eastern area' (Municipality of Naples 1996, p. 120). If the relocation of the petroleum area was successful, the Sebeto Park would become a reality: a vast park of 170 hectares, modelled on the course of the ancient river, drawing a five-kilometre-long green belt, covered with cycle paths, pedestrian and tramways (Municipality of Naples 1999, p. 361). A 'long walk' along the east-west

---

18   Law 183 of 1989 on the organisational and functional reorganisation for soil defence, had introduced hydrographic basin plans, binding for the general regulatory plans of municipalities, affirming the priority of the ecosystem boundaries of a territory over the administrative ones (Corona 2015, p. 93).

route would reunite the heart of the suburbs with the city centre, reaching the central station of the city and overcoming the barriers posed by infrastructural lines (such as the Tangenziale) and old industrial buildings, for many of which redevelopment interventions were planned (Municipality of Naples 1999, pp. 362–63). The ex-Cirio factory, for example, was destined for renovation into a university centre, thanks to the commitment of local authorities and the University of Naples 'Federico II' which included it in a unitary project that also extended to part of the ex-Corradini. In the project, the construction of the new university centre would be followed by the redevelopment of the public housing complex close to the former Snia textile factory, through the creation of a new equipped green area (Municipality of Naples 1999, pp. 463–64). Some of these planning areas actually saw rehabilitation and redevelopment, while some others remain abandoned to this day. If the Sebeto Park project had been pursued fully, things would be radically different today.

The most innovative element, however, was the interweaving of environmental redevelopment interventions and the promotion of economic activities. In the areas close to the Sebeto Park, about 500 hectares were earmarked for the new industrial settlements (Municipality of Naples 1999, p. 381). Obviously, the same precondition as for the park, namely the relocation of the oil area, recurs as a necessary condition for the production area and for the reclamation of brownfields. The new industrial area was to host 'clean industry' – that is, small, technologically advanced companies integrated with tertiary activities and with some horticultural and nursery activities. As proof of the importance of the intervention on a city scale, the historic centre of Naples would have offered most of small and artisanal industries the opportunity to relocate to the new eastern production area, in a new process of decongestion that recalled the nineteenth-twentieth century rehabilitation of the city centre, following which the first industrial area of eastern Naples originated. However, no space was reserved for noxious and heavy industrial activities: at most, the continuation of still-active non-polluting plants was guaranteed (Municipality of Naples 1999, pp. 362–70).

This first path (east-west) of the Park would cross a second axis, from the interior towards the sea: starting in the area of the former refineries, the park would reach the coast and the area of *pons paludis*, an ancient proto-industrial area, whose historical and monumental artefacts would have been, likewise, requalified. For the coastal area, however, it was necessary to deal with the strategic importance of the port of Naples, the seventh Italian port in terms of movement of petroleum products (Municipality of Naples 1996, p. 91). In

Assessing the Risks

other words, even the coastal redevelopment projects essentially depended on the disposal of the oil area. The Proposal of 1996 provides for the elimination of oil traffic through the conversion of the port's oil dock, a short distance from the coast of Vigliena, into a tourist port (*Porto Fiorito*) with about 2,000 berths, generating, among other things, 700 jobs. The decision was justified by the inactivity of the Q8 refinery and the aforementioned intention to relocate the oil depots. Secondly, the municipal administration was moving towards the removal of the old Enel thermoelectric power plant in Vigliena, 'a factor that would alter the environmental quality of the place', whose spaces would have been occupied by a large multifunctional centre for music and entertainment, which would also have involved the remaining part of the ex-Corradini factory. The aim of these interventions was to 'return the sea to the city', by generating a relation that could be simultaneously sustainable, productive and capable of triggering processes of territorial enhancement (Municipality of Naples 1996, p. 94).

Figure 3.10

General Development Plan, Municipality of Naples 2004. An overview of the projects for the eastern area. The project for the new urban park (Parco del Sebeto) is shown as a dark section at the centre of the map. Source: Archivi di UrbaNa - Urbanistica Napoli, via www.commune.napoli.it

Chapter 3

Ultimately, it can be said that the urban planning of the second half of the 1990s could have affected the reality of East Naples like the special law of 1904, re-establishing a link between the state, businesses and the territory. However, most of these designs have never been applied or have undergone radical changes. On the one hand, as an almost immediate consequence of the great public attention and private interests in the eastern area, we must consider a surge in the value of the land, which tripled over the course of just three years (1998–2000), even in cases of abandoned land and disused activities. The sudden increase in the price of land considerably slowed down recovery projects, the costs of which were also swollen by the immense size of abandoned areas such as the ex-Cirio or ex-Corradini factories. At the same time, speculation in land removed the investment prospects promoted, for example, by the Napoli Est company, which at the end of the 1990s had attracted the attention of major international brands such as Ikea and Wind, now put-off by the acquisition costs of sites. 'The future of East Naples' was then all in the hands of the public administration and the new Town Development Plan in progress (Russo, 29 June 2000), which would be approved in 2004. The new Plan recovered most of the aims of previous instruments and confirmed the leading role of the redevelopment of the eastern area, which, with its vast abandoned or at-risk spaces, offered the only possibility of 'expansion' to the city, once the revolutionary (especially for Naples) principle of zero land consumption has been affirmed as a priority (Recording n. 5). On paper, the transfer of the oil depots area was confirmed, as was the disposal of all equipment relating to maritime oil traffic: a new location would be identified outside the Gulf of Naples, in agreement with the Campania Region. However, in the years immediately preceding the definitive approval of the Plan, the most innovative proposals of urban planning instruments for the eastern area became the subject of wrangling between public and private, centred on the use of the coastline and on the definitive relocation of oil depots.

As far as the coastal area is concerned, there are some significant differences between the 1999 variant and the 1996 Proposal: the planned pleasure port is transferred from the area of the petrol dock to the coast in front of the ex-Corradini factory, and it is reduced in size to only 500 berths (Municipality of Naples 1999, p. 465). Furthermore, on the one hand the decommissioning of the old Enel thermoelectric plant is confirmed, but on the other its restructuring is envisaged: an evidently indistinct formula which clearly shows the current position on the ground. On the one hand,

Assessing the Risks

the renovation of the old Enel plant has not occurred. On the other, the restructuring of the second, smaller thermoelectric plant on site was carried out:[19] the second plant, named Napoli Levante, was originally built in the 1970s and renovated in 2007. A new turbogas thermoelectric power plant was thus built, owned by Tirreno Power Spa, in the Vigliena area, without waiting for the completion of the remediation works and, indeed, even omitting the necessary environmental impact assessments due to the widespread belief that the new structure was 'certainly less polluting' than the previous ones (Iannello, Morreale 2006, p. 14, pp. 27–28). The decommissioning of the Vigliena plants was instead limited to a smaller area, namely the former Enel plant. The latter was (and still is) public land, under the jurisdiction of the Harbour Authority of Naples. Furthermore, on the basis of the programme agreement of 23 December 2000 between local authorities, the University of Naples 'Federico II', the Ministry of Transport and the Ministry of Public Works, the construction of a freight yard on these spaces is foreseen, covering the coast with concrete and populating it with containers. This operation (still in progress) cannot fail to attract scepticism, if we consider the slim economic benefits that the area could derive from it.

With regard to oil depots, in 2004 these occupied about 150 hectares, a quarter of the entire industrial area, of which about half was unused. Since 2003, twelve of the oil plants still occupying the eastern area have been included in the national inventory of plants likely to cause major accidents, out of a total of thirteen plants with these characteristics in the entire Neapolitan area. In spite of the space covered and the associated risks, what remains of the oil area plays an insignificant productive role (Leone 2004, p. 12, pp. 44–46). Yet, in 2003 Neapolitan industrialists demanded the conservation of thirty per cent of the area occupied by the tanks for storage needs (*La Repubblica*, 8 July 2003). A compromise solution was then reached: in Articles 29 and 143 of the implementing rules, the 2004 Plan identified a very limited area intended for the temporary location of oil plants, prior to the definitive transfer. Along these lines, in 2005 Q8 Petroleum Italia announced itself ready to dispose of 37 hectares of the ninety it owned: this was the area occupied by the ex-MobilOil storage depots, mostly obsolete and dilapidated. The company proposed to concentrate the still useful fuel tanks on 53 hectares and to dedicate the remaining 37 hectares to the creation of a territorial redevelopment project including residences, services, sports

---

19   Approved by resolution of the City Council n. 137 of 7/22/2003.

Chapter 3

and commercial facilities and a park (Capua, 19 May 2005). In this way, a second compromise was reached with the institutions: with the memorandum of understanding of 30 November 2006, signed by local authorities and by Q8, the multinational obtained a guarantee of the permanence of its still-active plants still active in the area for at least another twenty years 'to satisfy the regional demand for petroleum products pending the definitive delocalisation'. During this long period of time, the company undertook to carry out the promised works and to secure the plants still active in those 53 hectares, defined as 'a smaller operational area',[20] pending the final transfer plan. Basically, a substantial reduction in the territorial area occupied by oil activities has been achieved and at least a partial redevelopment is expected, but, overall, the oil area has gained itself a few more decades of permanence. Consequently, the much more radical urban planning proposals of the 1990s, such as the Park of Sebeto, have been set aside.

3.3 Hopes and obstacles for an urban ecosystem

In the preceding pages, account has been taken of the processes and events that have left their mark on the territory of East Naples, or have profoundly hindered the prospects for sustainable redevelopment. Now we must turn to one of the questions posed since the introductory pages: how do the results of deindustrialisation affect the state of environmental degradation of East Naples? We should consider, first of all, that the economic decline, with the its whole spectrum of connected socio-cultural consequences, is still ongoing. The effects of the 2008–2009 crisis on the local productive fabric will reveal themselves to the historian's eye in years to come. Notwithstanding these, in the first decade of the new millennium the overall industrial birth rate remained zero (Celentano et al. 2010, p. 6), supressed by the area's lack of competitiveness, and the local economic system completed its transition from the secondary to the tertiary sector. However, the new service economy was anything but a propulsive force for local development; rather, it was a 'depowered' (Recording n. 4) economy. The hegemonic figure of the worker has been replaced by the less uniform one of the 'employee', engaged in public administration or services. Relatively few, just five per cent, of the local

---

20 Campania regional administration, Kuwait Petroleum Italia S.p.a., Kuwait Refining and Chimica S.p.a., Municipality of Naples, Napoli Orientale S.c.p.a, *Memorandum of Understanding*. 2006. Naples, arts. 1-4.

Assessing the Risks

workforce, find work in the spaces of logistics, transport and wholesale that are also invading the coastline, as we have seen. The spectre of unemployment hangs over all of them, averaging seventeen per cent in the eastern districts, to which must be added the unemployed looking for their first job, over 24 per cent (Celentano et al. 2010, pp. 153–61), and the incalculable mass of illegal workers.

In this context, the local secondary sector has profoundly transformed: between 1991 and 2010 the average number of employees in the secondary sector halved, going from thirty per cent (Simonetti 2003, table 4) to less than fifteen (Celentano et al. 2010, table 6). Due to the continuing crisis in the sector and the constant problem of sharing spaces, large industry, which had dominated the urban landscape during the twentieth century, has mostly given way to the very small artisan dimension:

> Small artisan shops appear in the tangle of streets and alleys of the historical centres, others are concentrated along the main communication routes, still others blend in with popular housing or develop close to large industrial plants ... The image that strikes the mind is of a 'leopard-skin' reality, in which busy streets, secondary streets and alleys, often heterogenous buildings (built up for housing or production purposes in different conditions and times), more and less prosperous and uneven, more and less liveable areas alternate and overlap in an atmosphere of ordinary confusion (Celentano et al. 2010, pp. 5–6)

Local production manages to survive in its own way, albeit with difficulty and within a critical and stagnant context. It adapts as it can to the changing times, but it cannot regenerate itself without an overall strategy, which has been drowned by the lack of ambition of the projects of the 1990s. This marks the definitive triumph of a spontaneous economy, through which an equally chaotic urban fabric is consolidated: a 'swamp', a mixed space halfway between the solid and liquid state, which alternates immense urban voids, small businesses and expanses on expanses of concrete. The elements that can give hope for a systemic and thoroughgoing requalification are still rare. To date, the future of East Naples still depends on the struggle with these brownfields, the material results of the historical sedimentation of the deindustrialisation process. In 1998 Roberto Parisi stated: 'as regards the eastern suburbs and in particular the industrial area ... we have been witnessing for about thirty years a constant depletion of the existing historical and architectural heritage' (Parisi 1998, p. 189). In that same year, 830 hectares of the eastern area were included in the Sites of National Interest (SIN, *Siti di Interesse Nazionale*)

Chapter 3

Figure 3.11

An overview of East Naples in 2017, showing a mixed urban fabric (factories, greenhouses, residences and cargo areas). Source: photograph by the author.

(identified by law n. 426 of 1998),[21] to be reclaimed under the direction of the Ministry of the Environment. The intervention, focused on the recovery of those former industrial areas that too often hide high concentrations of polluting materials, proceeded slowly and traumatically. Considering the redevelopment interventions carried out to date, a significant part of the erstwhile production space still awaits its own regeneration, generating a mixed space caught between immobility and development, sustainability and risk. In 1997, there were 34 abandoned areas, totalling 1,300,000 square metres, equal to five per cent of the total eastern area (Simonetti 2003, p. 592): to date, only some of these areas have undergone effective recovery and redevelopment interventions. Most continue to occupy the urban fabric

---

21   Article 1 outlined an environmental remediation and restoration programme for 14 areas in Italy (including East Naples) that hosted polluted sites and presented high environmental risks.

Assessing the Risks

and intertwine with the daily life of the neighbourhoods. In the words of Giovanni Dispoto, 'What you call dysfunctional urban disorder I see in this toleration of the coexistence of environmental risk, of brownfields, of residence. It's like an attic full of unwanted stuff [*laughing*]. That is, I have to do something about it, I have to eliminate what no longer has a reason to be, I clean up.' (Recording n. 5)

A new map of this disordered urban ecosystem can be drawn by abandoning the relative certainties of quantitative data and retracing in reverse the journey made in the introduction to this book. A reassuring starting point is found in the railway museum of Pietrarsa, inaugurated in 1989 but enhanced, after decades of neglect, and fully restored only in recent years, following a vast state investment approved in March 2017.[22] Crowds of visitors are attracted to the halls of the museum and to the magnificent spaces in front, once busy with the daily activities of this nineteenth-century metalworking giant. In the medium term, the redevelopment of Pietrarsa could act as a catalyst for the enhancement of the terminal stretch of the San Giovanni a Teduccio coast, which is already undergoing the (still improvable) redevelopment of the waterfront. Yet, behind it stands the shape of the ex-water purifier, 15,000 square metres that have been awaiting a reclamation operation since 2014 (Geremicca, 31 July 2014) and severely hinder access to the coastal area. Continuing along the coast, one notices the immense silhouette of the ex-Corradini war factory, which occupies seven hectares and has a total volume of 173,000 cubic metres (Simonetti 2003, p. 599). For seventy years, this giant has been waiting for new life: the tourist port project, after the endless negotiations previously mentioned, finally ran aground in 2012 in the absence of authorisation from the Ministry of the Environment, due to the failure to remove the asbestos buried in the area where the yacht club was supposed to be built. On the other hand, as regards the university residences and the event spaces, foreseen for the western part of the former factory, in 2013 the Municipality allocated twenty million euros for the restoration of the buildings, a sum that was insufficient (Quitadamo 2016, p. 74). The work remains unfinished, to date. Finally, the last stretch of the coastal strip, the Vigliena area, is today contested between the thermoelectric plants, one operational and the other decommissioned, and the expansion projects of the port of Naples, which aim to assign these spaces for logistics. The tourism and cultural potential of the area, although recognised in the

---

22   http://www.museopietrarsa.it/

Chapter 3

1990s schemes, is hopelessly humiliated. Between the containers and the fumes of the power stations, one can see the splendid shape of the former Cirio glassworks emerge, partially revitalised since 2011 by the new artistic workshops of the San Carlo Theatre,[23] behind which lies the rubble of the fort of Vigliena, a glorious memento of the resistance of the Neapolitan Jacobins in 1799, today preserved by the commitment of citizens' associations.[24] Observing such places, and bearing in mind the aesthetic value of the sea, more than a doubt arises about their current intended use.

If, on the other hand, you decide to go inland, you will keep coming across abandoned small and medium-sized warehouses, mostly a reminder of past tanning or agro-food businesses. Passing the popular district of Taverna del Ferro,[25] recently embellished by the immense murals of the artist Jorit, you reach the old productive heart of San Giovanni a Teduccio and the area of the ex-Cirio cannery. Part of the redevelopment project since the 1990s, and about thirty years after its disposal (1989), the plant has been regenerated by the futuristic structures of the new engineering centre of the 'Federico II' University of Naples and the Apple Development centre. A multifunctional complex capable of attracting new activities and a certain student presence, both indigenous and otherwise, could perhaps be a catalyst for local sustainable development in the near future. The university spaces, able to accommodate about 20,000 students and teachers, were inaugurated at the end of 2016 (De Fazio, 16 September 2016). The project, long-planned by the municipal administration, was promoted by the regional authority and the European

---

23   http://www.teatrosancarlo.it
24   During the day of 13 June 1799, the counter-revolutionary forces of the Bourbon reaction conquered the fort of Vigliena at a high price, its powder keg blown up by the few Jacobin defenders in a last desperate attempt to stop the assault (Lucarella 1992, pp. 276–87). The fort of Vigliena, site of heroic resistance of the Neapolitan revolutionaries, has been abandoned to neglect since then, an anonymous heap of rubble invaded by grass: in the summer of 2019 the Civic Committee of San Giovanni a Teduccio, after years of struggle, managed to obtain a commemorative plaque from the Municipality of Naples and is committed to revitalising the place. Nonetheless, the destiny of the old fort is still entirely intertwined with the city harbour's expansion. The Civic Committee, established in 2006, following the protest against the construction of the new thermoelectric plant in Vigliena, currently carries out information campaigns and fights against speculation and environmental degradation. At the forefront in this role of promoting the democratic participation of the neighbourhood are many former workers and former political activists, such as Vincenzo Morreale and Antonio Fondacaro.
25   Here a new Civic Committee was born in 2018, the former Taverna del Ferro struggle committee, fiercely animated by the desire for social redemption of a neighbourhood that wants to shake off the discriminating label of 'Bronx' or 'ghetto', starting with the essential, but too easily forgotten, values of democracy and ecology.

Assessing the Risks

Union and has recently been enriched by the arrival of the IT giant. The hope is that the conversion to a university space will allow the ex-Cirio site to recover its symbolic value for the neighbourhood and to play its role as a driving force for local development again. Likewise, Apple's investments could positively affect the image and competitiveness of the area.

A few hundred metres away from the ex-Cirio site, hidden in the concrete of the residential parks, stands the equally imposing silhouette of the ex-Snia-Viscosa factory, from 1998 onwards a business centre and wholesale shopping centre (Tropea, 13 July 1998): this brief outline of the redevelopments is then completed by entering the Gianturco district, where some of the warehouses of the former Mecfond foundry were converted, in 2013, into a shopping centre. However, it is enough to cross the other side of the road to come across the ghostly monument that is the ex-Tobacco Factory (Manifattura Tabacchi): 280,000 square metres (Simonetti 2003, p. 597) abandoned to themselves since the late 1990s and immediately included in the SIN Eastern Naples. In 2008, Manifattura Tabacchi was expected to undergo a revitalisation project aimed at creating a headquarters for the State Police, which ran aground (on paper) due to lack of funds. In the first months of that year, however, a serious crisis linked to the malfunctioning of the waste cycle in the city reached its peak and the municipal body identified in the skeleton of the large tobacco factory one of the emergency sites suitable for the storage of tens of thousands of eco-bales. On that occasion, representatives of local civic committees went to the site to assess the environmental conditions and suitability for a landfill, instead finding traces of chemicals, solidified tar and puddles of stagnant fuel everywhere (Manzo, 20 February 2008). The landfill was never implemented, because different solutions were found, and trust was placed in the redevelopment project, but in April inspections of the affected area by the Arpac (Regional Agency for Environmental Protection of Campania) confirmed the fears of citizens. Numerous contamination thresholds set for sites for private or residential use, were found to be exceeded, not only lead and other heavy metals but above all concentrations of hydrocarbons (Arpac 2008, pp. 173–93), in all probability connected to the proximity of the oil storage area. Entrusting the reclamation work to a semi-private company, in 2011 it was decided to carry out the redevelopment of the ex-tobacco building, partly recovering it for the construction of urban services and partly demolishing in order to construct 850 new residences (Cuozzo, 2 April 2011). In 2013 the first residences were completed, specially created for the students of the 'Parthenope'

Chapter 3

University: five years later the university residence was forced to close its doors, following a long investigation by the Ministry of the Environment which highlighted the impossibility of guaranteeing the healthiness of the area due to the industrial discharges of the old Q8 refinery (De Fazio, 3 October 2018). To date, the fate of the large structure seems to be a matter for optimism, thanks to the approval, on 8 October 2019, of a masterplan aimed at land reclamation and systemic redevelopment through infrastructural interventions, provision of public services and green areas and conservation of artefacts of historical value.[26]

A final mention, due to their persistent strategic importance, should be made of the fate of the inland areas, between Barra and San Giovanni, still marked by the presence of the oil area: although released from the burden of the refineries, the area is still crossed by oil pipelines and occupied by cisterns. After the 2006 memorandum of understanding, the actual implementation of the limited project contracted with the Q8 became muddled due to judicial inquiries that overwhelmed the multinational. In 2013, a simple customs check by the Port Authority of Naples allowed the launching of an investigation that shed light on the illicit nature of the multinational's oil waste management and disposal system. First of all, over 42,000 cubic metres of process water (special hazardous waste) from the crude oil that landed at the petroleum dock had not been disposed of properly: instead of being sent to the tanks for the treatment of oily water, they were stored in other tanks or even dispersed into the surrounding land. Furthermore, the tanks and other systems were outdated or had serious structural deficiencies that led to them contaminating the soil and aquifers and potentially at risk of infiltration and fires. Finally, a large section of the Q8 factory, apparently abandoned and, on paper, to be decommissioned, was paradoxically occupied by hundreds of illegal warehouses, owned by some companies connected to Q8 (in some cases even with work contracts), which carried out industrial processes on behalf of the parent company. All this took place in the area once occupied by the oldest oil plants, intended to be redeveloped according to the aforementioned agreements with local authorities (Chamber of Deputies, 19 January 2017). In December 2015, the Customs Agency and the Port Authority of Naples implemented a decree issued by the Court of Naples, at the request of the District Anti-Mafia Directorate, against Q8:

---

26   http://www.comune.napoli.it/flex/cm/pages/ServeBLOB.php/L/IT/IDPagina/14506 Last accessed 29 Apr. 2020.

Assessing the Risks

Figure 3.12

Former Corradini armament factory. September 2018. Source: photograph by the author.

on the basis of the actual sum saved by the company by using illicit waste disposal, over the past five years, a preventive seizure of approximately 240 million euros and of the disputed equipment and structures was carried out (Chamber of Deputies, 2 April 2016). The raids made it possible to discover the deliberate choices made by the top management of the oil company, in order to circumvent the tax burdens associated with ecological limitations (De Simone, 22 February 2017). The investigation, still in progress, stopped for the moment any possibility of intervention in the areas occupied by the activities or the skeletons of the oil structures. The territory of East Naples still awaits an overall and systemic redevelopment, impossible without being released from its most cumbersome and harmful tenant.

Ultimately, it is now necessary to insist on the issue of the limits still in place, as the failure in redeveloping abandoned areas and remediation of polluted sites not only materially prevents a different use of space but intensifies environmental risk factors and the perception of degradation,

Chapter 3

therefore impacts negatively on the possibilities of redeveloping the territory in its entirety. However, we should also highlight the 'glimmers of light'. These are initiatives and projects actively pursued by the most experienced exponents of local civic culture as well as by the new generations.[27] These rare points of light show that it is not impossible to achieve new and better conditions of life, nor to eradicate, once and for all, the factors of degradation and environmental disorder that block the area's development prospects. After all, decline and degradation have been the result of recurring choices, gradually bedding in over the course of history: in the same way, the present can choose to go the other way.

Conclusions

Observing it as a single, centuries-old process, the historical course of industrialisation, urbanisation and deindustrialisation covers the chronological span of local contemporary history in its entirety. The same historical perspective allows us, firstly, to grasp the most intimate links that exist between the structure of the territory and the economic structure as a whole. Over this long period, the genetic characteristics of economic and environmental decline and degradation can be observed. Unsustainability thus reveals itself as a structural element, or the result of the sedimentation of two interconnected processes, industrialisation and nineteenth-twentieth-century urbanisation, to which is added almost half a century of deindustrialisation. Of the three processes, the last, deindustrialisation, has not only triggered further potential but made visible that structural element of the area, environmental unsustainability, which industry and its perception as virtuous covered both materially and figuratively with a blanket of smoke. In other words, the deindustrial era intensifies pre-existing environmental problems and, above all, makes visible their implications for the urban fabric of eastern Naples. The industrial era almost uniformly hid these characteristics of environmental disorder, between the use of productive, residential and infrastructural spaces, allowing and accepting, for example, the adjacence of

---

27 Among the most active associations in the eastern Naples area, non-profit organisations such as the Maestri di Strada association, founded in 2003 and comprising volunteers, teachers, educators and professionals of all ages, stand out. The initiatives and projects of the association, often aimed at the youngest, occur daily and translate into both new educational proposals and the creation of associative networks. www.maestridistrada.it

Assessing the Risks

a house and a chimney, or a bathing area and an uncovered drain. Even the urban planning choices of the mid-nineteenth and early twentieth centuries were aligned with these convictions about what was acceptable, laying the material foundations for that mixed presence that the continuous attempts of the following decades could not to rationalise. If the planning of the area's growth arose with these specific characteristics and in line with certain and historicised convictions, in the same way the exaltation of industrial production, understood as a driving force for economic development, allowed the concealment of territorial and environmental problems under the blanket of the smoke of progress.

The critical decade of the 1970s, with its sudden global, national and local shocks, fully triggered the territory's negative potential, not generating but accelerating the impact of pre-existing factors. Hammered by the blows of the sector crises, directed by managements increasingly distant from the local scale, subjected to external interests and surrounded by other productive realities, by buildings and by the overlapping of infrastructural lines, local industries begin to lose profits and employees, or came to be located outside the boundaries of the old industrial area of east Naples. At this time, the fortunes of the economy were welded to those of the territory: due to its disordered and innately unsustainable nature, East Naples became less and less attractive in the eyes of new investors. The poor competitiveness of the territory prevented the industrial system from regenerating itself through physiological turnover. From here on, the constant presence of the vocabulary of crisis in the projects of local authorities, in business strategies, in media discourse and in collective opinion also tended to concentrate general attention on those limits to development that were all too apparent in the urban environment. Moreover, in the same years the skills and awareness necessary to identify the damage wrought on the territory by industry and urban disorder emerged, alongside analysis of the reverse process. This was partly due to some important personalities (such as Antonio Iannello) and partly the grew out of exasperation with ecological and hygienic problems (such as the 1973 cholera). Observed from a unitary perspective, the long 1970s perform the crucial function of 'piercing the veil' of illusion: the perception and awareness of economic decline and the perception and awareness of ecological degradation are intertwined. When, from the early 1970s but more consistently in the following decades, the legislation aligned itself with the new ecological awareness, the old principle according to which a house and a harmful plant could coexist close together was quickly overturned. At least on

Chapter 3

paper. In practice, only some of these plants had to abandon their traditional spaces in East Naples neighbourhoods for declaredly ecological reasons. Many others managed to adapt to the new conditions and to barely survive in the stagnant environment. Still others were able to successfully exploit the ecological discourse, guaranteeing their continued presence on site in spite of potential risks. It should be emphasised that, in the absence of effective and systemic public regulation, the possibility of fully applying these principles crumbles into a galaxy of specific and contingent cases: but, basically, this is where another structural characteristic of the territory of East Naples lies.

The history of the transformations of the eastern Naples area is mainly the result of individual 'exceptional' choices, extremely heterogeneous and distant from each other in space, time and motives. These choices are variously political, economic, speculative, but also ecological, social or ideological. What they have in common is the short or very short duration of the phenomenon, which in certain cases results in a rhetorical distortion of a real or artificial emergency, manipulated for contingent purposes. On the other hand, the outcome of the whole complex of these contingencies for the territorial fabric has structural consequences: which is why, for East Naples, 'pointing the finger' at urban planning errors is a misleading practice. We should discuss not errors but 'gaps', gaps generated not by the admittedly fallible mind of the planner but by opposing powers. From a privileged overall view, the continuous repetition of exceptional choices prevents not the definition (indeed, the history of local urban planning ideas is particularly lively) but the actual implementation of an overall urban plan – that is, an urban strategy that aspires to longevity. This obviously undermines any form of protection of the local environment, both built and natural: in the absence of a rational order imposed on the territory by the public actor, private, spontaneous or even illegal interests proliferate without obstacles, which in turn works to intensify risk situations and to undermine the future prospects of spatial planning, imposing individual priorities in a vicious circle.[28] If these dynamics are very evident in the approval of the Business Centre project in the early 1970s, in the failure to relocate the oil area in the second half of the same decade or in the continuous obstacles posed to the application of the adjusted urban plans from the 1990s to today, they can

---

28   Obviously, these are events specifically restricted to the local case, although I believe they can be inserted into the structure of the broader national trajectory, for which I can only refer to Vezio De Lucia, *If This is a City. The Urban Condition in Contemporary Italy* (Rome: Donzelli, 2006).

be easily retraced in the different phases of East Naples urban history, in the late-nineteenth and twentieth centuries. The general result is a constant urban anarchy, in which the principles underlying the sustainability of urban areas are drowned: the limitation of land consumption is superimposed on speculation and illegal activity; the redevelopment of abandoned areas alternates with the promotion of purely private interests; the provision of green areas and urban services overlaps with the presence of polluted and risky areas. Observed in a unitary perspective, like that proposed in this essay, the season of urban anarchy appears, however, anything but limited to the period of economic decline that coincided with the processes of deindustrialisation. What is significant, in this specific phase, is rather the intensity and the frequency of these contingent choices in a period marked by the declining arc of industry, by the widespread diffusion of new environmental awareness and by the emergence of local and national urban planning legislation that became increasingly attentive to ecosystem problems. In short, a profound hiatus between the actual decision-making mechanisms and the dominant economic, ideological and juridical climate recurs on several occasions, variously legitimised by conditions defined as exceptional or necessary, often more artificial than real. In fact, we can briefly reflect on the impact of those undoubtedly effective emergencies (such as cholera, the earthquake or the Agip explosion) on local urban planning to quickly draw a line between real and supposed: in this case it can be said that 'the exception creates the rule' – that is, it enriches both public opinion and the circle of decision-makers with experience, generating new urban planning solutions.

Undoubtedly, the new ecological awareness and the legislative achievements reached since the end of the 1960s has also managed to translate into some 'exceptional' phases (compared to a general rule marked by bargaining and anarchy) of public urban planning, at the end of the 1970s, in the early 1980s and 1990s. In these phases, new attention to the area and new forms of intervention emerged, aimed at solving the problem of environmental degradation at the root through the enhancement of the existing state, the provision of essential services, the creation of green areas and the redevelopment of spaces severely damaged or at risk. The undeniable successes of the post-earthquake season, albeit with some significant disappointments, at the same time demonstrate the dubious validity of over-superficial judgments on the reconstruction period. The 1990s phase, on the other hand, had the great merit of proposing a systemic alternative capable of integrating economic promotion and environmental redevelopment, perhaps essential to the definitive and holistic recovery of the spaces of east Naples, but it was demolished at the foundations by the usual physiological compromises which, to date, continue to limit any effective prospect of territorial regeneration. If the persistence in situ of the tank farm is the most visible manifestation of these arguments, the lack of capacity to regenerate most of the abandoned spaces demonstrates again how economic and territorial development or decline can intimately depend on contingent dynamics. It is therefore necessary to emphasise again how much the dismantling of factories, the material outcome of deindustrialisation, contributes to defining the new characteristics of the territory: in these terms it is evident that the processes of deindustrialisation physically accentuate the degradation of the landscape and unsustainability of the urban environment, through that swarm of skeletons of establishments of various sizes which in turn intensifies the dysfunctional environmental disorder, generating a vicious circle that continues to suppress the competitiveness of the territory. The failures of the past thus influence the potential successes of the future, and the rare successes of the most recent investments, local associations and committees and planning today are, for now, strongly characterised as merely puntal, 'glimmers of light' only, as we have seen in previous pages.

The 'swamp' is therefore the result of the solid interconnection, in historical processes, between economic dynamics and territorial changes, on multiple levels. A slow and progressive 'magmatic' sedimentation, which alternates phases of fusion and phases of solidification, amalgamates structural processes and contingent events and manifests itself in a territory with unsustainable characteristics that nevertheless hides the seed of its own regeneration. There is an ironic paradox between the order of the actual swamp of the early modern period, actually a system of gardens, and the current mental space enclosed in quotation marks, a metaphor for chaos, disorderly, but vital in its own way. Ultimately, this is an amphibious territory, hostile to order and made so by human choices, a sort of treacherous swamp in which it is too easy to get stuck. Or rather, to run aground, if you choose to ignore the rare passages through which to go back.

APPENDICES

The following interviews are the result of four[1] meetings with a category of witnesses that qualitative sociology would define as 'significant personalities of the local community'. However, here I mainly refer to the methodologies and *modus operandi* belonging to a partly different field of study, namely oral history. I acquired the necessary analytical tools and took inspiration from Italian historians, such as Alessandro Casellato, Gabriella Corona, Gilda Zazzara, Roberta Garruccio and Bruno Buonomo, and Anglo-Saxon historians and social scientists of deindustrialisation, such as Steven High and Tim Strangleman. As a consequence, the following interviews are characterised by a 'biographical' focus on the interviewees' memories and long interview times,[2] and by non-schematic and flexible questions. I never tried stopping the interviewees, and later on I deeply regretted the few situations when I actually had to. The uninterrupted flow of words allowed me to register opinions and information which I could have never foreseen, even if that meant straying from the original question. The choice to conduct some of the interviews with two interviewees worked similarly: on the one hand, their interaction exponentially increased the quality and quantity of their memories; on the other, it often led them away from the original question. All things considered, in these double interviews, the interviewees gifted me much more data to work on than I expected, and I think that's always a good thing.

Moreover, I did not want to put any kind of pressure on the interviewees and tried to make them as comfortable as possible by talking together about every distant memory, intimate thought or ideological stance. For the same reason, at the beginning of my research I thought that the choice for the context of the interviews was pivotal: by choosing a familiar context, such as public places or their own workplaces, I wanted to make each of the interviewees as comfortable as possible. Yet, I must confess that their extraordinary personalities actually helped me in that respect more than I expected, as they showed a huge amount of empathy for a novice researcher

---

1   I had to divide the first interview into two parts because of bad luck and because of the 'golden rule' in the methodological framework of oral history: never turn off the voice recorder. Unfortunately, the library that hosted the first part of the discussion with Enzo and Antonio had to close for the evening. Eventually we moved on and continued the interview outside, in the nearest square.

2   Furthermore, I always took some written notes on the locations, on the interviewees' facial expressions and gestures and on what I thought was most important, in order to adjust my original questions to the situation at hand.

such as myself. Incidentally, I think they revealed their personalities in the most fascinating and empathetic way during these not so rare moments when they managed to overcome 'formal' speech and started joking, or getting angry or passionate about the subject at hand, often switching from Italian to the Neapolitan dialect.[3]

Going back to the main topic, the selection criteria for the interviewees need to be clarified. What links the interviewees is a certain degree of experience and awareness of the historical topics in question, bestowed not only by age but by active participation in the historical processes I wanted to study. As I was interested in the links between deindustrialisation and environmental change, my choice criteria initially privileged former factory workers, but then extended to different categories as well as 'hybrid' personalities not categorisable in a single social group. Therefore, I contacted different types of witnesses, belonging to different social groups and with different work experiences, in order to extend the scope of possible responses and enrich the critical analysis through comparative methods. In the end, I think this choice worked well, and the reader will find different points of view on the same historical events and processes.

Now, allow me to sketch a brief introduction to each interview and interviewee. For the first and second interviews I contacted Vincenzo (or Enzo) Morreale and Antonio Fondacaro. Enzo Morreale embodies East Naples' contemporary history. He worked in different factories from his childhood to his thirties, when he joined the Neapolitan Communist Party Federation as an official. Later, he served as a provincial councillor in Naples for nine years and, today, is the driving force behind the San Giovanni a Teduccio Civic Committee. Over all these years, and up to the present, Enzo collected and studied a huge number of documents and other historical sources on the entire history of Naples, and East Naples in particular. Without his help, this research would not have been the same. Thus, reading his words you will find not only a testimony but an analysis of historical processes and events of the most disparate kind: his experience as a worker and a description of old factories; his memories of the Communist Party's organisation and opinion on political phases and social issues; last but not least, to-the-point

---

3   Sara and I tried to keep all of the dialect expressions in the text, but sadly we had to paraphrase some, for clarity's sake. I hope the reader will find these expressions as fascinating as I do: sometimes, the interviewees use old idioms that exemplify the extraordinary ability to synthesise conferred by the Neapolitan language.

Appendices

description of the environmental problems of the area and interpretation of the efficiency of the institutional responses. From a historian's point of view, the collaboration with Enzo was pivotal and his interviews clarify or deepen every aspect of this research, while touching many other subjects.

Antonio Fondacaro is definitely an important part of East Naples' soul. He is very well known in San Giovanni, where he has lived since his childhood: in fact, you can't take a walk with him in the streets of this district without constantly being greeted by people! His charming way of narrating his own memories will quickly prove that his popularity rests on a huge personality. His work experience in local factories is limited to his teenage years, but I doubt the reader will find more fascinating pages in this book than the ones where he collects his memories on the Cirio agri-food factory. His memories definitely widen the scope of the company history, which I recounted in chapters one and two. Antonio then worked as a railwayman for 43 years, but he did not linger on this subject: rather, he gave me an extensive account of his experiences as a political activist for the Communist Party and I think these political and cultural experiences characterise him as much as his work experiences. In the interviews, Antonio gives his opinions on the organisation of the Neapolitan cell of the Communist Party and the activity of its political leaders, but then complements his interpretation with stories on working-class culture and its principles, ideologies, songs. At the same time, he collects his numerous memories on specific strikes, demonstrations, factory occupations and even dangerous situations in which he was involved from time to time. Finally, Antonio is well versed in the historical sciences too, and his passionate studies on the history of Camorra translate into an interesting analysis of East Naples' social issues connected to delinquency and criminality.

I met Giovanni Moliterno thanks to Enzo, as they have known each other for a long time. The three of us met on the beach in San Giovanni a Teduccio, on a rainy day of December, while some volunteers were cleaning the shore of the debris regularly brought ashore by the tide. That was the perfect moment to talk about coastal pollution and, especially, the historical impact of the local tannery sector. Giovanni was the ideal figure to deal with these issues. Giovanni is a craftsman, more than a factory worker: he has been working wood and metal for forty years, in order to make technologically advanced tannery drums. In the interview, he describes in detail the processes connected to both tanning and tanning machinery, while highlighting local processes of technological innovation with tangible pride. At the same time, though, Giovanni is well aware of the environmental consequences connected to the tannery sector and gives a clear account of his (or his colleagues') experiences related to coastal pollution, human health and workplace safety. This information complements the account I gave in the second chapter. Finally, in this third interview Giovanni and Enzo discuss the delocalisation of the tannery sector and different historical events which characterised the local history in the 1970s and 1980s, to which I refer in chapters two and three.

According to Nino Daniele, political commitment is a life choice. A Communist Party official since his university years, Nino's career continued through the San Giovanni a Teduccio Communist Party cell, then the municipal council, the regional council (of which he has been the vice-president), the municipality of Ercolano (where he was mayor) and finally (at the time of the interview) the municipality of Naples once again. In January 2019, Nino served as councillor for Culture in the municipality of Naples and we met in the municipality seat, Palazzo San Giacomo, while Nino was enjoying a short break from work. Despite that, this fourth interview is all but restricted to the political topic. Nino's memories on specific factories and events are still fresh but it is on structural processes that his interpretation and opinion linger the most, with such clarity that I must confess I had to review some of my research questions. Therefore, Nino talks about local economic development, deindustrialisation and service economy as well as the post-earthquake and post-Agip explosion reconstructions, referred to in chapter three. In the end, Nino analyses present social issues and perspectives for redevelopment.

I got in touch with Giovanni Dispoto in the first place thanks to Gabriella Corona, for an informal talk on local urban planning history: Giovanni has more than four decades of experience in the subjects of architecture and urban planning. He was amongst 'I Ragazzi del Piano' ('the lads of the plan', described in Gabriella Corona's eponymous book) who drafted the Suburban Plan and the Extraordinary Programme for Residential Building, during the 1970s and early 1980s. His professional activity for the Urban Planning Bureau of the Municipality of Naples continued in the next decades, as he was the planner of, amongst others, the Urban Planning Variant of 1998 and the current GDP, approved in 2004. Between 2011 and 2012 he was director of the Urban Planning Bureau. From the very beginning of this research, Giovanni followed me and assisted me in understanding the urban history of East Naples. When we finally met, at the National Research Council seat of Naples, to record the interview, Giovanni helped me to understand the focal part of this history, the period between the early 1970s and the 2004 GDP. As such, this interview has the clarity of a proper lesson, as Giovanni

Appendices

schematically gives account of every phase of the contemporary urban planning for the city of Naples. Nonetheless, what fascinated me the most about Giovanni (and I hope the reader will agree on this point) was the emotive effect of the sum of his utmost professionalism and his view of urban planning as a means to achieve a higher degree of social equality, ecological sustainability, empowerment of local communities – in short, as a tool of modern democracy. This perspective manifests itself especially towards the end of our talk, where he expresses his opinion on present redevelopment projects.

Recording 1. First conversation with Antonio Fondacaro and Vincenzo Morreale

PLACE OF RECORDING: congress hall of the 'Antonio Labriola' municipal library, located in Piazza Giambattista Pacichelli, 10, Naples.

DATE OF RECORDING: 30 July 2018

INTERVIEWEES: Vincenzo Morreale, born in Naples on 19 April 1953 and Antonio Fondacaro, born in Naples on 15 October 1954.

Caruso: *First of all, I would like to ask for a brief summary of your work experiences; how you found a job; what your experiences are in the industrial sector.*
Morreale: My work experience has been very long. First, I was an assistant [*guaglione*, the young helper] of a tyre dealer in San Giovanni. I was curious about that activity, I wanted to tinker too. I was about seven, eight years old. My mother believed it was necessary and useful to learn a trade from a master craftsman (*mastro*). I also went to school, but then in the afternoon I worked. Then I found myself in a pastry shop, because my mother knew the owner somehow – he later became my confirmation godfather. Then I did something else, with my godfather, with whom I had a very intense and familiar relationship. He worked in a printing shop [*tries to remember the name*]. The owner was a senator of the Republic [*smiles*]. I don't remember the name, but he was a book author. I began to learn the trade of lithography and photoengraving. And I returned after a series of vicissitudes to carry out this job, I had finally chosen a path, that is, as an apprentice in an important business. Now let me talk about reconnecting with the history and industrial

traditions of this context. I worked in this place, the ex-Lattografica, an ancient industrial site.

Caruso: *Where was it?*
Morreale: In Ottaviano street, San Giovanni district. There were two different departments: one was innovative, the lithography, where I worked as an apprentice photoengraver; and then there was the old part of the factory, where the tinned tomato cans and olive oil containers were printed. I still remember these cans because, even though I was just a kid, they always fascinated me because there were very ancient presses. There were some really ancient electrical tools. There was a huge room full of star presses, one next to the other, connected through a large pulley to one of the first electric motors. You could see great leather belts coming down from the ceiling and spinning mechanised presses. Such a plant proves that the canning industry was very important here. I remember a friend recently asked me for pictures of old Metalgraf cans. The other thing that I remember very well (and I think that a real artistic heritage has been destroyed, since the old art of tin printing has been abandoned) is that there was an incredible number of lithograph stones, not all of the same shape but all more than ten centimetres thick, where the engravers manually drew the tomato and the writing. *Vall'a fa* ['it's not a simple thing']. The drawings went into the roller were printed with the press. Among other things, the factory still had wooden floors – I saw and experienced a true nineteenth-century factory. I moved in these very narrow spaces. I still have these images in my mind as a photograph; too bad I don't know how to draw very well.

Caruso: *Do you remember when the factory was closed?*
Morreale: Yes, right before the earthquake. At the end of the 1970s, they wanted to build a big parking lot for large vehicles and constructed a reinforced concrete platform. They totally destroyed what was inside it. Just think, in a few thousand years they will go digging and they will find the lithographic stones that I speak of. The process fascinated me a lot. I used to play with these star presses, but I was still a kid. Then the post-earthquake reconstruction demolished both the platform and what remained of the factory. Today in its place there are some houses, so all traces of this important industrial activity have been lost. I now remember the name of the old industrialist: Cavaliere Fichisecchi. In any case, the factory moved to Pazzigno and then

Appendices

I moved too. It was the summer of 1968. I landed in a large and important printing / graphics company in the eastern area, SAGRAF, which was located in via delle Industrie, San Giovanni district. When I started working there, it employed more than 230, between workers and technicians. A great business. A printing works generally has just five employees. It also had important publishers among its clients, and printed scientific editions. There is a textbook, a volume, which students still use today (later it may have been updated). It was called *Teodori*. Tens of thousands of copies of these volumes were printed, just to name one that most impressed me. And so there were large offset machines that churned out these texts. This type of activity was carried out for scientific publishing houses. I was even doing work for clients of international importance, such as FAO or the United Nations. Books for all over the world, even in Chinese or Arabic, in all the languages of the world. I entered with the status of apprentice, I must have been fourteen, fifteen years old and I'm confronted with this great business. The authorities were among the customers too; even driving licenses were printed. The activity was huge. There was both a lithographic plant and an older typographic plant. There was a department with incredible machines, about twenty of them. Since it was a large company, important publishers approached it. Putting down pages of lead type, in short, was a sight to behold. And it was conceived by two brothers who came from a small-town background and then moved. Caldarola, they were called. They had moved from a business they carried out in the ancient centre of Naples, a small company, before setting up this large graphics company. I dealt with the darkroom, photography, films, books, fumes [*laughs*]. In short, the working conditions, despite the status of the factory, were not exactly exciting. Among other things, I had to go to work half an hour earlier, because I had to turn on the machines and prepare other things, so that when the other workers arrived, they would find everything ready. And this wasn't all, because work ended at seven in the evening, but not for the young helper, the *guaglione*, who at that point had the task of cleaning. This was my working day.

Caruso: *What was your salary?*

Morreale: It was a big company, but the salaries were quite low. Then the trade union autumn arrived there as well.[4] I entered in 1968 and in 1969–70

---

4   The years 1968–69 in Italy were marked by working class demands over health, salary and working times. In their protests, workers often joined forces with students' movements.

the chaos began, the protest for better living conditions. I had no experience of this, despite my parents voting left-wing and my mother being a worker at Cirio. I somehow managed to understand that perhaps it was necessary to defend oneself and therefore I joined the union and started a long process of *unionisation* as well. I also played the role of unionised worker, member of the Internal Commission. Then my company became an avant-garde factory, which was a point of reference for other graphic companies in the sector. There was one, called Manzoni; there was another in the hinterland and other printing companies. I even think there was one owned by the current president of the Association of Industrialists [Vincenzo Boccia, managing director of Arti Grafiche Boccia S.p.A], which was almost as important as SAGRAF. It was a benchmark. Later, the subject of discussion was wage increase. The workers of my factory protested and were an inspiration (even if my colleagues will never admit it) for others, especially those who worked in the MobilOil refinery, who were also registered at the PCI, so we attended the same section; or for those of Ignis, who worked next to us. In short, my factory was in the vanguard from that point of view. This company, however, had a problem, as there wasn't, within the families of the employers, any heir who would take it over. One of the two employers only had daughters and he said that a girl couldn't take on such a responsibility [*ironically*], so it's complicated. The other had a son who was unfortunately involved in a motorway accident and that was how the troubled story of this company ended. It also began to have difficulties and to downsize. Actually, I offered to set up a cooperative management by the workers, and there were already significant and important examples of this in Italy, in Emilia for example, and the legislation that offered opportunities was there, at the time (I'm talking about the end of the 1980s). However, in order to set up a cooperative management, you had to invest your own salary. Therefore, many workers did not trust this kind of perspective of ...

Caruso: *Of self-management.*

Morreale: Self-management, yes. Perhaps there was a lack of self-confidence. I, on the other hand, was persuaded and convinced that it could and should be done. After all, we had already devised a plan to establish a working relationship with the employers on even terms: that is, we would have become the employers of our own employers and still managed to maintain a relationship with international clients, as I recalled at the beginning. It must also be said that in those years (now I'm talking about the mid-1970s, maybe 1973) I enrolled in the PCI, in the San Giovanni section, in a rather curious way: I

Appendices

asked a family of communists who lived upstairs how to make contact with the party and how to join, and they told me not to worry because from time to time a bus passed by to bring party cards, but it didn't happen. This was the official procedure [*laughs*]. After that, I went to the section and talked to a comrade [*compagno*] outside. He was called *Capemazzola*, that is 'hard head', and I told him: 'I want to join the party, the *compagno* who brings the cards didn't come', and he replied 'ah! now everybody comes here!' And I: 'oh well, *agg'pacienza* [lit. have a little patience – there's nothing I can do about it].'

Caruso: [*to Antonio Fondacaro, who is laughing*] *The same thing happened to you too?* [*Fondacaro nods and laughs*]

Morreale: this comrade had criminal records and he did not even know how to read or write, but after the war he hung posters. He had also had political experience, but he couldn't even read the political posters and sometimes he posted them upside down. Oh well, in any case, *me facette na cazziata* [he scolded me] because I wanted the card. When it arrived, I established a relationship with the party, then gradually entered the board of the local section. In 1983, they offered me a position as secretary of the party's local section. I gained more experience with time. After a while, an old comrade, his name was Vaiola, who was the head of the union [the CGIL] and had also been a partisan, offered me to become a union official. The word 'official' is frightening and I was frightened by the possibility. I used to say: 'I've always been in the factory', so this scared me a bit. Then, in the same period, the federation of the party asked me to work in the Neapolitan Communist Federation. I just didn't want to. I imagined it would be a difficult position, which required qualities that I did not think I had. They needed, in some way, to demonstrate to the party that there was attention to the working mass, that there was an effort at renewal in places as important as San Giovanni, which was a significant political locus, emblematic in many respects. They pissed me off. I didn't want to join the union, least of all the party federation. Then I wouldn't be able to decide or choose according to my own convenience, so in some respects I suffered from the decision when, from the end of 1984, I went to work in the Federation. This was the path of duty. There was chaos in the party ranks. It was a rather difficult life, complicated in some respects. Having started my career as an apprentice and a worker I found myself an official of the Communist Party. Then, with the dissolution of the PCI, a new question arose. We joined the Communist Refoundation, *Rifondazione Comunista*, and the decision was taken to stay within that party [...] Then later I made up my mind again, when this party found itself on the threshold of decline and it triggered a process that led it to question its social-democratic position and to move towards the democratic party. At that point, *se rumpettero e'giarretelle* ['that bond broke down'] completely and I had problems and difficulties. I found myself collaborating, only for a short time, with Rifondazione Comunista Party. I was a bit shaken by that experience because I had been used to a completely different type of path in life, I don't know how to say it. It was complicated. I was also in a fairly bitter controversy with the management of this party on a point that related to perspectives on the redevelopment of San Giovanni. In spite of myself, I found myself serving within a party, Rifondazione Comunista [...] I found myself supporting some very heavy commitments: for example, one of the reasons I clashed with the party was the question of the Tourist Port of Vigliena, so I sent a letter to *la Repubblica* and also made it the subject of a manifesto in which I criticised the speculative motive for placing it there. Soon after came the story of the thermoelectric power plant: I made a fuss, *nu burdello e'pazzi*, on these things and found the party against me again. I still keep these manifestos in which the parties I was involved with took a stand against me (a crazy situation). Then I was also a provincial councillor; I had nine years of institutional experience. I think I carried out this function, which I was well trained for, with dignity. ... Now, [*to Antonio*] it's up to you. Have I tired you out? [*laughs*]

Caruso: *Antonio, same question for you too – I mean, a summary of your work experiences.*
Fondacaro: Should I talk about my experiences in this area?

Caruso: *About your work experiences, in general.*
Fondacaro: I say this because I have also had work experience outwith the Neapolitan area, I had the good fortune or bad fortune to have a terrible experience of work in Turin at a young age. Let's say that I started doing a lot of jobs, even when still at school, because I was not much suited to studying ... That's why, while I was a student, I went to do odd jobs as well: I worked for a few years in a painting frame factory in the area, I learned how to make frames. Ten hours a day, 'super-exploited', moonlighting. I worked during the biggest period of production for the Cirio industry, this was illegal work as well: they would call you certain evenings, based on the production needs of the various departments.

Appendices

Caruso: *Do you remember who was contacting you?*

Fondacaro: There was a cooperative. The term 'cooperative' meant all 'Neapolitan style', not cooperative in the proper sense.

Caruso: *A sort of illegal hiring, in short.*

Fondacaro: It was a sort of intermediary, it was called 'Cooperative of Sant'Antonio' and I remember that this gentleman called himself *pizzeco e'rogna* [lit. 'pinch of the mange', referring to the scabies scars on his face]. And we went, all kids, in the afternoon, to the front of the entrance of this large factory and he chose us. 'You, you and you' [*points the finger*], in short, he chose a certain number of boys and sent us to various departments. We went there to work at night. You could end up in a department where the work was easier, such as the one where peaches in syrup or tomatoes were bottled. Or go to a department like the ice one. I remember the days when I and my brother, who shared my experiences with me, being more or less the same age as me, went to the department where we had to handle terrible blocks of ice and pass them on the rollers that carried them into various refrigerators. It was quite a tiring job for a boy of thirteen, fourteen. However, having family needs, because my father worked on the railway, we were four children, we didn't own a house, we paid rent ... so as a boy I already had a fairly strong sense of responsibility and I adapted to any type of job. In terms of work, then, I did many little things. The worst experience I had at work was during 1971, I had not yet turned seventeen, it was October, and I went around with dear companions (Ciro, *Fefé*, Peppe Zinno). It was the era of the *capelloni*, long-haired. By the age of fourteen I already had the first card of the Communist Youth Federation. My first card was in 1968, so let's say I was already 'floured' [politicised]. I had a very difficult relationship with school, I left it very early. My school was the party. But I had to accept, out of that sense of responsibility towards my father, the family, a situation that was unacceptable to me as a communist: that of being hired illegally by a Neapolitan intermediary who procured labour for the North and earned twice what I earned in a day, without doing anything. It was a form of mafia, I understood that. But I didn't have the courage not to do it, because I felt there was a need for it at home. I still remember my father in the train station. I was looking at him and I felt like crying because I had a lump in my throat but I wanted to show him that I was strong. And he said: 'come on, I'm telling you for the last time, don't go there. Here we always have something to eat, don't worry. What are you going to do?' But I went. As soon as the train left, I burst into tears. But I lasted four months in this ugly environment, working on metal pipes, in the city of Turin. There was this Turinese gentleman, very rich, who exploited we guys who came from the South, paying us 500 to 550 lire – I don't remember well, maybe I'm wrong – for every job we did. We had to go around Turin with a bag on our shoulders, alone, with a list of people: go around, knock, ask the ladies if we could enter. We had a list of names and we had to do this job of changing the gas meter seals. At the time, maybe because I was a boy, they showed me some kindness. But racism was perceptible, discrimination against Neapolitans was perceptible. Well, how that story ended: in short, we were a nice group of us, even my cousins worked there. This gentleman had a contract with Italgas which began to reduce the amount of work, and he reduced what he gave to us. We got to the point that, practically, with what little we earned we could not even pay for the pension where we slept. So, we were forced to organise a strike. I remember that my brother and I were seventeen and eighteen, but there was a comrade from Turin who, I will never forget, was called Della Pietra. He was sixty, I was seventeen. And the three of us organised this strike in front of the offices, all of them stopped. We convinced all the others, we were about forty people, from Calabria too, but mostly from Naples. With some firmness we resisted for ten or twelve days, to the point that we then went to the Chamber of Labour to ask for support. [The principal], when he received the document from the Chamber of Labour fired us all. He rehired those who accepted a reduced salary. Over time they came back, perhaps because they were more in need, perhaps they were less politicised or unionised, so we five or six were fired. At the Chamber of Labour, they gave us the account of our entitlements; despite our not having a contract because we worked illegally, they told us to present this document. When we went there to present this document to request the settlement due to us, we found two Camorra criminals from the Herculaneum area, I could tell from the accent. These two gentlemen stood behind the boss' desk and looked at us with a menacing gaze. When we brought this document then this 'bastard' master read everything and said – now I don't remember the figure, it would be absurd to remember it after fifty years – in short, he offered us a quarter, or rather less, much less than a quarter, just a pathetic amount of money, compared to what we were entitled to. We immediately said, 'it is not up to us, let's go back to the Chamber of Labour immediately'. At that moment the two unknown gentlemen intervened, tore

Appendices

up the paper, took the money and said: *si e' vulite chisti 'ccà sennò jatevenne proprio, è meglio pe'vuje* ['if you want this money, take it now, otherwise you better leave, for your own health's sake']. My brother and I returned, much to my father's delight. He hadn't wanted us to go, he absolutely didn't want it, but I was stubborn and the sense of responsibility made me go. This was the worst experience, but it has nothing to do with the Neapolitan area. Here we can talk about political experiences, like Enzo did; I remember perfectly when he came to the party, despite his being older than me. Enzo is a *compagno* for whom I have always had great esteem, from the first day I saw him and to this day, despite having political differences. Esteem is something different. I was fourteen and I was already in the party. But I came out two or three years after the communist-Christian democrats compromise that I did not agree with.[5] I had a perhaps more orthodox conception of the party. I stayed out of it but I always gravitated to the party area, I also participated in all the demonstrations, but I was not in the organisation and I was not even interested because I was not good at it, despite having had a few years' experience at the district council with *Rifondazione Comunista* as an advisor. It was the only time I approached the institutions because the institutional role is definitely not my kind, although I believe it is fundamental and, when the *compagni* have done it well, for years there have been great achievements. Because together with the role of protesting, the role of institutions is fundamental, even if not primary. In times of great struggle, such as the autumn of 1968, up to the end of the 1970s, this led to great improvements in working conditions for the working classes. So, I left the party. Then I don't know, traumatic political experiences ... I suffered two attacks from fascists, one in my neighbourhood [San Giovanni a Teduccio] around 1978–1979; having a character that is a bit – shall we say – disobedient, I always had to fight off someone who provoked me, even the fascists. As a result of a quarrel that I had with one of these 'gentlemen', a month later they waited for me by my house and they beat me up thoroughly. Being a bit thin and not very accustomed [*laughs*] to fight, I let you imagine how it ended. But I believe that our neighbourhood has been a reservoir of ... [*searches for words*], and Enzo is one of the

---

5 The PCI-DC compromise or 'historic compromise' was a progressive political accommodation between the two parties, which represented the two opposite sides of the Cold War in Italy. It lasted from 1973 to 1980 and marked the distancing of the PCI from the USSR, but was not accepted by the far left.

noblest examples of working-class culture. Of worker dignity. We are talking about the end of the 1970s here ... people had their own identity, there was work for everyone, the great workers' achievements led to the application of national employment contracts. We moved from internal commissions to works councils. There were links between businesses and the party, the so-called 'cells'. There were parties. The party [the PCI] in particular was a garrison of training, employment, aggregation.

Caruso: *Of democracy, in short.*

Fondacaro: Of democracy. All citizens, even non-communists, saw in the Communist Party a point of reference, where they could resolve their own issues, personal but above all collective. It was a real school, in which we trained. Myself and dear Enzo as well.

Recording n. 2. Second conversation with Antonio Fondacaro and Vincenzo Morreale

PLACE OF RECORDING: Giambattista Pacichelli square, Napoli

DATE OF RECORDING: 30 July 2018

INTERVIEWED: Vincenzo Morreale and Antonio Fondacaro

Fondacaro: [*takes up the discussion on the local Communist Party*] I experienced the foundation in San Giovanni of the Communist Youth Federation; the main section was effectively used as a recreational club. There were billiards and pinball machines. In short, it was a source of income for the party. Later on, there would be a huge increase in the number of party members. I was a boy when I started frequenting the section. And I remember the first *compagni* (at the time I was a kid, I was fourteen), who helped us understand what the Communist Party was and all the rest. They organised a party school, whose teachers I remember well: Maurizio Valenzi ...

Caruso: *Ah, the future mayor of Naples.*
Fondacaro: Yes and Pietro Valenza, senator, Paolo Vicchia, Umberto Minopoli. We were kids and they schooled us. And from there the first nucleus

Appendices

of the Youth Federation was founded. We were about fifteen kids; some others were university students. And that's how the San Giovanni Youth Federation began and, let's say, systematic militancy became understood as a continuous presence in the quarter, with activities and all the rest. It was around the end of 1967 and the beginning of 1968. It was the climate that was brewing almost everywhere, not only in Italy but in Europe, the sweltering autumn of 1968 was beginning.

Caruso: *Antonio, tell me about your relations with the union, as well as with the party. How was it? Both your personal relations and the relations within the party. Lastly, what were the relations between the party and the union in those years?*

Fondacaro: Let's say that the CGIL union has always had a very close relationship with the Communist Party. At least the majority of it. There were officials and union activists who were also in the Party bodies, because at that time the party was organised into sections, not circles, and had its own cells in neighbourhoods and factories. Factories that were located in the territory of San Giovanni a Teduccio, Ponticelli or Barra referred to the San Giovanni section. They had their own cell secretary who was included in the executive bodies of the section, in the steering committee or even in the secretariat, because it was believed that direct contact with the productive reality, with the reality of workers and factories, should be constant. It was a perfect organisation. Perfect in every part. Not only technical and organisational but also human and existential. We were like a big family, we helped each other. We were always together. Personal life and political life had almost become one. This was the party. I remember the first formation of the FGC, the first battles, the first factory occupations in which kids of the Youth Federation were allowed to enter the occupied factories. The first factory, I remember, was the Nicolò here in Bernardino Martirano street.

Caruso: *Was it near the place where there's a school now?*

Fondacaro: No, the factory is now abandoned. And I remember that the workers occupied it once. We were a group of boys from the Youth Federation, all minors, and the police, directed by two marshals of the time, Rametta and Cofi, whom we knew well because they were from San Giovanni and were good people, but they had to obey certain orders: they gave us an ultimatum; if we hadn't cleared the factory, they would have had to clear it. They prepared the fire hydrants. I remember the secretary of the section at the time, who was called Giovanni Sodano ... later a colleague of mine, because at the age of 22 I won a competition for a railway job and I was there for 43 years. I retired in January [2018] after 45 years and six months of contributions and 43 years of actual work.

Caruso: *My grandfather was also a colleague, he worked at ATAN, but he stopped several years ago.*

Fondacaro: Your grandfather was a tram driver, I knew him. Back to the topic, I remember that the secretary of that time, Giovanni Sodano, said: 'all the FGC boys who are not yet eighteen years old must leave!' And I remember this escape through the walls of the factory and we jumped down ... we wanted, for the spirit of belonging, to stay, but he felt responsible for us minors. After that there was a confrontation with the police but the occupation remained. And I remember well the occupation of Cirio, which lasted four months.

Caruso: *When?*

Fondacaro: Cirio... [*tries to remember*] 1973 or 1974 ... but maybe I'm confused.

Caruso: *What do you remember about that occupation?*

Fondacaro: The occupation of Cirio was beautiful because a solidarity network of all the factories in the industrial area was created to support the families of the workers and we of the party stayed there night and day. I remember that I strummed the guitar and I had a repertoire, mostly unknown militant songwriters.

Caruso: *Do you remember what the reasons were for this occupation of Cirio?*

Fondacaro: They wanted to relocate Cirio to Caivano, and then they succeeded. Employment cuts as well. Later it was relocated. Then I remember Rivetti, a pharmaceutical company near the beach of Vigliena: I remember the wonderful evenings spent with all the workers and I was there for hours singing songs. Which I also did when I was in the military in Asti, among other things. There my political passion also led me to risk jail. It was when Forlani was Minister of Defence and filled military prisons with political militants. And I unconsciously gave him the chance, or rather consciously because I knew what I was doing and I also knew the dangers I ran. I'm

Appendices

talking about 1975, the year of the municipal elections, when Valenzi won in Naples, Novelli in Turin, Aniasi in Milan. We, both Communist and the Socialist Party, took all the big municipalities in Italy.

Caruso: *Was that a great illusion?*

Fondacaro: A great illusion, yes. The army did not send me to vote, of course, because they knew how I'd vote. And I, out of spite, began to sing in a group close to the Communist Party, a musical collective that made shows during the election campaign. I finished the election campaign in Nizza Monferrato on stage singing the Neapolitan song *Sacco e Vanzetti* by Anonimo and it was very satisfying. We were singing political songs.

Caruso: *Antonio, before we talked about ethics, civic sense and respect for the urban spaces of this district and more generally of what is now the former industrial area. When did you begin to perceive a change? In your opinion, when did this area begin to fall into degradation? When did this area change from an industrial area to a new reality, today's reality? Or what was the transition phase towards this 'swamp' that we see today?*

Fondacaro: I believe that the second half of the 1960s and the whole decade of the 1970s, including the early 1980s, were years of great growth and emancipation for both workers and districts. And I believe that the degradation, not only environmental but political, social, of ethical values too, began in the second half of the 1980s, with deindustrialisation. The Communist Party became bourgeois, too. Hence the choosing the compromise with the Christian democrats, which turned out to be a choice, in my opinion, that gave rise to behaviours that were no longer radical. The idea that we had about a real alternative to capitalism, it declined more and more. The party presence in the territory lost the spirit it had once had, as the garrison for control of the area, of democracy, of relations with the neighbourhood and of workers' struggle, mainly. And I believe that the decline started there, then it was progressive ... today we are completely abandoned by the institutions. This also leads to widespread antisocial behaviour, disrespectful of common areas and of the environment. The state of the coast, and Enzo can give us all the institutional paths that have led there, is a prime example.

Caruso: *Enzo, we were talking about decay in the neighbourhood after deindustrialisation. The question is, when did you begin to perceive a process of decay, of* *degradation of this quarter, and more generally of what was once the industrial area.*

Morreale: I think that this decay isn't a recent process. Actually, it was caused by very same industrialisation processes that have affected the area. There is a beautiful map, by Luigi Marchese, from 1814, which is kept at the Institute of Homeland History (Storia Patria). I asked for a copy, they gave it to me. There is also a previous one, that of the Duke of Noja, but I am very interested in Marchese's one, because of its colours, because it is effective, because it is an overall picture. And you realise, looking at that 1814 paper, that we were practically inhabiting a piece of the earthly paradise. This is the truth. There was not even the railway in Pietrarsa.

Caruso: *That came in 1839.*

Morreale: Actually, there were already the Granili, for example. You realise what has happened over two hundred years. A huge disaster. At least that's how I consider it.

Caruso: *In the sense of environmental disaster?*

Morreale: Yes, of environmental disaster, especially as regards the state of the sea. What remains after this long cycle? One word: degradation. And despair. One asks whether another model would have given more? What I know is that in Portici, San Giorgio, [not industrial] – neighbours to San Giovanni – despite the conurbation and other serious problems that exist, the degradation that we see here, somewhere that started off as a similar small town in the Neapolitan belt, does not exist. In my opinion, it is a long-term issue, accelerated in the 1920s. It's not a matter of political prejudice but facts: in via Alveo Artificiale [In San Giovanni. Formerly an artificial riverbed, now covered by concrete] hundreds of thousands of tonnes of sludge go into the sea, to this day. That decision dates back to the 1920s. Few know that. Because the artificial riverbed had a completely different path and was built for quite different reasons, namely to convey and control water runoff from the hills and convey it towards the sea. And so ...

Caruso: *It was a land reclamation operation.*

Morreale: A necessary one, because we were in the swamps here and the channel was apparently even navigable. You could also fish there but you needed a licence. After that it became a sewer. In 1920 there were legislative measures, let's call them, which further developed the port and this

Appendices

channel, which had already changed its characteristics, was diverted and brought into the neighbourhood of San Giovanni. Other riverbeds, too, that started out as protective measures for the area, became sewers. In those years, San Giovanni also lost its municipal autonomy [1925] and provided Naples with a dumping ground for its complex problems. In truth, it was a long-standing process: for example, the leatherworking factories were moved from the centre and brought over the Granili bridge. It was a part of San Giovanni, and in 1920s the quarter lost it. For example, in these years the choices for the oil area were made and the port expansion towards the east decided. There were problems of silting at the entrance to the port, so they developed the port and took it to the borders of Vigliena. Then they started building thermo-electric power plants, a trend I am very passionate about. Then the EAV plant with law 1904, the Capuano power plant and so on.[6] It has been a long-standing choice.

Caruso: *Excuse me if I interrupt you. Concerning ethical degradation and the loss of values linked to workers' identity, what can you tell me?*

Morreale: This is very interesting. The degradation has ancient origins and when San Giovanni was deprived of its municipal autonomy it was put under direct government control. The thing is that San Giovanni has never been considered Naples. That is, Naples ends at the Ponte della Maddalena. We are effectively still in the seventeenth century, when the cartographer Baratta indicated the end of the city there ... Then there came something new: the novelty of the 1970s. With decentralisation, there was hope for the establishment of neighbourhood councils, and therefore direct democracy. And to tell the truth, the PCI formed its own local ruling class through the local cell. It was imagined that this could also correspond with a growth in participation and democracy. In my opinion things went differently. Paradoxically, there has been neither a growth nor a development of democratic life but ... let's say degenerative phenomena.

Fondacaro: But don't you see one of the causes in the transformation of the Communist Party?

Morreale: Yes, then things went hand in hand. For example, in the initial phase the party had – and it is a bad thing that I am about to say but I would also like to clarify – supremacy. That is, the board decided, had greater re-

---

6   See Ch. 1 p. 21.

sponsibility and power in deciding and determining things. This can also be criticised in some respects because in an institution, we would say today, one is with one's own conscience, despite the programmes of the parties to which one belongs. However, there's a new contradiction arising, when individuals count more than parties. I mean [*laughing*], 'if I bring in two hundred votes, how many can you bring?' Or maybe you won't get a single vote.

Fondacaro: There is also the abandonment of democratic centralism.

Morreale: Right there is also that. These are transformations, for me, which we need to go into and discuss cautiously, so we don't simply imagine a centralised party with democratic centralism, but a party where we can discuss, where we can compare ... Honestly, one of the most challenging lessons learned in the party is that you constantly have to refer to your autonomy, in order not to disturb your own conscience, which is even more demanding, but in any case, there is a degenerative element there. Then let's discuss it, let's go into it in depth, let's see the causes. So, I have two documents, two dossiers. I collaborated in the drafting of these two documents among other things, but I was young so I kept little or nothing. Being a typographer, I took care of the graphic part. I was also a secretary of the party cell, though. Two documents in which we said, in 1983, 'we have done these things, we plan to do others'. And that document had a runaway success. So much so that I intend to gift it to the municipal library. From a very simple reading of those documents, you understand one thing: that there is a ruling class that is within a process and a national dynamic but that wants to improve its context, while discussing its issues. One of the themes is the redevelopment and recovery of the suburbs, and this is the first dossier. Then the second dossier marks another phase, the waning phase, that of the earthquake, of decisions and there is a defeat. Hence the reconstruction. The reconstruction model through which we have never had a critical part in the decisions and choices that have changed the face of the neighbourhood. These choices were supported, by the way, by scientists and academics. It is enough to say that immediately after the reconstruction there was an article, I do not know if I still have it from *la Repubblica*. It was signed, undersigned, by one of the most important urban planners in the country, the one who wrote *I vandali in casa* [Antonio Cederna, the book is from 1956], criticising all the urban planning choices that had impoverished the Italian territory. Cederna said: 'a piece of Scandinavia has been created here in Naples'. That too was a choice, an evaluation. If someone like Cederna was wrong, we can be wrong too

Appendices

[*laughing*]. And through those choices in the post-earthquake period, we communists suffered a heavy blow.

Caruso: *Taking a cue from what you've told me, I want to ask you both a question, then you are free both to respond. How much do you think the earthquake and post-earthquake reconstruction influenced the subsequent situation in the neighbourhood? From the economic point of view, that of social aggregation, political cohesion...*

Fondacaro: I think that the earthquake was a turning point, not just for Naples but for the whole of Campania and for the political relations it generated. I always return to the same theme. The Communist Party was a great political force as long as it was able to maintain certain principles and certain values and control and combat ill-conceived policies. I am convinced that if the Communist Party of that time had had the strength and ability it had always had to counter certain drifts, it could have changed the course of events that then generated a cascade: behaviours that then 'polluted', if not ideologically corrupted, people inside the Communist Party. Previously I was speaking of the abandonment of democratic centralism and the compromise with Christian democrats: these were the elements that gave way to a negative transformation of the Communist Party. And all of this has sparked in individuals and even militants, let's say some of them, the possibility of only thinking about yourself, at the expense of the principles you always followed. Just grow your own little garden. Starting with little gardens we reached large estates. And from the large estates we arrived at exploitative work conditions and positions. And then careerism, a deleterious element that we have always fought, led you to believe that the exploitation of work was not a problem. Let's say a 'power failure'. In the end, Vincenzo and I lived it first-hand, right? He's not saying random things. We have seen how people's behaviours changed from the 1980s onwards. Behaviours that had nothing to do with the principles, not just of communism, but of the Left itself. Then various polluting elements, unclear relations with characters who had nothing to do with our history, or with other political forces such as Christian Democracy, which in this neighbourhood has always done its business through the most efficient use of clientelism, which we always opposed. And these forms of collusion have undermined the foundations of the party.

Caruso: *Antonio, we are now in Pacichelli square, we are also surrounded by people of my generation, some a little older, some a little younger. You told me, in* *the course of the interviews, that you had experienced illegal work. What do you think is the fundamental difference between the world of labour, thirty or forty years ago and today? What you think was the attitude of people who were your age at the time towards illegal work and what attitude do young people have today?*

Fondacaro: it depends on the period you are referring to. If we talk about the period preceding 1968–69 then we were in worse working conditions than the current ones. Then, there was a great period of struggle, with the sweltering autumn that aimed to tear down the processes that capitalism puts in place, because capitalism is inhuman and exploits as far as it can; we know that is the evil of society. At least from our communist point of view. I repeat, the second half of the 1960s and the entire decade of the 1970s marked a period of great achievements, in which working conditions improved, as much as economic conditions and consequently social, environmental, behavioural and civilisation conditions as well. People lived in a condition of dignity and not of… [*looks around*]. With the transformations we talked about earlier, I think working conditions are getting even worse than before. Even worse. Right now, this proper slavery … The destruction of national collective agreements … and here the union and the party are responsible … The total destruction of national contracts. This myriad of casual contracts, lasting ten, five, six days. As if the job market had become a cow market. We are no longer human elements that produce, not even through the relationship with a machine, we have become producing machines ourselves. And as such, we're exposed to wear and tear and become just trash to throw away. We are in total catastrophe, worse than those years. The current conditions can be found at the beginning of the twentieth century and up to the years of fascism. Working conditions were already improving after the war, even before 1968, but they can't be compared to current ones. The current ones are of total slavery, in my opinion.

Morreale: these aspects are substantially different. At the beginning of industrialisation, you still had a development of the productive forces and therefore the conflict between capital and labour was also based on this development. In the 1980s, which was also the moment of crisis here in Naples, for example, you had a coincidence of the crisis, as it were, of a social and economic model with the welfare crisis. And therefore, for me the crisis of the Left started in the 1980s, when you had a restructuring, a relocation of production systems, restructuring even at a global level. This is the historical stage I'm talking about. And the Left did not withstand this change from

Appendices

the point of view of the dynamics of work and innovations. The Left did not stand up to this clash and a difficult crisis began. In this context of crisis of the Neapolitan industrial fabric, the earthquake was an accelerating factor. And in that phase the Socialist Party represented a destabilising element, from my point of view, since it did not manage to shift the attention of the Italian Left, or of the State, towards social-democratic claims and reforms but, in many respects, I think, contributed to producing an even more complicated situation. San Giovanni, for example, which had had this electoral history, lost its majority [PCI majority] in the municipal council and centre parties gained it. It was a novelty. An amazing thing had happened. In those years then, there is the story of the march of the 40,000 [great protest of the FIAT workers of Turin, October 1980], which is still being discussed now. And then there is the death of Berlinguer [Secretary of the PCI, 1984]. I mean, the vortex of the crisis sucked up the left, which has not withstood the fight. Then there are other degenerative elements inside the crisis. *Je addeviento sempre chiù realista d'o 'Rré* ['I feel more and more cynical']. If this is the new way of life, I am following it. Human dynamics led to that. People said after these events 'well, I have never been a communist', with a certain nonchalance. We are still in this crisis and due to its evolution, we have reached the breaking point of this story. I remember there was a book that talked about the Chinese revolution, saying 'you have to read the last four hundred years to understand this process'. To understand the current process, more modestly, based on the things I have experienced, we need to reread the last thirty or forty years.

Caruso: *Enzo, a question specifically for you. You have been very interested in the petrochemical area in recent decades. Since we have talked about the party dimension, the political dimension and the popular, city, and civic dimension of the neighbourhood, the only thing missing is the discussion of companies and businesses. Reading some essays by Roberto Parisi, in particular 'Lo spazio della produzione', he speaks of a 'petrochemical siege', or a decision-making vacuum connected to the presence of a strategic sector such as oil. In your opinion, both today and, above all, in the key situation of the 1980s (thinking also of the Agip explosion in 1985), how much do you think this presence / non-presence has influenced the economic dynamics of the neighbourhood?*

Morreale: Present, present [*laughing*]. That one is alive and fighting with us. The SAGRAF was only tens of metres from the refinery. I won't tell you about the alarms I've heard over the course of my working life. Every now and then the sirens could be heard. I remember one in particular, where there was a fume leak and many of my colleagues fainted or got sick. *Je rimanett'allerta* ['I endured it without problems']) in that circumstance. It's a thing that has accompanied and accompanies production. In some areas, there are people who still complain about the fumes. What happens is, when the gas carrier arrives – and there are practically always several of them moored in the port, waiting to unload – some gas is released into the air even when there is no accident. Those who studied the thermo-electric power plant said, 'look, you can use all the tricks you want, a certain percentage will always be lost in the air anyway'. Then there are some things that really make you angry and smile at the same time. The problem of the presence of chemicals, of the oil area, because before there was the refinery, was linked to the port of Naples which has a strategic importance because it not only supplies the city and its hinterland but is important on the supra-regional scale as well. It is very complicated to solve this 'problem'. Yesterday, joking a bit with a friend of mine about the risks, I said, 'okay, where do we want to put it [the oil area]?' This stuff has to be put somewhere in the end. Obviously, constant processes of rationalisation, delocalisation, reduction should be favoured, but the idea that you … [can remove it permanently] They tried, but they failed and the oil area remains in situ. The General Development Plan [of 2004, the current GDP of Naples] takes a strong line and calls for delocalisation … There is a statement: the oil area must go away. But no one has yet explained how, where and when. It remains a petition of principle. Now, the ridiculous thing that can even raise a laugh in a wretch like me, is that in 2012 there was a proposal for a variant to the General Plan. What did this variant anticipate? Since the harbour needs to expand, let's take the area of sea beyond the oil docks, fill it in, get another 400,000 square metres from this operation, move the oil area beyond the breakwater and effectively build an oil platform. Like they do in the North Sea. Imagine an oil platform in the middle of the Gulf of Naples [*laughing*]. And this proposal was so improvised that the Superior Council of Public Works just had to say, 'clarify yourselves, because we have not understood how you want to proceed. Give us the characteristics and all the necessary studies, behind creating something of this kind.' The sea of Naples may seem so calm and serene but when there is a storm it destroys everything. And no breakwater can hold up. Several times over the centuries it has been broken down and smashed. They want to do something in the Gulf, which would maintain the existing situation: an enlarged port, in addition to the oil platform placed in the middle of the sea, and in

Appendices

any case all the coastal depots would remain unchanged. This presence is a nightmare, from which it is difficult to imagine being relieved in the near future. I personally think that it will be necessary to implement a coherent, lasting initiative and over the years to work continuously in stages, step by step. Start reorganising this sector. I repeat, it would be very easy for me to say, 'let's take it to another place, who cares, let's just solve the problem', but things are not exactly like that. There is a lot of propaganda.

Caruso: *Of course, strategic importance must be taken into account.*

Morreale: The question is how not to further burden this area. Start the redevelopment, now. This should be a new policy: the redevelopment starts tomorrow morning, you don't even put in another spoonful of concrete, you use a jackhammer to knock down a piece instead, then the following year another piece and so on. This is the way to stay anchored to reality. Instead they want to invite another disaster.

Caruso: *Enzo, how long has the oil sector been at a standstill, or at least reduced production to a minimum?*

Morreale: The crude oil arrived there [*points towards the old refinery tower*] and it was refined. There was a perennial flame on that contraption that still stands, the tower. This activity is now decommissioned but the storage area is still used, an immense storage area. In some streets you can still see fuel tanks that are burned, deformed. Those sirens that I heard as a boy ... I'll tell you about a misadventure I had in the oil area: we wanted to make a movie (on the thermo-electric plant, we finished it recently), so I went there alone in the morning and I started to film the Q8 depot. Outside the gate, in complete tranquillity. At a certain point a surveillance car arrives, screeches to a halt and asks me what I am doing there: 'you can't stand there, what are you doing here?' I replied 'but I'm outside the building, I'm making a movie and there is no prohibition'. Conclusion: 'we alerted the police'; and there was also a haulier who helped them. I seriously risked being beaten up. At one point the police arrived. I, on the other hand, called the *carabinieri* on the phone and said 'there is an idiot who has arrested me', I mean the vigilante. Conclusion: these policemen invited me to go to the police station in Ponticelli. I said: 'I want to understand, what's my position, have I been arrested, stopped?' They replied: 'absolutely not, the police officer just wants to talk to you'. I went there to the police station in Ponticelli, it was 2006

I remember, and there was an official in the way, a person who understood the situation and said to me: 'look, since we are worried, because there is an alarm situation, what have you filmed?' I said: 'I went there and there was no prohibition, I did not enter the private property. Of course, if you really want to know, I was very interested in a little dog that somehow was something incredible because it inspired me with a certain tenderness [*very ironically*].' The official then said to me: 'Can we see it?' and I handed over the camera, turned it on and there was this little dog running around among the articulated lorries. General laughter. They handed me the camera, but they didn't want to give me a copy of the report.

Caruso: *Amazing. Thanks Enzo. A very last question for both of you, feel free to talk together if you want. On delinquency, both organised, juvenile and spontaneous. How do you perceive the delinquency of forty years ago, when the neighbourhood was an industrial area, compared to the current crime?*

Morreale: [*laughing*] This is another provocation. Go on Antonio, you first.

Fondacaro: and this is a sore point because I personally have been dealing with the history of Naples for some years. It's an old passion of mine. I am very fond of nineteenth-century and later Camorra history. I know very well the mechanisms of the Camorra organisations. Wanting to talk about our neighbourhood specifically and address this issue, the discussion becomes difficult. First of all, because the Camorra families whose names we hear on television are there, but ... it may be that we live in a different reality despite being in the neighbourhood, but I physically *nun'e saccio proprio* ['don't know them at all']. But I can say that the neighbourhood where I grew up did not experience this phenomenon so badly. Not as much as today, at least. Of course, the Camorra is now something else entirely. Defining it as Camorra is also improper, because the term 'Camorra' presupposes a certain type of organisation that hasn't existed since the end of the Second World War. We can only speak of hundreds and hundreds of gangs that split the various neighbourhoods amongst themselves. But I can say that we did not live the problem of the underworld in our neighbourhood with such fear in the past. There were phenomena of widespread crime, and so on. But I don't remember such a big problem in the 1970s. We started living it in the early 1980s, with the war between Cutolo people and *nuova famiglia*.

Appendices

Caruso: *The 'famous' scissione, split?*[7]
Fondacaro: Yes, we really felt it here. There were many murders all over Naples, even in San Giovanni. I have seen many shootings. Today I don't know how to define it: I don't feel the problem of the underworld as my own, here in San Giovanni. I have never experienced it first-hand. I know it exists, I know it exists. But I don't see it. I don't hear of micro-crime phenomena in San Giovanni (you, Enzo, correct me on this). I hear the current reports, shootings and all, but I don't experience them.

Morreale: I think it is the epilogue of an extremely explosive situation. Unbearable, in some respects. I recall the story of the area that was destined to be built on … [the project for the new auditorium in Taverna del Ferro street] Emblematically it has also become a symbolic place, the one where they buried… [18-year-old killed and buried, February 2016] is something creepy. It must be said that the San Giovanni working class had always had energy, it was a deterrent, from my point of view. For example, the PCI section was not in New York but in San Giovanni. And in any case tens and dozens of people gravitated around the section of the PCI, hundreds at the end. That is, I never felt this criminal presence, I'm talking about the 1970s and 1980s. They were two separate worlds and it was an expression of the culture of work. Now, in such a situation, so ramshackle, so complicated … it is clear that this presence has found its legitimacy. Do you understand? And therefore, it is a palpable presence. It is a presence that is felt. Now, it is clear that we live in a certain context and in a certain reality, so we know the neighbourhood from the point of view of our context and our reality. I know very well what could happen to me if I walked by there, or if I met this or that person. What helps us is habit and a life spent in this context. But those energies of the world of work have totally run out. There have always been two different worlds. In the Enel archive, I noticed a flyer, dated 1958, in which the workers said, 'stop the fascist dealers and the Camorra'.

Caruso: *You spoke to me another time about the fact that the Camorra members also entered factories such as Cirio to put pressure on the workers.*
Morreale: Right, so as you can see they were two different worlds. But the first world, that of work, was preponderant. It had hegemony. That's the

---

7   A violent and long-standing feud between two *camorra* organisations over cigarette smuggling and Sicilian mafia interests in Naples. It lasted from the 1970s to the 1990s.

point. This hegemony is lost and now there is only one hegemony: despair.

Fondacaro: However, the problem of widespread crime is closely linked to unemployment. We have said that in the 1970s there was great development and almost full employment in San Giovanni. Automatically, criminality was reduced to a minimum. And since there was also such a strong and identifying worker presence, that small element was marginal. Then, as we have said, in the early 1980s, deindustrialisation began, the Camorra war, the explosion of the heroin market ... therefore, the underworld found fertile ground.

Caruso: *In summary, let's say that the Camorra and crime in general in the area is the spearhead of all the processes we have talked about?*

Morreale: [*laughing*] If you sow peppers, you'll find peppers. The sowing here is human despair. The responsibility lies with a State that has liquified, which does not exist, which you never or rarely encounter. You just need to go to certain areas and there is a very real risk of being involved... how can you say... a witness to these realities. Among other things, in San Giovanni we have the *Carabinieri* barracks, the barracks of the Custom Corps (Guardia di Finanza), a very large garrison of the traffic police. The police are here, two hundred metres away ... you can't even say, 'open another barracks'. It would probably be better to say, 'open another factory'.

Caruso: *Gentlemen, thank you both for your availability.*

Recording n. 3. Conversation with Giovanni Moliterno and Vincenzo Morreale.

PLACE OF RECORDING: Giambattista Pacichelli square and the public beach of San Giovanni a Teduccio, Naples.

RECORDING DATE: 1 December 2018

INTERVIEWED: Vincenzo Morreale and Giovanni Moliterno, born in Naples on 12 March 1947.

Caruso: *Giovanni, the first thing I would like to ask you is to give a summary of your work experiences in the factory and other places.*

Appendices

Moliterno: I have forty years of experience. I started by selecting timber that came from Africa, iroko timber, from the Ivory Coast. You first chose the boards that were compatible to do a job and then you started cutting. It was cut according to the size. It ranged from one metre to four metres in diameter and four metres in length. Then we continued according to the measurements that the customer chose.

Caruso: *Which local factories did you work in?*

Moliterno: Always in the same place, Vertmac. Now it is gone. In Gianturco. We made tools for tanneries.

Caruso: *Do you remember from what year to what year?*

Moliterno: From 1968 to 2005. Then I retired.

Morreale: And where did you learn this job, Giovanni?

Moliterno: To do these things? First, I worked in other companies that did other types of work, then when I went to Vertmac I learnt how to make equipment for tanneries.

Caruso: *Do you remember when all the tanneries that were here on the coast started to close?*

Moliterno: In my opinion it began as early as 2003 or 2004, so let's say from 2000.

Caruso: *So very recent?*

Moliterno: Yes.

Caruso: *What was the situation in the 1970s?*

Moliterno: There was a *boom*, between Gianturco and San Giovanni they were full.

Caruso: *Do you remember what the effects of the pollution produced by these factories were and also some popular demonstrations against pollution?*

Moliterno: I don't remember the demonstrations, but I know that the dye, the tannin they used and all this stuff here ... the meat that remained attached to the hides ... it all ended up in the sea. They skinned and the rest went to sea.

Valerio Caruso

Caruso: *Two more questions, what do you remember about the 1980 earthquake?*

Moliterno: I remember from the 1980 earthquake that we all had to escape and we left the factory for three or four days and then returned later. For us, most of the orders came from Irpinia, from Solofra, so we had to stop for a while and then we started again.

Caruso: *The second question, do you remember the project to create a tannery centre in Ponticelli in the 1980s?*

Moliterno: Yes, but nothing was done, in the end. That was a promise that was not kept. I remember that. As regards my work in these years, I remember that I had to make a huge tannery drum for a Chinese client and some Chinese people came and filmed me.

Morreale: This drum was truly huge, it could hold 5,000 skins.

Moliterno: We exported drums to China, Saudi Arabia. But it had to be shipped in a disassembled state. Then one of our workers went there and assembled it.

Morreale: It was not an easy process, but possible with specialised equipment.

Moliterno: It wore a three-metre toothed crown. Made with six arms. Then it used a large geared motor. And it had the speed one wanted, from three gears.

Caruso: *Do you remember how many were employed in the factory?*

Moliterno: At the height of our factory's glory, we were twenty. Later on, just seven or eight of us were left.

Morreale: And the drums, were they made of wood?

Moliterno: Yes, because it maintained a stable temperature. Each plank was seven centimetres thick and we crafted these wooden staves with different diameters, so they would fit into each other.

Morreale: Sorry for interrupting, Valerio, but he told me about this process many times and it was not a simple job but a rather complex thing. A technology that defined this place and made it highly specialised in the sector.

Moliterno: There were also machines for buffing the hides, for polishing. The velvet wheels. They were wooden wheels, sixty centimetres in diameter and forty in width. They were covered with red velvet, or felt. Then there were others made with blades that were used to scrape the hides, they were called 'buffers'.

Appendices

Morreale: Was your factory supplying other local enterprises? And do you remember which ones?

Moliterno: Yes, the Vergona in Gianturco, or the Muscariello firm, many years ago.

Caruso: *How many years ago?*

Moliterno: Eh, in the 1960s and 1970s. Muscariello was at the Gianturco intersection. Do you remember the Honorable Muscariello? [*to Morreale*]. But there were many of them … the Osci firm. The largest one was the Russo firm, which remains active in the hinterland and has two or three hundred workers.

Caruso: *So they delocalised?*

Moliterno: It is in the hinterland and mostly processes the skins of cattle and cows.

Morreale: What about those that were on the Vigliena coast? They were also pretty big.

Moliterno: I don't remember the names. However, there were three or four.

Morreale: They were quite large. Today, it's a brownfield site.

Moliterno: There was also another one between the Ponte dei Francesi and Ponte dei Granili. Then several in Herculaneum. Some in Nola.

Caruso: *What about the Sant'Erasmo area?*

Moliterno: Sant'Erasmo was full.

Morreale: The factory where he worked was in Sant'Erasmo.

Moliterno: Yes, next to Mecfond.

Morreale: When was it founded?

Moliterno: A hundred years ago. First there was the father, then the children, then the grandchildren.

Caruso: *A family business?*

Moliterno: Yes.

Morreale: It was specialised because there was a lot of this activity going on.

Caruso: *And technological specialisation.*

Moliterno: However, we also worked with more ancient tools, such as easels. They put them [the hides] on an easel and then they removed the attached meat with a crescent-shaped knife.

Morreale: It is a workshop that lived through the entire industrial period.

Moliterno: Then we also made tilting tanks. They removed the hides from vats filled with lime, they threw them into another vat which was called the 'reel'. We invented it, there was also a patent. It was a tip-up tub. Inside, a reel turned and made all the water move together with the hides. We invented it ourselves and we had the patent. It had pistons that gradually rose and unloaded the hides on the ground.

Morreale: Have you ever gone to Saudi Arabia to assemble these tanks?

Moliterno: No, your cousin went there though, your cousin Vincenzo.

Morreale: He was your *guaglione* [apprentice], you taught him the job.

Moliterno: He went to Saudi Arabia and also to Morocco. In Morocco they still had tanks on the ground. In Tunisia too.

Caruso: *A quality export, in short. Proper 'made in Italy'.*

Moliterno: I agree. But the timber came from Africa. So, we used iroko timber. We also used oak, however, it did not work so well, after some time it would pulp and *infracecava* [was easily soaked with water]. A timber that lasted a long time instead came from South Tyrol, the larch. The larches, maintained their non-permeability, they did not let the water flow. To make a tannery drum it took an average of twenty days, between blacksmiths, carpenters, electricians and mechanics. We also used a mechanical lock.

Morreale: In short, a device made of wood and metal.

Caruso: *And everyone worked in the same factory?*

Moliterno: That's right.

Morreale: The first time Giovanni told me about this I realised that when he speaks of a 'drum' it's than a container, it is a sort of 'space capsule'.

Moliterno: A tank, in a nutshell.

Morreale: But a huge one. How many metres wide was it?

Moliterno: For the most part we made them three metres wide and three metres long. It had a wooden porthole attached, then we modernised and made sliding steel doors.

Appendices

Morreale: And who were the competitors?

Moliterno: The competitors were a company that came from Santa Croce sull'Arno, in Tuscany. The Gozzini company, which still exists. Towards Vicenza there was another competitor. In Naples there was only us.

Caruso: *In Solofra?*

Moliterno: There is one in Solofra, but … just now he wanted to hire me [*laughs*]

Caruso: *And you didn't go?*

Moliterno: No, now I'm 71 years old.

Morreale: We could have gone there together, Giovanni, so you could have taught me the job [*laughing*].

Caruso: *Enzo, what do you remember of the local tanning centre?*

Morreale: I can't remember the exact timing. There was the Merli law which essentially changed the rules, making it no longer possible to carry out tanning activities, to discharge into the sea, specially-equipped areas were needed and so on. As a result of these provisions the tanning sector entered a crisis and the administration, realising that it was a sector with many employees, tried to define a solution. The solution was to create a tanning hub in the eastern area of the city of Naples, in the Ponticelli area. In the initial phase, this proposal aroused great interest, because it could have been an opportunity for development. After the proposal was launched, the environmentalist associations led an initiative to prevent the project. After which, the companies changed their mind, partly due to the relocation, partly on the basis that these activities had become illegal due to the Merli law. The entire sector of tanning then faced a crisis, because it could not expand, or stay in this district. Some of them would have resisted less than a decade ago but then gradually, one by one, they were hit by the crisis and now I think not even small workshops remain. Some of these always remained at the artisanal level, even individual level, because it was clearly a profitable sector at the time. There is this first aspect. Then in my opinion the other aspect is connected to changes in the general market, and in the leather one in particular… all those hides coming from China and other countries …

Caruso: *Competition.*

Morreale: Yes, global competition has definitively 'solved' the problem.

Moliterno: However, if I remember correctly in San Giovanni there is still a tannery in via Nuova Villa. You know, where the radar was, *aret'a furnaria* ['behind the furnace'] shortly after the entrance to the new University. On the right there is a tannery. I remember well because I've been there lately.

Morreale: And they still process raw hides?

Moliterno: Yes, and they do so with the tannery drums and all the rest, to this day. I know this because I made my last drum for them. Big, it was not three metres but about two and a half metres. So, the workshop is still there.

Caruso: *What's the name of the firm?*

Moliterno: I don't remember the name, but it's still there.

Caruso: *It's the last one, right?*

Moliterno: In the area, yes. It should still be active

Caruso: *Earlier we were talking about pollutants. In terms of effects on health, both yours and of other people you know, what can you tell me?*

Moliterno: I can tell you only one thing. We had a driver. We went to Solofra every day. And this driver, in addition to being a driver, was also an assistant in leather factories. He had to go inside the drums, cleaned, removed the residues of leather that blocked the machinery and so on. And this driver soon died of ... what's the name of that disease ...

Morreale: Cancer?

Moliterno: Blood cancer, leukaemia. He was a dear friend, from Ponticelli. In addition to being a driver, he was also forced to be an assistant. You know, in small factories it is not like in big factories where you have only one job. Sometimes I went into those drums to assemble the double bottoms, because the drums had these double bottoms and when they unloaded the hides and then opened the valves, only the water came down and the hides remained inside. Then they opened the doors when they had finished unloading and went to the trolleys. Then from the trolleys they put them on the benches. Then from the stalls they put them to dry. And then they went to the processing, the dry cleaners. There are several processes in leatherwork.

Caruso: *Another question. Compared to the years when you started working, that*

Appendices

is, the late 1960s and 1970s, in years afterwards do you think that the tanneries centre changed from a larger dimension to an artisan dimension?
Moliterno: It evolved more to an industrial dimension. From artisanal to industrial.

Caruso: *The opposite process, therefore, from artisanal to industrial?*
Moliterno: Because they emancipated themselves.

Caruso: *I also speak of employees within each factory.*
Moliterno: Yes, the smaller factories disappeared and became ...

Caruso: *Amalgamated, but here in this area or outside?*
Moliterno: The most part in Solofra.

Caruso: *Therefore, relocation.*
Moliterno: Yes, some in the city's hinterland as well

Caruso: *The artisan workshops disappeared from here and went elsewhere and became industrial, is it right?*
Moliterno: Yes, but on local context you have to understand something else. The pins we used to shoe the lumber to the ring gear, their heads had to be made of bronze, because otherwise the acid of the hides would corrode them. Bronze resists acids. Fortunately, next to my factory there was a foundry that did all these jobs. A foundry involved in making propellers for motorboats. But it also used to make the pins for the drums.

Caruso: *When did you start exporting abroad, to Tunisia and Saudi Arabia?*
Moliterno: Late 1970s and 1980s. The decline came with the 2000s.

Caruso: *Do you remember some of your trade union movements before closing?*
Moliterno: Yes, we were registered with the CGIL. The contract for us was the same as 'woodworkers and cork workers'. Imagine, we did a lot of metalworking and ended up being 'wood and cork' [*smiling*].
Morreale: Not even the contract for leatherworkers?
Moliterno: No, because the other contract was more advantageous for the employer.

Caruso: *Enzo, would you like to add something?*

Morreale: Yes, I don't know if you have considered the fact that there were large companies of this type in San Giovanni. But now I'm talking about the nineteenth century. As far as I know, the Boutillon company, inside the Corradini complex, was one of those. And there were also others on site.

Moliterno: There was one in Primo Vico Marina, where you go down to the seafront. On the right there was a tannery. Just before going down to the underpass that goes to the seafront.

Caruso: *A small tannery?*

Moliterno: Yes, but it discharged so much polluted water into the sea! [*laughs*]. Grey, brown and sea water.

Morreale: The impression I've kept most strongly is the stench of this water and the fact that it was generally whitish. Milky white, more or less, even if faded. And it was unmistakable. You had a mixture, a compost, made of sewage, of leather and then of who knows what more. The incredible thing that we discovered some time ago, not so long ago, was the fact that tankers were still dumping into the sea coming from who knows where, and they were discharging this hexavalent chromium into the sea, which has devastating effects on health.

Caruso: *And the raw sewage was in the open air?*

Morreale: Yes.

Caruso: *Do you remember when they began to cover riverbeds and raw sewers with concrete?*

Morreale: I remember Croce del Lagno, that point there *abbasc'a'ddo mariuolo* [literally 'down from the criminal' but it is a toponymic]. It's a fantastic name, I know, [*laughing*] but so it was called. There was this drain known by most as the *lavarella*, a perennial drain. This perennial drain discharged sewage and tanning water into the sea. But the same thing happened in Vigliena. We saw one of these drains together [when we visited the beach at Vigliena] but now it is mainly sewage water rather than industrial waste. And then there were the large drains like the Pollena riverbed and the Sannicandro riverbed that were once visible, there was no gravel, no rocks but you could see this stuff coming directly into the sea and you saw …

Appendices

Moliterno: You could have stepped into it while you bathed.

Morreale: Yes, while you tried to remove the sand from your feet. [*laughing*]

Moliterno: Just imagine that right here, on the beach where we stand, there was the restaurant and next to that wall made of lava stone there was a flooring factory, it was called the Ferraro flooring factory. And it dumped into the sea. Sometimes red water, sometimes white water, depending on the floors they were making.

Morreale: At this very moment, the beach is being cleaned [*points at the volunteers surrounding us*], but there are parliamentary questions dating from the 1950s on this very same matter. I don't remember what the parliamentarian was called but I still have his name somewhere. I thought he was a leftist, instead he was Christian Democrat. I do not remember the name. He raised the question that the sand was being stolen from the beach, the sand was removed.

Caruso: *To do what?*

Morreale: It was used for construction or to introduce it into other things. Apart from the fact that putting sand in buildings is a wicked thing ...

Moliterno: My wife's grandfather was from Castellammare di Stabia. They moved here, near the beach, but there was dumping of building waste material. The trucks came and unloaded here on the shore. There was a proper mountain of rubbish.

Morreale: A month ago, I crossed paths on the Facebook page with Angela Restaino, who had been a teacher here in San Giovanni and secretary of the PCI of Croce del Lagno. I'm talking about the years before the earthquake. She organised the first cleaning of the beach, in which I participated, and bear in mind that here now seems like being in Hawaii compared to how it was at that time.

Moliterno: The sea always carries residues. Every so often the sea brings them here during storms.

Morreale: So there was this first cleaning of the beach at the end of the 1970s and we were in the midst of the Valenzi administration, after which the municipality established a daily beach cleaning service. And somehow this cleaning has been going on for twenty years and there is still a lot of garbage.

Moliterno: Much of it is remnants of post-war reconstruction materials that ended up on the beach. Here there was the Sapio beach, then there was the Rosa beach, then there was the Santé beach and then there was ...

Morreale: The Catuogno beach, you have forgotten.

Moliterno: And there was a municipal beach, in front of the Boutillon building.

Caruso: *How long ago?*

Moliterno: In 1950 or 1952, until the first Enel power plant was opened on the other side, the beaches were still there. Then Enel expanded ... I remember that Alcide de Gasperi came to inaugurate the Capuano power plant.

Morreale: The film is also in the LUCE institute archives.

Caruso: *Vincenzo and Giovanni, a question for both of you. What are your views on the dynamics of the oil sector of the 1980s and 1990s?*

Morreale: Well first of all, more than the 1980s we should talk about the 1970s ...

Caruso: *Yes, but skipping the 1970s question for a moment and going directly to the moment before the Agip explosion ...*

Morreale: In the 1980s the characteristics for the oil depots had already been decided. The oil docks, with attendant pipelines, were not expanded as the companies planned. Previously there had been the intention to expand this area, to implement coastal fuel depots and one of these areas was designated and purchased by the oil company ...

Moliterno: It was English, BP.

Morreale: ... it was on *terra re'parule* ['the land of the swamps'] as it was known in our part of the world, namely a swathe of open countryside. After the companies acquired this land, we knew nothing more about it. When we were young, we used to go there frequently, but then we could not anymore...

Moliterno: It was also planned to expropriate the houses.

Morreale: Indeed, so there was a rampant enlargement process that affected us and of which we had no knowledge or awareness. We only saw that this area of the *parule* had been cleared, where it was still cultivated among other things.

Caruso: *When did BP buy this land?*

Morreale: At the end of the 1970s.

Moliterno: In my opinion at the end of the 1960s, Enzo, because I had a friend who was worked on that land and also had a job in BP.

Appendices

Morreale: People were left a little to themselves, despite these cultural roots, no one knew what was happening there. Then obviously this project to further expand the coastal depots must have been really problematic and therefore for years we had this abandoned land which became effectively a football field, where we went to play football. In fact someone actually set up a proper football pitch with goals, nets, etc. I remember that the owners obviously tried to inhibit this activity and sent an excavator to dig furrows so people couldn't play. Then a ditch was dug but it was gradually filled up. Then of course there were other illegal activities, such as scavenging for scrap metal. With the earthquake the occupants of this area were moved and then compensated. However, this grassroots project was wrecked, as it were, without the need for anyone to have knowledge or awareness of it. Of course, if one reads the literature of those years one realises what was happening… what their plans were…another environmental damage on the list … [the oil area expansion projects; see Chapter 2] at this point it must have been divine intervention that somehow mitigated these truly abominable intentions.

Moliterno: A ticking bomb in the city.

Morreale: Which by the way is still there. It was a question of moving thousands of other families, of driving them out. Then the area was freed up, as it happens, as a result of an explosion. After they destroyed the old district of Pazzigno, in order to redevelop it, I always tried to find something that could be a link with its lost memories. After the earthquake, then the Agip explosion, they decided to demolish part of this district. Among other things, the area was affected by a urban redevelopment project [The Suburb Plan] and it was said this was a way to accelerate things…

Caruso: *Are you talking about 167?*

Morreale: Yes, there were some pieces of this urban settlement that, however dilapidated, might be amazing like *o' Palazzo ra birr* ['the beer palace']. It was clearly torn down. There was a certain Pecoraro there – if you read some nineteenth-century advertising stuff, you realise it's a very old enterprise – who made carbonated drinks. They made soda, there were pine cone-shaped glass bottles and, before Coca-Cola existed, they offered something else, the Legger Soda. I remember that when they told me 'go and buy two or three sodas' I went to Pecoraro and when he didn't have any in stock, he made them on the spot. Then it seemed like watching a cartoon. At a certain point the pulleys, the tables came into operation [*makes hand gestures to mimic the* *process*] ... and the bottle with the soda came out. That building was pulled down. Recently a friend of mine was looking for a map of Pazzigno but it has disappeared, it has been erased. But he gave me a card from the 1960s where the new district and the so-called *finance buildings* was already built. And in any case, there is at least the layout of those buildings.

Moliterno: Nearby there was the IMPLA plant, which produced plastics.

Morreale: We talked about these substances the other day.

Caruso: *Like plexiglass, the company was German.*

Morreale: Now the plant belongs to the former president of the Industrialists Union and it no longer produces plexiglass but plastic containers. Indeed, when you go to take the train or pass along the *strada e' fierro* ['iron road'], you smell a solvent smell from that part. Among other things, that factory went on fire once, because of course we didn't have enough risky activities around there already! It is close to the Pazzigno park, on one side, the highway on the other. However, from what I remember at a certain point someone came and expropriated the land because it was evidently the intention to proceed in that direction ... then if you ask me today why nothing has been done, I do not know what to tell you. Evidently the enormity of the project was such that they had to give up. The land remained as it was, abandoned, or used as football or for unhealthy activities such as scavenging and so on. Then the earthquake hit and this land was purchased by the government and there is now what you see, residences, a housing estate where the land of *parule* was.

Caruso: *And what do you both remember of the 1985 Agip explosion?*

Moliterno: I remember that I had to go to work and since I live on the third floor you could see a huge blaze. 'How am I going to work this morning?' I reached the *Ponte dei Francesi* on foot and they didn't let me pass. The next day I managed to pass and there were guards ... everyone was running away. It was thought that it would explode again. So, we fled to the harbour.

Caruso: *Why another time?*

Moliterno: Because it was thought that another four tanks would catch fire.

Caruso: *A chain reaction?*

Moliterno: Yes, and there was also someone who died

Appendices

Caruso: *Five, that I remember.*

Moliterno: For one of them, they found only the outline on the ground.

Morreale: Raffaele Zinno always told me that he was associated with the group that managed the emergency on the ground, also because hundreds and hundreds of families from Pazzigno had to be evacuated and were put on ships, or sent in the hinterland of the city (in Sant'Arpino town). In short, a mess. And he told me about his relationship with one of these engineers who was head of the fire brigade and about a tank in particular that he couldn't figure out: what the hell was in that tank, I'd like to know? It was a hard thing to understand and manage.

Moliterno: It was too full.

Caruso: *Too full?*

Morreale: There are fuels there, but also chemicals. In this oil dock there isn't just refined material being unloaded but other elements arrive for the chemical industry or for what remains of it.

Moliterno: Yes, however, crude oil arrived at the time for the refinery. It was not refined.

Morreale: Raffaele Zinno never knew how to explain. I just know it was more complicated to manage.

Caruso: *So, the much-touted line that some smugglers were stealing gasoline and that this was the ultimate cause of the explosion doesn't convince you?*

Moliterno: For me it's more likely that the workers of the plant itself tried to get petrol.

Morreale: I don't know. Human behaviour must also be placed among the elements that can possibly cause harm and danger. One person throwing a butt is enough ... it is one of the risk factors that you must consider. It can't be said that it was an individual ... if a madman comes and pulls something on an oil tanker of that type ... if you go to a place where there is no one within a radius of five kilometres, it's a thing, but if it is densely inhabited this causes thousands of deaths. Then I don't know if what happened can only be attributed to thefts or things of this kind ... The emergency plan for the port of Naples, as it is called, plan required by national law and still on the Prefect's website, what does it show? That from the oil docks to the hinterland of Poggioreale there is a series of branches and pipelines and in the event of a fire it can become a huge fuse. I don't know if it's clear. If a port ship explodes, the entire Poggioreale district will burn, and vice versa. In case of danger the ship must be immediately removed. As if it were a car [*laughing*]. And in fact, I always imagine a scenario of this kind, even with respect to projects that are under construction. It is complicated already, and if you increase these activities, the risks will increase too. Among other things, in this square, according to the provisions of the plan, we should have a notice that says 'dear gentlemen, this is the air quality, this is the situation and in case of an emergency *fujetevenne*' ['run away']. What does this plan tell us today, after more than twenty years? In case of danger, if the board in the middle of the square has not yet been placed, a loudspeaker will pass and inform us that there is a dangerous situation. Just imagine it [*laughing*]. Here petroleum activities are profitable, they are still flourishing, they don't weigh on the coffers of the Municipality of Naples. So – damn the infamous misery – if you just put up a board where you inform about the quality of the air … Among other things, these aren't sporadic events. Whenever there is loading and unloading of ships and so on, there are leaks. Some scientists say they cannot be entirely prevented. You can put in all the gaskets you want, a couple of per cent always ends up in the atmosphere. Now this material that ends up in the atmosphere mingling with other materials and other activities, such as the plants or the tanks, can be a very complicated mixture to manage. But, lucky them, people are so unaware …

Moliterno: Enzo, but have you forgotten that in the past when you arrived in San Giovanni you smelled a smell of broccoli?

Morreale: And that was actually gas and crude oil.

Moliterno: As soon as you crossed the Ponte dei Granili: 'we have finally arrived in San Giovanni'. Why was there that stink?

Morreale: The riverbeds and that other smell. I saw a nice aerial photograph of the army central office, what's it called … the IGM, where we can see our riverbed. There is this Pollena riverbed that begins in the hills and arrives with a straight course, namely Argine street, to the sea. It was made with a ruler and it looks like this in the aerial photo. At a certain point they decided to divert this nineteenth-century riverbed and move it to the heart of the San Giovanni district, where it has caused all these disasters: because it created problems in the port, it carried debris that blocked the port. The solution was to take it to San Giovanni. And from this photo you notice the dangerous curve it makes. That type of solution led to further degradation of the neighbourhood, which in the meantime became a proper sewer. Not surprisingly, now I'm reading a lot of things about cholera which is a subject that fascinates me a lot. It is no coincidence, then, that in 1973 San Giovanni once again became a crucial focal point due to this discharge.

Caruso: *One last question, a bit uncomfortable for both of us. I say uncomfortable because it has nothing to do with what we have talked about now but instead I am talking about politics. What do you remember of the 1983 elections and of the victory of centre parties in San Giovanni and in the eastern area in general?*

Morreale: Yes, but I wanted to say one last thing about accidents that I have just mentioned.

Caruso: *Back to the previous question, okay.*

Morreale: I lived in a building opposite to the port area, a little before Pazzigno. Once I heard a roar and saw very high flames: bear in mind that in front of my apartment there were very tall buildings but despite them it seemed like the sea was burning. Imagine, now I have tried to find something, some reference to that accident, before the one of 1985.

Caruso: *Are you talking about the fire of 1978?*

Morreale: No, yet another. During the fire of 1978 I was in the factory, many colleagues got overcome by fumes but nothing happened to me. This one happened in the middle of the sea. There was an oil spill of fuel and flammable substances. We don't know why, it is said that the fishermen triggered ... imagine the sea on fire. The flames spread over the water.

Caruso: *Chemicals?*

Morreale: Right, hydrocarbons. There was a flash. I was a teenager then... it was the early 1970s. This is about accidents. Back to the elections of 1983 ... I lived them in a 'privileged position', that is, the party section. That time was hard, perhaps we have already talked about this. The earthquake changed local reality considerably. There was a process of further degeneration in social relationships as well, then the general economic crisis, relocations, world capitalist restructuring, layoffs and the consequences in the social fabric. These things together created an explosive mixture for both the dispossessed and workers. Then another degenerative element was introduced: the general context and the political system pursued by centre parties in the

1980s created a hostile political environment for the Left. In those years this aggressive initiative was led by the head of the socialist party, Bettino Craxi, and it became very tough to bear, for the Italian Left.

Moliterno: Who was the mayor, Lezzi?

Morreale: No, Lezzi came later and, in some way, he was also welcomed with a certain open-minded attitude within the left. Actually, degeneration began earlier. There was a faction of the council that become 'rampants' [individualists], this is the name. Then there was this very strange mixture, the tool of democratic participation and the neighbourhood council became a factor and a distorting element ... at that point individual candidates made profit. The theme of local political representation ... you are a neighbourhood councillor, how many votes you get, how many votes you give ... if you bring me the votes, if you respond to this dynamic and this intertwining you will have recognition, a counterpart ...

Caruso: *Clientelism.*

Morreale: Yes. I tried to say it ... the dynamic was this. After that, hell broke loose here. Even pieces of the social body began to become jagged. Problems, earthquake and socio-economic crisis, a new political situation, 'rampantism' did the rest. Then imagine if you evaluate from the national point of view what was happening ... The period of the 1980s was a watershed. It [the shift from Keynesianism to neo-liberalism, Fordism to post-Fordism] was a focal point for the Italian political system, and probably for other countries too; social, political, economic profiles and even ideal perspectives were profoundly redesigned. This happened in those years. The climate of the polling stations, I remembered yesterday with two fellows of the party. One of them now lives in northern Italy and is interested in healthcare. We had a presence in all the polling stations. At that point in the election campaign we were hundreds and in real time we were able to understand what was happening in the polling stations. And it was a real tragedy. Then, a moment later, the AGIP issue also came along and that was it. Then a piece of San Giovanni was transferred to Sant'Arpino. Among other things, I was one of the militants who made the party cards, I had the responsibility of staying in touch with those who went to Sant'Arpino. I endured *mazzate e morte* ['strong criticism'] both personally and politically.

Caruso: *You're not talking about the party cell?*

Appendices

Morreale: No, the inhabitants.

Caruso: *You are talking about the post-explosion context, of course.*
Morreale: When the Agip exploded, it was necessary to provide housing for the displaced and the first houses that became available were some public housing built in Sant'Arpino, between Casoria and Poggioreale. People didn't really take it well. Then, I never understood why these urban settlements didn't work. There must be a problem. Although people had received a new home, all the degrading factors reproduced themselves successively. Paradoxically. In Pazzigno they were already there. After that, paradoxically, these degrading factors multiplied in public housing, through phenomena that were new and unknown in some respects.
Moliterno: However, many asked to return to San Giovanni and returned.
Morreale: A relative of mine didn't want to, but in the initial phase it was terrible. Think about the fact that many of these people later had to come and vote here, because they had their residence in San Giovanni and the other was considered temporary? Imagine one of those from Sant'Arpino, so pissed off, rightly or wrongly so … The Agip explosion caused another explosion in the social and political body of the Left.
Moliterno: That neighbourhood was also out of the way.
Morreale: It was a mess. It is behind the airport. The connecting road was then a small underpass for a settlement of thousands of people. The access to the main street from Poggioreale passed through a small bridge. Then subsequently they made openings and alternative routes. I was there last year and it continues to be quite abandoned as a neighbourhood.

Caruso: *Giovanni, same question for you too, that is, what do you remember about the 1983 elections.*
Moliterno: What do I remember, who was elected mayor that year, Valenzi?
Morreale: No, the Valenzi council ended then.
Moliterno: Yes, then came the socialist councillor, the one who later became president of the EAV. An opportunist…
[*they don't remember*]
Morreale: He was so important that we don't even remember the name [*laughing*]. At least I remember what he looks like, if I see him passing by, I'll recognise him.

Moliterno: Until recently he was director of the EAV

Morreale: That's right, but he also was involved in a long legal case, then he was acquitted I think. And then he was given that job.

Moliterno: And then later he returned during the Bassolino era.

Morreale: Well, Bassolino arrived in 1993

Moliterno: Bassolino's first words: 'in a year San Giovanni will become suitable for bathing'. *Nun m'o pozzo mai scurdà* ['I will never forget it'].

Morreale: People believed it, though.

Moliterno: The only good thing he did was the opening of the Troisi Park, which had been closed for many years.

Morreale: Too easy. The problem of the park is connected with its management. Before it was created you could already sense that something was not right ... anyway, if you create a public enterprise, the municipality should manage it ... but its political efficiency is much reduced ... if I go for private management, instead, I can postpone the opening of the park ... [and save on operating costs]. As a matter of fact, when they finally opened the park, you could have found many fish, brought by the seagulls from the sea to the artificial lake: in other words, this park was left to itself for so much time and became such a wild place that you could find sea fish and sea water in the artificial lake. Then, the first thing Bassolino did, and also an important one, was the opening of this park, in 1993: it was built in 1986–87 and was closed for seven or eight years, a period during which people could only see it was nice but couldn't access it. But it was easy to open it. It is also discussed in de Lucia's book [*Se questa è una città*].

Moliterno: And now the lake is abandoned anyway because there is no money to make the hydraulic pumps work.

Morreale: This park has been open for thirty years, but the pumps only worked for very short periods.

Moliterno: There was also a beautiful fountain in the centre, remember?

Morreale: Of course, once in the *Corriere* I had the opportunity to criticise the councillor of the time because someone put in ducks and geese, which proliferated, but when the municipality decided to do maintenance on the tank and dry it out, some of these were taken elsewhere, and the others ended up being mauled by some dogs. That hurt me a little. I remember that I took pictures and sent them to the newspaper and it was published. The theme was roughly 'where have the ducks gone'?

Appendices

Moliterno: But it was a nice park, my children had a lot of fun.

Caruso: *I remember it as well, though I was very young. Thank you both for your availability.*

Recording n. 4. Conversation with Nino Daniele.

PLACE OF RECORDING: Palazzo San Giacomo, Piazza Municipio, Naples.

RECORDING DATE: 7 January 2019

INTERVIEWED: Gaetano Daniele, born in Naples on 31 July 1953.

Caruso: *The first question concerns your personal work experiences and your party and public positions and commitments.*
Daniele: My profession is a party official, in the sense that since my university years I have been an employee, an official of the PCI. That's the only profession. I've been committed in politics my entire life. Once, I was given the opportunity to work for the Municipality of Naples, but I refused because I wanted to continue on the path of militancy. Back then, political commitment was a life choice for us all. You devoted all your commitment, all your energies, all your activity to militancy. To this day. I have had a lot of public offices. Obviously, my career started in San Giovanni a Teduccio. I was secretary of the local section and district councillor, but at that time the district councillors were nominated, they were not elected. Then I also became the neighbourhood party leader. And then I was elected to the municipal council in Naples, when I was still very young – in the mid-1970s – when Maurizio Valenzi was elected mayor of Naples. I was there for a long time, then I was regional councillor, vice president of the regional council, mayor [in Herculaneum] and currently I am councillor for De Magistris. In the eastern area at that time the PCI had a particular organisation. San Giovanni, Barra, Ponticelli, which were the industrial area, had this institutional body, the 'party zone', which coordinated the various sections of the territory. For example, in San Giovanni there were five sections, or rather a section that was divided into four other territorial cells, territorial cells, and then there were the factory cells. We are talking, at a guess, at certain times, between

two and three thousand members of the PCI. I was also area manager for Barra, San Giovanni and Ponticelli.

Caruso: *The second question I would like to ask concerns your personal memories of the tanning centre in the San Giovanni a Teduccio area. Do you remember anything?*

Daniele: I remember a little. These small companies in the tanning industry, which supplied raw materials for the entire production of leather in Naples – and I think also for a large part of the metropolitan area, of Campania – were small businesses, but very consistent. Obviously, they had very polluting processing procedures. At a certain point, I think at the beginning of the 1970s, the problem of this very polluting presence arose. For a long time, they worked around the notion of a specific water purifying plant for tanneries, which could solve this pollution problem and safeguard… but nothing more was done, so it was never achieved. In the meantime, tannery products became unprofitable due to market dynamics, and this type of processing began to move towards third world countries. Keep in mind that in Naples, let's say in the post-war period up to the 1960s and 1970s there was a lot of production of gloves and shoes. *Naples does not remember.* Now we remember it because we celebrated the fiftieth anniversary of Rocco Barocco or Valentino. That is, Naples also had very important brands in the field of fashion, which then established themselves nationally.

Caruso: *What do you mean when you say 'Naples does not remember'?*

Daniele: Naples doesn't remember because it seems that *made in Italy* is just a product of the North, particularly of Milan. Now I would not say that it was born in Naples, because we always have this (partly justified) tendency to boast about our own records, even in the many fields that we no longer remember were characteristic of our city. Most of all, many of these jobs were done at home. Much of the production, a bit like the English textile manufactories of the industrial revolution, many of these factories used homeworking. So the production of gloves and other objects …

Caruso: *Was it artisanal work?*

Daniele: no, home-work. Housewives or artisans, families and so on. At that time there was a fairly significant market, at least for semi-finished products. Back to the topic, I remember this water purifying plant was not built, due to

Appendices

the usual bureaucratic complications of financing, now I don't remember. But at this point all these activities, despite our failed battle to safeguard them, they were closed, partly because they were polluting, therefore they were subject to sanctions by the health authority, and partly because – already in the 1970s – a series of enterprises with little added value began to move to other areas.

Caruso: *My third question concerns the Snia Viscosa dispute of the late 1970s. Do you remember? Personal opinions?*

Daniele: The Snia Viscosa dispute concerns something else. In other words, the restructuring processes that have always involved the Italian chemical industry suffered a series of problems over time. I believe Snia Viscosa, which produced this very innovative fibre, entered that game of restructuring, of ownership changes. I believe that, rather than a market reason – having no outlets – I believe it entered these restructuring mechanisms.

Caruso: *Was it a public procedure?*

Daniele: Public and private. There was a long war around the Italian chemical industry, first public and then private, that involved Italian capitalism. Throughout the 1970s and 1980s, up to *Mani pulite,* when it was discovered that the famous 'mother of all bribes' was just… and then the protagonists' suicides, then the political failure that followed. The history of the Italian chemistry sector is a very complicated history, which concerns the structures of national and international capitalism. Snia Viscosa, more than anything to do with local reasons, in my opinion ventured onto this chessboard. The fibre that Snia Viscosa produced was very innovative at the time, so it was never clear why they finally decided to close the plant.

Caruso: *The same goes for Cirio of San Giovanni a Teduccio?*

Daniele: In my opinion, yes. I repeat, I think it applies to all the deindustrialisation processes in Naples, in particular in the eastern area … then there are even more emblematic issues, because at a certain point all these companies lost – in the processes of centralisation and to the detriment of the South – the management centres and research centres were lost. In other words, the company know-how. The real damage that we have suffered is that gradually these management centres were moved to the North in the processes of 'concentration'. So, the segments that remained in Naples were departments where there was only a piece of the production process but no longer the entire company strategy: research, the selection of products to be brought to market. To 'build a business centralisation' and give shape to a single company dimension, the business centres were moved either to Rome or to other parts of the North. At this point what remained ... when the crises began, a series of departments were cut that were no longer strategic. When you deprive a production plant of its mind – let's say, of its direction – it is evident that it is no longer strategic, in the sense that whoever makes the strategy, the directionality, does it in another place that he considers a priority. Hence the dependency that gradually ... Obviously, our system was already dependent in some way, in the sense that it depended on an industrialisation process coming 'from above', in other words born mainly from public impulse and not from an endogenous force. Then, with the passing of time, political and economic projects for the South lost their centrality, this was the outcome. I am thinking of another sector where we had an important role, the aerospace sector, and they gradually took the essential departments away from here as well. I am led to read this process of deindustrialisation of Naples as a gradual subtraction of directionality. And then the peripheralisation. And therefore, the marginality that then obviously suffers harder blows with the crises. Especially when, with decentralisation, the widening of the global markets, global delocalisation to non-European countries of a series of productions...

Caruso: *This obviously resolves the fourth question I wanted to ask you: your opinions on subordination and the 'headless nature' of the local economy.*
Daniele: Yes, it also happened with finance, with the Bank of Naples, very recently. Even with the *Risanamento* [The Post-Earthquake Recovery plan], all the real estate assets go to private individuals. When we say privatisation is in fashion... The state centralises it and then transfers it to private individuals.

Caruso: *Then I will move on to other questions relating to personal opinions and memories of the Agip fire in 1985 and the 1980 earthquake.*
Daniele: The earthquake of the 1980s was actually a catastrophic moment for the history of the city. The Camorra war began in the same years. The whole theme of reconstruction has taken on certain characteristics. This is a very negative story.

Caruso: *What are your views on reconstruction?*
Daniele: The reconstruction was a tragedy ... a tragedy.

Appendices

Caruso: *What about the eastern area?*

Daniele: In the eastern area, above all. Certainly. The recovery of the old town centres, which was also a part [of the Suburban Plan] ... and also the provision of infrastructure, which were the two positive parts, but then turned out to be too grandiose. In the sense that they were made on demographic forecasts that then did not occur. And at the same time the type of building chosen was ... really ... another case of subordination, in the interest of the builders. The mistake, a cultural mistake for which I also feel responsibility, of the 167, was repeated. In the sense that we thought that giving a house was 'the way of emancipation', of redemption and so on. Instead that was a mistake, because in the end we concentrated the margins all in the same point. We created a mechanism for reproducing marginality. While, on the other hand, the character of the historic centre – because the historic centre is one of the few in the world that has within itself its own 'peripheries' that is, areas of extensive degradation and social marginalisation – with all its problems and social complexity and opportunities, works in some way as a mechanism for social integration. Instead, when you have assignment mechanisms whereby you put all 'poor people' in a single place ... both in the idea of social housing and in the assignment of those houses to the same social typology, you create a self-reproducing mechanism. It hasn't redeemed anything. Then obviously there was also the collapse of a series of training agencies, then consumerism, cultural degradation and a whole series of things that were intertwined, but fundamentally there was a conceptual mistake. In short, transferring a part of the local society to 20,000 new houses in the metropolitan area meant that it was just left behind.

Caruso: *As in the case of Sant'Arpino?*

Daniele: Everywhere, everywhere. In the area of Nola, in Marigliano, wherever there have been new settlements, no integration has been created. People transferred from the city centre were isolated for a long time, because the connecting infrastructures – that were supposed to be built – came twenty or thirty years later. And they have not yet been completed. There was no actual mobility. Therefore, Naples does not yet have a metropolitan dimension. This is the truth. So these inhabitants felt removed and never integrated into a new system of social relationships.

Caruso: *Referring to this question, I would like to ask you for some opinions on* *the changes in social structure and collective identity. Above all, in the eastern area. Think, for example, of the perception of crime, changes in the labour market and territorial, environmental and ecological degradation.*

Daniele: With deindustrialisation, of course. Let's say that once the workers, clerks and small professionals disappeared, they moved to the surrounding municipalities, such as San Giorgio, Portici or others towards the North area. The workers were gone, because the factories were gone. In addition, 'poor' groups from the historic centre were forced to move after the post-reconstruction projects. These are neighbourhoods that have undergone a de-proletarianisation process.

Caruso: *Would you define the eastern area identity as underclass?*

Daniele: Basically yes. Except in some cases. But that was the process. Barra, San Giovanni, are neighbourhoods that have become ... except for some timid signs ... but substantially from the 1990s onwards, but maybe already in the mid-1980s ... what happened to the social standing of those neighbourhoods? The large training agencies, schools, parties, Catholic church schools, then the factories, the workers' associations. When the workers are organised and there is a discipline, there are trade union battles, there is an emancipatory factor, collective life, being part of a struggle to construct social mechanisms based on rational relations. When all of this disperses, what is left? There is nothing left. Hence also the political degradation, in my opinion.

Caruso: *What is the cause of political degradation?*

Daniele: That there are no more parties. There is not much left. Everything is based on the personality of the leaders. But then, locally, let's say not too much.

Caruso: *And what about the perception of crime?*

Daniele: Consequently crime grew. With the characteristics that the Camorra has, with its fragmentation, the infighting of families. The Camorra families of San Giovanni, I think of the Mazzarella family, even ascended to the zenith of the mafia. They had reached a significant level in the criminal hierarchy not only in Naples but all of Italy. But then this is basically evident. The clans in our territory are numerous and constantly changing. But they are there, they occupy a space and take control of the social system. Although they have suffered – like all of our reality – quite hard blows over the last few years,

Appendices

many have been consigned to their deserved habitat – prison – but there is no doubt that it is a phenomenon that persists with heavy social influence.

Caruso: *Do you think that crime is today more 'spectacularised' than in the past? Or is it given more space in newspapers, more space on television, more space in collective perception?*

Daniele: I wouldn't say that. I repeat, they have suffered severe blows, so there is progress. What characteristics this change has and what is happening, I don't know. It is a thing for further study. Then in general the understanding of phenomena, especially mafia ones, occurs after the fact, on the basis of judicial acts, of the investigations carried out and so on. In Naples the anti-mafia prosecutor has been producing exceptional results for years, I believe that it is no coincidence that the last two national anti-mafia prosecutors, Franco Roberti and Cafiero de Rao, have both been Neapolitans and have come from the battle against the Neapolitan clans. We have to give credit to an investigative capacity that has led to an in-depth knowledge of the phenomenon. But it is difficult to say in this flux what has happened and what is happening. How much is there still of the mafia bourgeoisie, of capital, how they are moving, because obviously much mafia capital is untraceable, sent to foreign integral tax havens. So, it is clear that there are networks of interests or social sectors that in any case are in some way these same mechanisms. But let's say that the Neapolitan Camorra has never been centralised like the Mafia, namely it has never had an apex. It has always been a lot ...

Caruso: *'Feudal' [laughing]*

Daniele: Very 'atomistic', let's put it this way. The Camorra cartels were born in our territory during the wars, the *Nuova Famiglia* against Cutolo ... the big cartels were formed especially in these phases. Each territory has its own settled clan that contracts and negotiates with the other clans, but there is no hierarchical pyramid. Every now and then a dominant cartel comes out and takes centre stage.

Caruso: *I would like to know your opinion on the function of factories and, more generally, of workers' aggregation in the eastern area in limiting and stemming criminal phenomena, in the past. What do you think of this role of 'democratic embankment'?*

Daniele: It is fundamental. I'm not saying that when there were workers' groups there were no criminal groups. But let's say that there was no undisputed dominion over the territory. For example, even at Cirio there were many workers' struggles against Camorra. For example, the Camorra settled in commercial distribution: in one place, only the ice cream of one vendor was distributed, and not the ice cream of another, if you went to buy an ice cream, you only bought that ice cream. Because the Camorra, in that neighbourhood, in that area, controlled the distribution circuit. In general, the struggles of the workers always have this function: the active democratic life is always this, I mean to break these mechanisms of control, of absolute domination over the territory. It has always been a struggle, but in short ...

Caruso: *Even daily activities, assemblies...*

Daniele: Meetings, cultural life, books, posters ... these are all things that are no longer there. Or in a really minimal way. Fortunately, if there's something that the city is very rich and gifted with, it is volunteering. There is a lot of volunteering, a lot of solidarity. But mainly organised by the church. Earlier, there were also the 'people's houses', the workers' mutual aid societies, the consumer cooperatives, a whole solidarity fabric that was born around the union and that is no longer there. There is a space of solidarity and voluntary service, of strong religious inspiration, but that's it.

Caruso: *So, if I ask you about the 'virtuous exceptions' that can be traced today within the eastern area, what would you indicate? From a civil point of view.*

Daniele: In the eastern area the surprising thing is the cultural activities, the theatre, the experience of the Nest, Ikbal, in short, solidarity associations. Before there was the Arci, Olimpia 71. These are the only points of aggregation and collective life. And the school of course.

Caruso: *The last two questions I would like to ask you concern, first and foremost, the 'forced tertiarisation' of the territory that you write about in an article in* l'Unità.

Daniele: Degraded tertiarisation. In the sense that the tertiarisation that characterises industrial areas is usually an 'advanced' tertiarisation, its businesses are functions of the quality production cycle. Our tertiarisation is 'degraded', in the sense that it is often a disguised unemployment, they are small activities that replace ... even trade is a disguised unemployment, you can't find a job so you go into small business, the small shop, the mini-market.

Appendices

There was a time when fry shops opened. By degraded tertiarisation I mean this: small bureaucratic businesses began to proliferate when those general services that used to be in the hands of the public administration were not performed any more because of lack of funds. But they were not big businesses, big design studios...

Caruso: *This does not create development...*
Daniele: Yes, if we also think about the port, what about the containers? The Chinese Cosco brought them to the Neapolitan area. Productive development has not been replaced by a modern, new productive fabric. There are many young people and even good start-ups, especially in recent years, not to mention the past years. Small IT activities ... all very fragmented, all very individualistic, constantly changing, but not the expression of an advanced tertiary system at the service of a solid economy.

Caruso: *The last question concerns the perception of congestion and the saturation of spaces in the eastern area, increased by the presence of many brownfields. What is your opinion, crossing the eastern area, by car, by train, on foot, and seeing this mixed use of territorial spaces?*
Daniele: We have never paid attention to implementing an urban plan. The truth is that after the phase of industrial crisis and deindustrialisation – which all the European cities that had a more or less strong industrial vocation have gone through – other cities, in the thirty years in the forty years that lie behind us, they have experienced one or even two phases of urban transformation, of changes in urban destinations and change of urban functions. Naples did not. The eastern area, if you remember at the beginning the 'urban transformation company' [Napoli Est, 1992], with that famous manager whose name I can't remember [Fabiano Fabiani], but then nothing changed. The oil depots have not moved. Earlier there were processing activities too, now there are just the depots. All those brownfields, huge spaces, abandoned, desolate. That is, there has been no urban plan, nor have there been any major investments. The city then had a huge crisis, the waste crisis [in 2006], and so on, and was no longer able to attract new investments. Let us not forget that for more than a decade and even before we have been going through the most serious global crisis the world has known since the war. So also attracting investments that weren't ... well, I gave the example of Cosco. The Chinese people invest in the area, but they

don't invest 'for charity', they don't export communism, let's say [*laughing*]. They export something else.

Caruso: *Referring to what has been said, I actually skipped a question. Earlier I also asked you about the oil sector in general, now I'd like to ask for your opinions on the Agip fire in 1985.*

Daniele: I remember the Agip fire well, right. I remember that it exploded and we had to evacuate a lot of people there. How difficult it was to find alternative accommodation, because we were in the aftermath of the earthquake and we already had tens of thousands of people who had to be relocated. We arranged ships in the port to shelter these poor people who had suffered the Agip explosion. However, even then the area remained as it was, it did not have any further destination. Then they were placed in houses. I remember very well all the time they were on the ships and there were these ships anchored in the port. Imagine living in a ship in the port, with all the discomforts, humidity, health problems. Then they were transferred to hotels and then to Sant'Arpino.

Caruso: *Okay, thank you very much for your availability.*
Daniele: You are welcome. Thanks to you.

Recording n. 5. Conversation with Giovanni Dispoto.

Place of recording: National Research Council, Piazza Bovio, Naples.

Date of recording: 28 January 2019

Interviewed: Giovanni Dispoto, born in Naples on 24 February 1947

Caruso: *Giovanni, the first question I would like to ask you concerns the General Town Development Plan of 1972, and in particular the impact of this master plan on the territorial structure of east Naples.*
Dispoto: The main limitation of the 1972 GDP was the postponement of its implementation to the 29 areas into which the whole territory was divided, intended to have as many executive urban plans (now deemed 'effective plans'). This never happened, because it was up to the Public Administra-

Appendices

tion to provide them. Therefore, only some initiatives that had already been decided, such as the Business Centre, went ahead. Let's say that there has been no development of the contents of the 1972 plan, starting, for example, with services, whose scale was not related to the areas identified for their construction. For this reason, there was a commission specifically appointed by the Valenzi council to draw up the Framework Plan for Services consisting of a census of the areas to be allocated to meet the standards set by the plan of 1972. The Framework Plan for Services was completed but did not result in updating the PRG of 1972.

Before talking about the impact that the PRG of 1972 had on the eastern area, we could talk about the historic centre or the western area. Indeed, perhaps the historic centre is one of the most significant topics of the 1972 plan, because there were very significant amendments to the plan by the Superior Council of Public Works, which then approved the town plans of the municipalities. In particular, the Council expanded the perimeter of the historic centre to include the *Quartieri Spagnoli* which the plan envisaged dividing by the construction of a new road upstream of via Toledo, a projection that was therefore cancelled by the Council.

Shortly after, with the first decentralisation of the 1970s and the establishment of the regions, to which urban planning was devolved, things changed. The change made it possible to reintroduce and get approved by the Campania Region, with its new competences, the project rejected by the Superior Council of Public Works, of a new university centre in Monte S.Angelo, to be built in the western suburbs between the Rione Traiano, then nearing completion, and the Agnano basin. The plan's provision to preserve an area of environmental value falling within the Phlegraean Fields had been rejected. We know how it ended up, the new hub was built, works and will soon be served by the new Monte S-Angelo station of line 7 of the Naples underground network.

For the eastern area, what I certainly remember is how there were significant forecasts in the 1972 plan connected to the presence of the port: the definition of its perimeter and the identification of retro-port areas.

The post-war master plan of the port dates back to 1958 and provided for its extension to the east with four new docks, almost certainly to cover the entire stretch of coast between the eastern limit and the boundaries of the municipality of Portici. The 1972 master plan does not incorporate this provision but limits the expansion of the port to the east to a single new dock. The limiting of the expansion of the port towards the east would then be confirmed by the 2004 master plan, as we will see later. What is significant are the forecasts of the 1972 plan for the rear port area, also in the eastern area, which I illustrate here [*he shows a map of the plan*] with a map that shows you which areas were destined as zone F2, that is to support port activities (logistics, headquarters of shipping companies, etc.).

In fact this did not come to much, or rather I cannot tell you to what extent it occurred but certainly there was no possibility of port operators acquiring these areas and using them for their own activities. This situation changed completely with the 2004 plan; there has been a complete revision of the relationship between the port and the city and in particular the eastern area, a relationship that the plan of 1972 fitted into an eminently productive-industrial vision of the eastern area as a whole.

It is certainly not wrong to think that the whole of San Giovanni, Pazzigno, Barra, Poggioreale, even partially Ponticelli, constitute the so-called eastern city, a single large basin (the basin of the Sebeto river) which is actually, from the geographical point of view a wide coastal plain, bordering on the Vesuvian area. This area has over time been characterised by its relationship with the wider territory of the metropolitan area through the development of a delusional infrastructural network: railways, highways, interchanges, viaducts, oil pipelines, etc., which 'cross' the area, in fact not serving it and even 'jumping over' it. Therefore, this territory was influenced by infrastructure indifferent to the identity of and historical distinctions that exist between San Giovanni, Pazzigno, Barra, and Ponticelli. From this point of view, the territory was unified, but in a vision that overall confirmed its characteristics as an industrial periphery. Nor have any other corrective actions been taken, as intended in the new land use plan of 2004, to redefine the original characteristics of the landscape of the eastern area, starting with the 'empty' or still-cultivated land (the gardens called the marshes), to complement the historical centres and urbanised areas. This is an important premise.

It is evident that between the 1970s and 1990s, when a new urban planning era began in Naples, many things changed: the ending of existing productive activities, the new environmental culture, the prevalence of disorderly urban growth and land consumption. This disorder has many faces: hydraulic, environmental, urban in the strict sense. What you call 'mingling' or 'promiscuity' is a fair definition. At the beginning it did not seem so correct, perhaps it is not really technical, but in a sense it sufficiently gives the idea of the disorder that found here and therefore of the need to restore a defined physiognomy to these places. Which is addressed with the

Appendices

2004 plan. Even if the actual implementation has not yet taken place, or at least only in a very limited way. This profound transformation hypothesised by the 2004 plan results from the need to remove activities with high land consumption and a lowimpact on employment, as in the case of oil depots which heavily affect the redemption – in terms of safety and pollution – and urban planning of an area that actually constitutes the only real potential 'expansion' area of the city. It is no coincidence that recent expansion, both in the nineteenth-twentieth century with the first renovation and, much more recently, with the Business Centre – among other things not yet completed – all took place in the eastern area.

Let's now move on to deal with the western area, which compared to the eastern area has a very different story, because it is entirely part of an area environmentally characterised by volcanic activity: the Phlegraean Fields. In particular, it can be said that Bagnoli constitutes the eastern edge of the Phlegraean Fields rather than the western outskirts of Naples, separated from it by the Posillipo hill. This natural barrier has been overtaken over time by Posillipo street / Coroglio, crossed by the Neapolitan Crypt and the Seiano Cave built in Roman times; and by modern tunnels for trains (Naples-Rome railway link) and motor vehicles (Vittoria tunnel and Lazio tunnel) built in the twentieth century; but the sense of discontinuity and impediment has remained, even in the denomination that still preserves the two parts into which the city is separated by the Posillipo promontory: Piedigrotta on one side, Fuorigrotta on the other.

On the contrary, in the eastern area, except for the discontinuity formed by the barrier of the railway yard, a coastal plain extends, mainly occupied by oil depots, which borders seamlessly with the Vesuvian area and along the coast up to Castellamare. The reconversion, redevelopment, re-urbanisation of this area, of approximately 800 hectares, is the only possibility for urban 'expansion' of Naples. Although it is more accurate to speak of recovery and redevelopment than of expansion, as the 2004 plan does not provide for any territorially homogeneous 'C' area (i.e. use of free land for new settlements), in pursuit of one of the main objectives of the plan – zero consumption of land.

Caruso: *We will return to the 2004 regulatory plan, and to talking about the previous interventions.*

Dispoto: But, sorry, I have to say one thing otherwise I'll forget it. The relationship between the plan of 1972 and the one that came later and paved the way for the 2004 GDP, is that in the plan of 1972 the theme of the environment does not yet manifest itself in all its importance, although certainly the theme of safeguarding valuable environmental areas was considered, albeit limited to the identification of homogeneous zones I and L: namely wider green areas and private green areas, which had in part survived the impetuous urban growth. However, in the plan of 1972, certainly for the eastern area, there was no significant or even qualitative element referring to the landscape. That is, the real difference with the 2004 plan lies in the fact that the GDP did not consider the eastern area a compromised area, devoid of identity or, at best, an area to be reclaimed. The 2004 plan recognised the original landscape features of the eastern area, which, in sequence, pass from the Sebeto basin to the foothills of Somma-Vesuvius, from the coastal plain to the slopes of the volcano. The perspective on the Neapolitan landscape, as well as being from the urban centre or from the hills, can also be taken from the outskirts of the eastern area, from where you can enjoy a magnificent view of the Somma Vesuvio, the hill of San Martino and the Camaldoli, and from Poggioreale even of Capri. Therefore, the spatial characteristics are considered structuring elements of the physical identity of the territory. In particular, the theme of water also emerges in all its importance, and not only in a metaphorical sense. The hydraulic history of the eastern area is perhaps also at the origin of its chronic disorder.

Caruso: *However, one of the first steps taken by the 1972 GDP is to recognise the polluting contribution of the factories on site. Hence the 'N' scope of the 1972 GDP which greatly limits the expansion, in the end, of polluting activities. How much do you think this has influenced, in one way or another, the processes of deindustrialisation proper in the eastern area?*

Dispoto: This is a question that I can't answer, I do not know to what extent, really, these limitations have had consequences, or how much other factors have intervened. For example, the question of the refinery and oil depots, of the connection between the oil docks and the depots, has created a knot, an umbilical cord: a concentration of issues, in which I do not know to what extent the limitations set by the 1972 plan could intervene. There has never been – because the laws that provided for it did not exist at the time, and neither do they to this day, it seems – a regional energy plan that would deal with the presence of a petrochemical industry with supra-regional dimensions and functions in the heart of the urban area, occupying a lot of space and separating the city centre from the eastern suburbs. The pipelines that connect the oil dock to the depots cut across the plain, going up from

Appendices

the port to the internal areas, following the path originally traced by water in the opposite direction. From this point of view, it seems to me that the problems of safety were underestimated by the 1972 plan, problems which then tragically manifested themselves with the explosion of the Agip tanks in the 1980s; there were victims and enormous damages, buildings evacuated and inhabitants moved. Since then, the refinery has been closed, but the presence of the tanks carries the 'risk of major accidents' to this day.

This leads us to look at the eastern area, in my opinion, as one of the densest areas of problems concerning the environment and safety. There is the red area of Vesuvius eruption risk, which previously did not include the Naples area and instead now includes the Ponticelli area and takes in the area of the new hospital; we have the aforementioned presence of oil depots; to all this is added the fact that, due to lack of hydraulic pumping, the aquifer is once again emerging and at risk of overflowing with consequent flooding of the depressed areas (areas below the Headquarters, underground floors of the Luzzatti district, etc.). Last but not least, there is the other great topic, in a certain sense a unifying one, that of the Site of National Interest, the SIN: one of the fifty polluted sites considered to be of national interest, whose remediation involves, among other things, a significant intervention.

Caruso: *I propose moving on to the second block of questions, which have to do with the Suburban Plan. More generally, the Reconstruction, the PSER and the Suburban Plan. Much has been said about the Reconstruction, actually. Maybe too much. And on the Suburban Plan, regarding East Naples, there are many elements that have completely transformed the territory: looking at the previous and subsequent images there is a big difference. So, I would like to ask you what were, in your opinion, the greatest successes of the Suburban Plan and more generally of the period of the 1980s, for East Naples, and what, in your opinion, were the greatest failures?*

Dispoto: This is certainly a good question. Beautiful because it was asked 35 years on, more or less, from 1980s. Almost forty. It is useful to make an assessment. The Extraordinary Residential Building Program (PSER) was based on an urban planning tool – namely the Suburban Plan – that the Administration of the time, the Mayor Valenzi, had approved a few months before the terrible earthquake occurred. The innovative element, highly innovative and avant-garde for the time – there is no doubt about this because comparisons cannot be made with other cases, even in Italy – was to concentrate the redevelopment of urban interventions in the areas of the suburbs where, however, by periphery we also meant the ancient villages of eighteenth-century and rural origin. Places inhabited without interruption from their foundation until today. The famous *casali* that surrounded Naples were autonomous municipalities with their own territorial identity, so much so that it was only in 1926 that there was an administrative and urban reform with the 'great Naples' that led them to be definitively integrated within the city. This event, with the subsequent urban expansion after World War II, was the premise for the transformation of these places in the indistinct suburbs we know today.

When the Suburban Plan was drawn up, we were in the 1980s and there had not yet been a change in the GDP in force at the time – since 1972 – which identified the historic centre of Naples with the oldest part, but did not take into consideration the historic centres of suburban towns, namely the Casali. Therefore, the Suburban Plan managed to modify the prescriptions set by the 1972 GDP, or at least revise them. Rereading these centres in terms of recovery (law 457/78 on recovery plans was approved a few years earlier) was a significant turning point, even if we must consider the difficulty of re-reading places that had meanwhile transformed into the suburbs we know today as a result of everything that had arisen around them: from public and private building districts, to uses of all kinds (motorway junctions, warehouses, parking lots, shopping centres), illegal construction, etc. This urban disorder had ended up completely emptying these villages, the hamlets, of value, thus rendering them the periphery of the periphery. There were no more degraded places in the suburbs than these: poor, unhealthy, left to fend for themselves. In the photographs of the time, we see not only the deterioration of buildings but the miserable conditions in which these people lived. The original historical centres had dissolved due to neglect and decay. It is easy to think that such a reality should be 'healed' by demolishing everything, erasing all traces and starting again. Exactly the opposite of the principle affirmed in the Suburban Plan – namely the recovery of what already existed, following the example of other cities like Bologna, that had started this new experiment even in the urban centre.

The principle that the historic city was a monument to be respected as a whole with its stratifications has established itself over time with a series of successes, but also of defeats, up to this day. The conservation of historic centres alone is not enough, it risks being limited to the survival of the buildings alone, but not to the protection of inhabitants and activities. Today, there is a big risk of seeing the historic centre transformed by tourism into a Disneyland-like theme park, preserving its buildings but not its soul.

Appendices

Caruso: *A bit like Venice.*

Dispoto: Venice is certainly the most poignant example. But I don't know if Naples in this sense doesn't run some risk of 'gentrification', as things are going now. Surely in the 1970s and 1980s there was still the need to defend the historic centre, as evidenced by the commitment that the Assizes of Palazzo Marigliano lavished to counter the initiative of Neapolitan private entrepreneurs called the 'Kingdom of the Possible', an initiative whose objective was an essential building transformation of the historic centre: the asset to be protected was not the historic centre as a whole, but only its monuments, opening up to massive replacement interventions. The people who tried to affirm this position are no longer there, nor do I think they have heirs. It does not seem to me that today there is great interest in this approach, also given the touristic success that the historic city has had in recent years, albeit at the risk of expelling inhabitants and an excessive commercialisation of the same.

But let's go back to the extraordinary programme that started with the Suburban Plan. We start there, with the idea of restoring these areas, replacing where necessary, but safeguarding the urban fabric, avoiding new buildings that could be isolated and unrelated to the context. However, the projection to build about 13,000 houses in the city was not enough to meet the need for a total of about 20,000 houses. Then 12,750 apartments were built in Naples starting with the Suburban Plan, also with the completion of the still not built-up areas in the '167' of Scampia and the '167' of Ponticelli. The remainder, up to the 20,000 mark, were planned by the commissioner-president of the Region, for the province of Naples. Thus, we managed to preserve the idea of working through normal urban planning instruments, even if we had to respond to extraordinary events and a state of emergency.

In addition, puntal interventions were tested in the urban centre, where areas of decay and unresolved abandonment were identified. In this way, public facilities were also created in the historic city (schools, green spaces, gyms, etc.) whose effect on the context after almost forty years is demonstrated by their continuing usefulness, in some cases also creating connection between areas that were not communicating.

In ten years, the entire programme was closed and completed. As early as 1984, the interim solutions adopted immediately after the earthquake had already been eliminated. The operation of the programme was guaranteed through the appointment of the Mayor Commissioner, the mechanism of concessions, the public calls in which important Italian companies participated, the establishment of the Technical Office, directed first by Vezio De Lucia and then by Roberto Giannì and Laura Travaglini. I, who participated in this operation, am more than convinced of its results, indeed I am proud of it. In Naples there have not been many of the problems that unfortunately happened elsewhere due to other calamitous events: solutions considered provisional later becoming definitive, accommodation not being built, etc. The 20,000 lodgings were built with all services, people were moved, the lodgings assigned. The assignments had an impeccable but also very particular and complicated management, because, among other things, it was necessary to allow those who lived in accommodation that was expropriated and then repaired the possibility of a return to their places of origin. So, there was a turnover.

Finally, for the sake of completeness of information, I remind you that the Parliamentary Commission of Inquiry (president Senator Oscar Luigi Scalfaro) appointed to ascertain the proper conduct of the PSER in Naples, carried out its task scrupulously but concluded its investigation without detecting any anomalies.

Certainly, we should not forget the squatting that happened even before these developments were completed, with consequent delays and inconvenience for the legitimate assignees. In short, there were some problems but frankly I don't think they compromised the fundamental clarity with which the housing was allocated. And I can say, because I participated in it, that some of the squatting was solved with evictions carried out with great care and full success, without any accidents occurring. I believe that on the whole it is not possible, even from this point of view, to make significant criticisms of the extraordinary programme.

However, precisely because I am convinced of the success of the PSER, I'll try to say what in my opinion did not go too well, taking stock after so many years and considering what happened in the places where the interventions were carried out – from this point of view there are very different situations from area to area.

For the first time in our city's public planning history, all urban services (many new urban services, even for the outskirts of Naples that had previously lacked them all) had been put in place by the extraordinary programme. These services were needed, in order to satisfy the entire area's requirements. For once, even the public green space was not neglected: indeed, public green and open spaces (courtyards, squares, streets), but more generally urban services overall, were conceived as the foundation of the new public city system. The

Appendices

various parts into which the plans were divided (recovery, replacement, completion, new building) were integrated and connected through urban spaces, in which green was a significant, not a marginal or residual, element. Each of the twelve neighbourhoods had a park of at least two or three hectares on average, not to mention the large parks built in Taverna del Ferro, Scampia and Ponticelli, which are up to fifteen hectares. After a long time, we can see that the interventions carried out have survived, some in the best, some in worse conditions, even in spite of poor maintenance, not to mention, at least in some cases, of real abandonment by the Public Administration.

The problem arose immediately. Who would be in charge of managing all this new heritage? Then we made a suicidal choice in my opinion. It was all assigned to a private company, Romeo Gestioni Spa, a Neapolitan company of national standing to which all the real estate assets created through the PSER were entrusted. Their job was to collect the fees and manage all the maintenance. The contract signed by the parties exposed the Public Administration to a huge dispute that dragged on for years, because the concessionaire argued that the maintenance works and the solutions adopted did not guarantee the proper functioning or durability of the housing, that the operating costs were therefore higher than expected, and so on. This dispute lasted a long time, finally at the expiry of the contract the concession was not renewed and now the management of the assets is back in the hands of the Municipality, though I have not yet seen improvements from the point of view of management efficiency. Management is an important issue: nothing is preserved without adequate maintenance. Another critical aspect arose due to the non-use of parts of premises created to house commercial activities on the ground floors. Premises that were left unused were then either vandalised or illegally occupied and also used as makeshift accommodation. These interventions to foster trade, craftsmanship, production should have contributed to the rebirth and redevelopment of the areas in a broader and deeper sense, what today comes under the abused term regeneration. This has occurred but in a very partial way. Beyond the mere assignment and collection of rentals, the Public Administration did not manage to trigger new development processes, or new policies that could improve what the PSER had created, for the purpose of preserving social cohesion.

I think that, with the 2004 plan, these shortcomings have been reconsidered, not only in reference to the experience of the post-earthquake reconstruction, but precisely because of the role that the peripheries can and must assume in combatting inequalities. Perhaps it can be said that the greatest novelty, with extraordinary transformative effects on the centre-periphery relationship, in particular as regards the northern suburbs, was the construction and commissioning of Line 1 of the underground, which connects Scampia with the Central Station, passing through the historic centre, connecting the upper town with the lower town. From this point of view, a radical change in the perception of the distance between the centre and the periphery has occurred.

Caruso: *The extension towards the eastern area of line 2 of the underground, too.*

Dispoto: Surely, however, for the eastern area, I would say that today we are still in a stalemate, as regards urbanisation and the implementation of the plan's provisions.

Returning again to the Suburban Plan and the criticism that can be made, I would say that the main one is that the PSER was a lost opportunity to address the issue of the suburbs as a whole, rather than limiting it only to historical centres. These critiques fail to assess the complexity of the situation, due to the state of emergency. However, it should also be emphasised that, among other things, there was also an involution of the Plan, because the programme managed by the Region, from a certain point, was directed towards important infrastructural works, which sometimes had connections with the original Plan, but many other times completely unrelated to it. What would later be called a 'second reconstruction' was implemented, but perhaps it would be better to call it 'the other reconstruction' in every sense. In this regard, it is enough to mention a sample intervention that was the subject of investigations by the judiciary and consequent trials: the regimentation of the *Regi Lagni*. Sixty kilometres of what remained of the legendary Clanis river, transformed by into a canal with cemented banks, which in recent times was the subject of a superficial re-naturalisation process with new plantings, but no intervention on water pollution. So, there was some waste. However, I repeat, this was another reconstruction. In Naples with the PSER there were no such cases.

Finally, noting the current situation and the unsatisfactory quality of life in the suburbs, let us also remember that when the extraordinary programme was implemented, the suburbs, especially the eastern ones, still had a large number of activities and occupations in place, there were still industries and workers. So, socially speaking, the situation has changed a lot today. I don't know what the levels of unemployment are in the east, but I think they're very high.

Appendices

Caruso: *Between sixteen and nineteen per cent. If we add young people's occupations we arrive at around thirty per cent. Instead, forgive me, you mentioned Taverna del Ferro and that specific area, on the border between Barra and San Giovanni a Teduccio. Let's take it as a specific sample. There is all the school complex and equipment of Viale Due Giugno, there is the Troisi Park, and then there is the so-called 'Bronx' of Taverna del Ferro. Here, from a purely planning and urban planning point of view, how would you describe the situation from a territorial point of view? Considering both the past and the present?*

Dispoto: Fundamentally, there are technical, technological and industrial issues. We are talking about the fact that in the 'Bronx' the building typology of the PSER residences is completely different from that adopted everywhere else. That is to say, what the French call 'grands ensembles' were built, namely large residential complexes of industrialised construction, large containers or beehives, call them whatever you want, the terms perhaps tends too much towards derogatory tones. The decision to concentrate a large part of the housing needs of Taverna del Ferro in these complexes was also dictated by the opportunity to save in terms of time and land also to create the adjacent park of more than ten hectares, now named after Massimo Troisi.

But undoubtedly these achievements present some negative aspects, of management if nothing else. To manage a building that houses about 200 families, I would like to know which condominium administrator would take up this position, when, moreover, there are cases of arrears, squatting, even illegal activities. Let's consider this: the social unease in these places existed even before the post-earthquake works were carried out, the reconstruction did not bring it. The extraordinary programme was unable to redevelop places from a social point of view, for example by imagining initiatives that could create employment and therefore alternatives to illegality.

In the end, I see the balance as extremely positive for having managed to do something that I don't think has ever been done anywhere, at this scale and with this commitment. I certainly see the limits as concerns management, and the lack of social policies on the part of the Public Administration that would foster greater participation by citizens.

If the construction of large residential complexes presented serious management, social and sustainability problems, for example the two large buildings of Taverna del Ferro in S. Giovanni, or the Vele in Scampia (not built by the extraordinary programme), the remedy of proceeding with their destruction is also questionable (and in fact it has been discussed), fuelling the idea that social recovery can essentially depend on the wrong choice of building typology. In this regard, I would like to point out that, unlike the cases mentioned above, no committee has ever formed to demand the demolition of residential buildings built with the recovery [*laughing*] or the demolition of the new buildings, or to reduce the population density etc. Thus, it seems to me that, as there were no protests, things went pretty well, almost everywhere. I went there many times. There are delightful places, such as San Pietro a Patierno, or the historic centre of Ponticelli and that of Piscinola. They are not very well maintained, because management is obviously always a problem. But not bad ...

Caruso: *It's not 167.*

Dispoto: I would say no, it's not 167, absolutely. I would like to clarify the topic raised by the so-called Bronx (the two buildings of Taverna del Ferro, aka the 'big steak'). There was not one mistake but a concatenation of issues. At that time a first aim was to provide not only San Giovanni but also Barra and Pazzigno with adequate services, but the three districts did not have much space available. So, the big opportunity was Taverna del Ferro, with that large available area, already used for horticulture, which could satisfy the needs for greenery and other services in all three areas. Another factor was the constraint of the buffer zone of the cemetery placed next to this large area, which limited its construction possibilities. At this point, the conditions were all there to carry out an intensive intervention, entrusted to the architect Pietro Barucci, whose project established a balance between the building and the park, between intensive and extensive spaces, between the built and the unbuilt. If we see the building from the park it seems to us in proportion, they are in balance with each other. Perhaps the flaw is that there is insufficient distance between the two buildings, almost forming an alley, so they shade each other. There are no shops, even if the premises have been built, but not used, and then illegally occupied and also used as homes.

Caruso: *The Troisi Park faces the same problems, after so many years. So, Giovanni, I would go directly to the third question under consideration, which has to do with the proposed Variation to the General Plan, of 1996, with the Variation to the General Plan approved in 1999 and with that of 2004. Therefore, both differences between the two urban plans, and, above all, which are, in your opinion, the greatest strengths of what is probably the most revolutionary project for the redevelopment of the eastern area.*

Appendices

Dispoto: You will remember that we started with the western variant approved in 1998, then the historic centre and then everything was put together with the eastern and north-western areas, in a single variant approved in 2004. The eastern area is the one that, in my opinion, inspired, together with the historic centre and the environmental system, of course, the most ambitious aspects of the plan. A total rethinking in a plan that wanted to re-establish a relationship, a spatial and functional link, between the historic centre and the eastern periphery. Ambitious because it has always been considered a challenge, with solutions that are difficult to implement, starting with that of the Piccinato plan of 1939 which provided for the transfer of the railway station to the East, transforming it from a terminus to a stop on the line, a retreat to make room for the city to advance in that direction.

But let's go back to the plan approved in 2004, which envisages reaching Ponticelli with an axis that can connect it directly to the historic centre, and also symbolically represents plan's aim to overcome the dichotomy between centre and eastern suburbs. An axis adaptable to existing conditions, capable of overcoming the numerous obstacles in the area: the strip of railtracks, motorway junctions, oil pipelines, and a whole series of barriers, which increase the distance between the centre and the eastern suburbs. As the crow flies between the centre and Ponticelli there are a few kilometres, very few, but to get there you have to go around the area of the oil depots and the distances multiply. So, in fact the possibilities in the eastern area have been thought about very deeply, because I believe that there are significant opportunities for the environmental and urban redemption of the area. As I said before, it is the only coastal plain for the city, so you have to consider it as an expansion area. And the cornerstone, the keystone of all this, was certainly the displacement of oil depots, the problematic nature of which had already been stigmatised in the plan of 1972, as you said earlier when reflecting on this topic.

Caruso: *Yes, it is a topic introduced by Professor Parisi.*

Dispoto: And not only by him, I think I have also reread it on some other occasion. Then, oh well, just take the plan of 1972. It should not be considered a static situation. While the Port of Naples continued the expand to its east, oil activities tried to expand as well. Therefore, it was a struggle over the inner coastal spaces, divided by the 1972 GDP between the industrial activities of the port and the oil industry. In short, everyone wanted space.

Valerio Caruso

Caruso: *Forgive me Giovanni, here, on the map, you can clearly see this sort of 'barrier' that separates Naples proper, Naples city, from the eastern area. So, it can be seen that Poggioreale, although historically part of the eastern area – is one of the four districts in the area – it is part of Naples city. Then there is this barrier which also involves Gianturco and which separates the city proper from the eastern area. There is a watershed, so to speak, that goes from Poggioreale to Ponte della Maddalena, in fact. What do you think about it?*

Dispoto: But I would say that the presence of this very relevant and significant element in the problems of the eastern area cannot be avoided. The railway tracks have roughly the shape of a capital T lying down, with the tracks that, coming from the north and south, cross at Gianturco and, rotating ninety degrees, continue their run ending at the Piazza Garibaldi station. The T-shape of the track layout therefore defines two quadrants separated from each other and from the eastern area: the upper quadrant from the industrial area; the lower quadrant from the area of San Giovanni and Villa. Two enclaves are created comprising above: the Vasto, Poggioreale and the Business Centre; below: the market area, Galileo Ferraris street, Corso Arnaldo Lucci, the Maddalena bridge. This barrier is overcome, limitedly, in a north-south direction, by the following road axes: Corso Novara / Piazza Garibaldi / Corso Arnaldo Lucci to the west; via Gianturco in the centre, which connects the two quadrants under passing the railway; via Traccia / via Ferrante Imperato to the east connecting Poggioreale with San Giovanni.

The connection above and below the airport should certainly be improved by underpassing the railway at least one other point near the Business Centre. Which I believe would still be possible.

The east-west connection, of which I have already spoken, that is to say the city centre with Ponticelli, is envisaged by creating a route that connects existing road sections (via Galileo Ferraris, via Di Tocco, via Argine), also creating a short tunnel that underpasses the railway at the intersection of via Ferrante Imperato and via Nuova delle Brecce. Getting past the railway is possible, in this way you would exit onto Nuova delle Brecce, which takes you to via Argine, which in turn leads to the historic centre of Ponticelli.

Unfortunately, you see, today due to this tangle, to reach Ponticelli from the centre you have to go all round the houses, because there is a railway.

Caruso: *Behind the industrial area, running parallel to via delle Repubbliche Marinare? Climbing steeply...*

Appendices

Dispoto: I would rather say a parallel and almost symmetrical route to that of via De Roberto and the overlying viaduct of the State Street 162. The subject is still, unfortunately, unresolved and accounts for the failure of the great project for the eastern area and its 're-urbanisation', that is to create the conditions, the premises for the reuse of the whole eastern area.

Caruso: *This is the visible element of that promiscuity, the mixture we are talking about. This dysfunctionality.*

Dispoto: I would say yes. The overall picture that I have made still says little about the possibility of a project (now I might be exaggerating) from the ground up, a project that starts from the territory to rediscover or redefine the shape of the city, an urban project that has to do with the landscape, with the physical elements that allow those who live in the suburbs to have the same material experiences as those who live in the city. We need to rediscover the ancient historical sites and promote new places, in a disordered place such as this, dominated by large infrastructure (trains, motorway junctions, viaducts, etc.) and by the fences of those empty urban spaces that once were factories.

In the eastern coastal area there are indistinct infrastructural tangles involving viaducts, oil pipelines, trains, motorways, interchanges, etc., which arise between the houses, with consequent levels of insecurity, risk, pollution. I believe that this is the fundamental fact that distinguishes the awareness of this plan from everything that preceded it. What you call dysfunctional urban disorder I see in this toleration of the coexistence of environmental risk, of brownfields, of residence. It's like going into the attic at home [*laughing*]. That is, I have to do something about it, I have to eliminate what no longer has a reason to be, I clean up.

Caruso: *Giovanni I also wanted to ask you this: what do you think was the essential reason that the projects of 1996 and 1999, acknowleding their differences, were not entirely applied?*

Dispoto: But look, as regards the coastal strip in particular, that of San Giovanni we are facing ... ah wait, I have it here. This is the preliminary urban plan for San Giovanni a Teduccio. Here you will find [*he shows me the Plan's index*] a history of urban planning and transport. It tells something of the things I have partly told you but with more specific elements on the role of the ex-Cirio, of Corradini, of the port. It must be said that in the preliminary version, in the proposal, issues were addressed in a more decisive way. For example: the decommissioning of the Vigliena thermoelectric plant. Another thing that was said in the preliminary plan regarding the boundaries of the Port, is that it had to move back to the west with the customs barrier, (defined with the reconstruction of Piazza del Municipio and the area in front of the Stazione Marittima) and not expand to the east. That is, the port was supposed to allow the city to rediscover its relationship with the sea, at least in part. In the case of San Giovanni this is one of the fundamental themes, regaining the possibility, as a place located on the coast, to feel at one with its natural geographical condition. Which is totally denied.

Caruso: *Yes, in fact the only accessible place on the coast is the last one, the terminal one before Pietrarsa.*
Dispoto: In fact, if the promenade between Pietrarsa and the disused water plant purifier was then carried out – whatever the result, which I don't even know [*laughing*] – it must be recognised that the then-president of the municipality, Tonino Borriello, wanted it with great determination.

This attempt of the plan to 'contain' the Port (with a sea front of about five kilometres) at both ends, but also inland, has not yet been successful, so unsuccessful that now the new Port Authority has approved a Master Plan that is again trying to promote some outdated views, namely another expansion of the port towards the East. The cause is to be found in some facts that have failed to guarantee the containment of the Port. For example, the Project Financing of a tourist port between Vigliena and Pietrarsa was a well-designed project which then saw the contracting company bankrupt; the presence and redevelopment of the Napoli Levante thermoelectric plant (known as Vigliena power plant), a plant whose relocation was assumed as part of the planned recovery of the site, in order to return these places to common use; the redevelopment of the Corradini brownfield, owned by the Municipality of Naples, has not happened yet: this place could be pivotal if we want to support the Tourist Port project, which is supposed to be built on the adjacent coast. Plus, the Corradini brownfield could host some of the Universities' activities that could be shared with the new Federico II building in San Giovanni, where the former Cirio used to be. All of these projects for the Corradini brownfields are promoted by the 2004 GDP. The preliminary project for the recovery of Corradini is there and perhaps also the economic resources to carry it out.

Caruso: *Thirty million.*
Dispoto: 'Only' thirty million, I remembered more. But Corradini, if you go

Appendices

to the port site now and see their masterplan, they presuppose the destruction of Corradini and the use of the area for container terminals and logistics.

Caruso: *Not from a design point of view but on a more general level: what do you think were the factor, (political, contractual, of various types) that may have influenced these Plans.*

Dispoto: I think that in the eastern area there are public and private entities that are decisive for its redemption: the Municipality, the University, the Port, the Railways, the oil companies, etc. These same actors who can determine the redevelopment can also prevent it. There has certainly been a lack, despite signed programme agreements, of that form of institutional collaboration that should place collective interests at the centre of the governance of an area, not particular interests. The interventions already carried out or in progress are limited: the recovery of the MecFond by Neapolitan entrepreneurs; the former Tobacco Factory; the new Faculty of Engineering in the ex-Cirio factory in San Giovanni. And numerous Urban Implementation Plans were proposed by private individuals, some dozen of which were also approved, but their implementation has only been partial, partly due to the unfavourable economic situation that occurred in 2008.

Among these plans, that presented by the Q8 company would have had a strategic role in the redevelopment of the oil area and the entire eastern area, but for now only the preliminary plan has been approved. Nonetheless, it is to be considered an excellent signal for the conversion of the eastern area. But I don't know the reasons things aren't moving; everyone tells me that the process is still in progress and that 'it will continue and go on' but …

Caruso: *… was suspended for judicial inquiries.*

Dispoto: In this regard, I recall that an entire study was carried out by a specialised company which was given the task of investigating the possibility of making a pontoon along the Domitian coast [North of Naples] and therefore transferring ship traffic there with a marine pipeline to discharge cargo in a production and industrial area located inland from the Domitian coast. There were no major objections on this issue, but no consensus was expressed either. Pending a definitive solution, an intermediate stage was at least considered, consisting of the possibility of reusing the inactive refinery areas and of reorganising the existing oil depots of all the companies in the area, so as to occupy only part of the current space.

Valerio Caruso

The real problem is that we're still living a patchy situation today, not rationalised by an intermediate solution such as concentrating everything in one location and freeing the rest of the area. This means that there is still a territory full of activities that involve the risk of a major accident. Connecting, managing, coordinating all this is a real long-term commitment that involves many public and private subjects. It's much easier to deal with the restyling of Partenope street.

Caruso: *I think, at least this was my opinion from analysing the various sources, that since the core of the intervention, which has to do with the oil hub, was abandoned, it is no longer possible to reconnect the eastern area with the centre of Naples. That is, that axis that you designed earlier, literally placed inside the eastern area, fails, or at least you have to do it somewhere else, right?*

Dispoto: I think that the solution of problems does not necessarily have to go through demolishing entire areas, also because it is impossible. Here we aren't lacking in urban projects, but they connect portions of the territory together without creating an integrated system at the various scales [*he describes in detail the main road axes of the area, indicating them on paper*]. So, this is what we need to work on, also because the large industrial sites, which constitute real barriers, have meant that compared to the normal fabric of a city, even an industrial one, the districts lack the small fabric of urban relations, based on urban places where citizens can live and with which they can identify themselves. The prospect – for now only hypothesised by the port authority – of obtaining other spaces to accommodate containers on the seafront and elsewhere means having new visual barriers and the definitive separation of San Giovanni from the sea.

Caruso: *It practically reaches the coast of San Giovanni a Teduccio.*

Dispoto: That's far more important than the problem of the railway. You will find a physical barrier because you have seen what these container depots are, there isn't much turnover, they remain there for a long time.

Caruso: *Yes, we see the dress rehearsal in Vigliena, where the containers are already. That is another barrier between the land and the sea.*

Dispoto: That is even more looming. At this point one wonders why the port of Naples should work like this, as if it has the paramount right to carry out its activity while ignoring the urban context. The whole area of

Appendices

the most central port corresponds to the perimeter of the seafront of the historic centre from which, through the so-called 'calate' (descent to the sea), in the past you could have reached the sea, but now this possibility has been denied, as if it were still an off-limits military zone. I would also add that, despite the retreat of the so-called customs barrier envisaged by the plan to the west, with the in-progress reconstruction of Piazza del Municipio and the Stazione Marittima area, there was no environmental improvement in the east. On the contrary, bulky containers accumulate. As usual, the eastern area is at the end of the line, the final part, the 'attic' of the city.

Caruso: *This metaphor of the attic is beautiful. Thanks, Giovanni.*
Dispoto: You're very welcome.

BIBLIOGRAPHY

Adorno, Salvatore and Simone Neri Serneri (eds). 2009. *Industria, Ambiente e Territorio. Per una storia ambientale delle aree industriali in Italia* (il Mulino: Bologna).

Adorno, S. 2017. 'Alla radice della questione ambientale nel Mezzogiorno. Cassa, industria, territorio e ambiente negli anni Sessanta e Settanta', in Gabriella Corona and Riccardo Realfonzo (eds), *Le politiche per l'ambiente in Italia* (FrancoAngeli: Milano).

Afan De Rivera, Carlo. 1832–33 [edition 2018]. *Considerazioni sui mezzi da restituire il valore proprio ai doni che la natura ha largamente conceduto al regno delle due Sicilie.* (Forgotten Books: London [2018]).

Amatori, Franco, Duccio Bigazzi, Renato Giannetti and Luciano Segreto (eds). 1999. *Storia d'Italia. Annali 15. L'industria* (Einaudi: Torino).

Arpac. 2008. *Servizi di caratterizzazione delle aree residenziali, sociali ed agricole nel sito di interesse nazionale di Napoli Orientale - SIN 3* (Campania Regional Administration).

Barbagallo, Francesco. 2015. *Napoli, Belle Époque* (Laterza Editori: Roma-Bari).

Barca, S. 2005. 'Napoli orientale: la città del rischio', *I Frutti di Demetra: Bollettino di Storia e Ambiente* **7**.

Belli, A. 2001. 'Attività produttive ed ecosistemi. Strategie d'intervento sostenibili a Napoli', *Meridiana. Rivista di storia e scienze sociali* **42**.

Bevilacqua, Piero and Gabriella Corona (eds). *Ambiente e risorse nei Mezzogiorno contemporaneo* (Meridiana Libri: Corigliano Calabro).

Buccaro, A. 1992. 'L'area industriale orientale nel secolo scorso: origini dei luoghi e interventi fino all'unità', in Augusto Vitale (ed.), *Napoli, un destino industriale* (Cuen Editore: Napoli).

Campania regional administration, Kuwait Petroleum Italia S.p.a., Kuwait Raffinazione e Chimica S.p.a., Municipality of Naples, Napoli Orientale S.c.p.a. 2006. *Protocollo d'intesa* (Napoli).

Cardillo, Enrico. 2006. *Napoli. L'occasione post-industriale. Da Nitti al piano strategico* (Guida: Napoli).

Ceci, F. 2016. 'Vent'anni di pianificazione urbanistica', in Luca Rossomando (ed.), *Lo stato della città. Napoli e la sua area metropolitana* (Napoli Monitor: Napoli).

Celentano, R., L. Guadagno, L. Meldolesi, M. Palesacandolo, S. Scognamiglio and S. Sposito. 2010. *Piccole imprese e tessuto socio-economico di Napoli Est* (Comitato NEST: Napoli).

Centro Studi Investimenti Sociali (CENSIS). 1984. *Evoluzione e governo dell'area napoletana. Società, economia e comportamenti familiari* (Società Editrice Napoletana: Napoli).

Corona, Gabriella. 2001. 'La sostenibilità urbana a Napoli. Caratteri strutturali e dinamiche storiche', *Meridiana. Rivista di storia e scienze sociali* **42**.

Corona, Gabriella. 2007. *I Ragazzi del Piano. Napoli e le ragioni dell'ambientalismo urbano* (Donzelli editore: Roma).

Corona, Gabriella. 2015. *Breve storia dell'ambiente in Italia* (Il Mulino: Bologna).

Corona, Gabriella. 2016. 'Volti e risvolti della deindustrializzazione. Alcuni interrogativi sulla contemporaneità'. *Meridiana. Rivista di storia e scienze sociali* **85**.

Corona, Gabriella, and Simone Neri Serneri. 2007. *Storia e ambiente. Città, risorse e territori nell'Italia contemporanea* (Carocci editore: Roma).

Dal Piaz, A. 1982. 'Il programma straordinario nel quadro delle vicende urbanistiche della città', *Edilizia Popolare* **166**.

D'Antonio, M. 1990. 'L'industria in Campania tra politica e mercato', in Paolo Macry and Pasquale Villani (eds), *Storia d'Italia. Le regioni dall'Unità ad oggi. La Campania* (Einaudi: Torino).

De Lucia, Vezio. 2006. *Se questa è una città. La condizione urbana nell'Italia contemporanea* (Donzelli: Roma).

Erbani, F. 1998. 'Vita di Antonio Iannello: difensore del Belpaese', *Meridiana. Rivista di storia e scienze sociali* **31**.

Esposito, E.D. 2015. 'L'alba senza sole di San Giovanni: 30 anni fa l'esplosione al deposito Agip', *Napoli Today* (https://www.napolitoday.it/zone/ponticelli/san-giovanni-a-teduccio/esplosione-incendio-deposito-agip-vigliena-21-dicembre-1985.html) (retrieved 5 May 2021).

Frascani, Paolo. 2012. *Le crisi economiche in Italia. Dall'Ottocento a oggi* (Laterza: Roma-Bari).

Frascani, Paolo. 2017. *Napoli. Viaggio nella città reale* (Laterza: Roma-Bari).

Garruccio, R. 2016. 'Chiedi alla ruggine. Studi e storiografia della deindustrializzazione', *Meridiana. Rivista di storia e scienze sociali* **85**.

Gasparrini, G. 2010. 'Il recupero urbano', in Sergio Stenti and Vito Cappiello (eds), *Napoli Guida e dintorni* (Clean: Napoli) pp. 275–290.

Grippo, Ugo. 1971. 'Il potenziamento della Mobil Oil', *Campania Dc* **1**.

Iannello, Francesco and Vincenzo Morreale (eds). 2006. *Il destino di Napoli est. Dai progetti di delocalizzazione industriale e riqualificazione ambientale alla costruzione della nuova centrale turbogas di Vigliena* (Istituto Italiano per gli Studi Filosofici: Napoli).

Istituto d'Igiene, II facoltà di Medicina e Chirurgia dell'Università di Napoli. 1975. *Archivio Monaldi per la tisiologia e le malattie dell'apparato respiratorio* **2**.

Leone, Ugo (ed.). 2004. *L'area orientale di Napoli. Contributi per un progetto* (Università di Napoli 'Federico II' – Amra: Napoli).

Lucarella, Cristoforo. 1992. *San Giovanni a Teduccio. Storia di una borgata napoletana.* (Arti Grafiche Meridionali – Masi: Portici).

Migliaccio, A. 2004. 'Terre d'acqua. La rete idrografica come matrice insediativa della piana orientale di Napoli', in Ugo Leone (ed.), *L'area orientale di Napoli. Contributi per un progetto* (Università di Napoli Federico II – Amra: Napoli).

Mitchell, Timothy. 2013. *Carbon Democracy: Political Power in the Age of Oil* (Verso: London-N.Y.).

Morreale, Milena and Vincenzo Morreale. 2015. *Un quadro sintetico sulla storia della fabbrica Cirio di San Giovanni a Teduccio in Frammenti di storia della 'Società Generale delle Conserve Alimentari Cirio sede sociale di San Giovanni a Teduccio'* (Paper for the Municipal Library 'Antonio Labriola', San Giovanni a Teduccio).

Municipality of Naples. 1972. *Piano Regolatore Generale 1972. Norme di attuazione* (Napoli).

Bibliography

Municipality of Naples. 1980. *Seduta straordinaria del Consiglio Comunale* (Napoli).

Municipality of Naples. 1988. *Relazione dei gruppi PCI e PSI al consiglio circoscrizionale. Riattazioni e ricostruzioni* (Napoli).

Municipality of Naples. 1996. *Proposta di modifica al Prg: centro storico e area orientale* (Napoli).

Municipality of Naples. 1999. *Variante al Prg di Napoli. Centro storico, zona orientale, zona nord-occidentale. Relazione* (Napoli).

Municipality of Naples. 2000. *Piano della rete stradale* (Napoli).

Municipality of Naples. 2004. *Variante al piano regolatore generale, centro storico, zona orientale, zona nord-occidentale. Norme d'attuazione* (Napoli).

Municipality of Naples. 2011. *IX Censimento generale dell'industria e dei servizi* (Napoli).

Municipality of Naples. 2011. *XV Censimento generale della popolazione e delle abitazioni* (Napoli).

Municipality of Naples. 2014. *Piano città per la rigenerazione delle aree degradate. Recupero ex complesso industriale Corradini* (Napoli).

Muto, G. 2009. 'Le tante città di una capitale: Napoli nella prima età moderna'. *Storia urbana* **123**.

Neri Serneri, Simone. 2005. *Incorporare la natura. Storie ambientali del Novecento* (Carocci Editore: Roma).

Parisi, Roberto. 1998. *Lo Spazio della Produzione. Napoli: la periferia orientale.* (Edizioni Athena: Napoli).

Parisi, Roberto. 2001. 'Verso una città salubre. Lo spazio produttivo a Napoli tra storia e progetto', *Meridiana. Rivista di storia e scienze sociali* **42**.

Parisi, Roberto. 2017. 'Tra acciaio e petrolio. Storia dello spazio urbano-industriale di Napoli (1945–1985)', *Italia Contemporanea* **285**.

Partito Comunista Italiano, Sezioni di San Giovanni a Teduccio. 1980. *Dossier 1980. S. Giovanni a Teduccio: un quartiere che cambia.* (Napoli).

Quitadamo, M. 2016. 'Presente e futuro dell'area orientale', in Luca Rossomando (ed.), *Lo stato della città. Napoli e la sua area metropolitana* (Napoli Monitor: Napoli).

Rossi, P. 1992. 'L'area industriale orientale nel secolo scorso: progetti e trasformazioni urbanistiche dopo il 1860', in Augusto Vitale (ed.), *Napoli, un destino industriale* (Cuen Editore: Napoli).

Sereni, Emilio. 2013. *I napoletani da 'mangiafoglia' a 'mangiamaccheroni'. Note di storia dell'alimentazione nel Mezzogiorno* [1958] (Edizioni Istituto Alcide Cervi: Reggio Emilia).

Signorini, Peter. 2016. *Come Natura Crea. Cirio, una storia italiana* (Mondadori: Milano).

Simonetti, L. 2003. 'Deindustrializzazione e vuoti urbani nell'area orientale di Napoli', in Ugo Leone (ed.), *Aree dismesse e verde urbano* (Patron Editore: Bologna).

Spadoni, Marcella. 2007. *SNIA. Storia* (Centro Online Storia e Cultura dell'Industria: Torino).

Tino, P. 1993. 'Napoli e i suoi dintorni. Consumi alimentari e sistemi colturali nell'Ottocento', *Meridiana. Rivista di Storia e Scienze Sociali* **18**.

Vitale, Augusto (ed.). 1992. *Napoli, un destino industriale* (Cuen Editore: Napoli).

Vergallo, Luigi. 2011. *Una nuova era? 'Deindustrializzazione' e nuovi assetti produttivi nel mondo (1945–2005)* (Aracne Editrice: Roma).

ARCHIVAL SOURCES

Digital Archives of the Italian Chamber of Deputies. 'Acts, XII Permanent Commission', 23/9/1980.

Digital Archives of the Italian Chamber of Deputies. 'Acts of the parliamentary session. Annex B', 4/2/2016.

Digital Archives of the Italian Chamber of Deputies. 'Commissione Parlamentare di inchiesta sulle attività illecite connesse al ciclo dei rifiuti e su illeciti ambientali ad esse correlati. Resoconto stenografico', 'Parliamentary committee of inquiry regarding illegal activities connected to the waste cycle and related environmental crimes. Stenographic transcript', 19/1/2017.

Digital Archives of the Italian Chamber of Deputies. 'Interrogazione a risposta scritta 4/17991 presentata da Gambale Giuseppe', 'Parliamentary question 4/17991 presented by deputy Giuseppe Gambale', 23/9/1993.

CIPE digital archives. 'CIPE resolution on request for expansion of the Snia Viscosa plant', 20/9/1974.

Il Corriere della Sera digital archives. A. De Simone. 'L'inquinamento ambientale a Napoli, le immagini mai viste', 'Environmental pollution in Naples, unseen images', 22/2/2017.

Il Corriere del Mezzogiorno digital archives. P. Cuozzo. 'Nell'ex Manifattura tabacchi 850 alloggi', '850 homes in the ex-Tobacco Factory', 2/4/2011.

Il Corriere del Mezzogiorno digital archives. F. Geremicca. 'In pensione il depuratore dello scandalo San Giovanni a Teduccio rivede il mare', 'The scandalous water purifying plant is no more. San Giovanni a Teduccio sees the sea again', 31/7/2014.

La Repubblica digital archives. E. Borriello. 'La Mobil Oil Italiana è stata venduta alla Kuwait Petroleum', 'Italian Mobil Oil sold to Kuwait Petroleum', 21/3/1990.

La Repubblica digital archives. C. Cambi. 'Napoli adesso è più europea', 'Naples is now more European', 4/8/1997.

La Repubblica digital archives. P. Capua. 'Piano Q8 per l'area orientale un parco al posto delle raffinerie', 'Plan Q8 for the eastern area, a park instead of the refineries', 19/5/2005.

La Repubblica digital archives. A. Cederna. 'Lo scudetto della ricostruzione', 'The championship of reconstruction', 20/5/1987.

La Repubblica digital archives. A. Cederna. 'Quei miracoli del dopo-terremoto', 'Miracles after the earthquake', 1/12/1990.

La Repubblica digital archives. B. De Fazio. 'Gianturco, area non salubre: chiude la residenza universitaria', 'Gianturco, an unhealthy area: university residence closes', 3/10/2018.

La Repubblica digital archives. B. De Fazio. San Giovanni a Teduccio, festa aperta a tutti per il nuovo polo di Ingegneria', 'San Giovanni a Teduccio, party open to all for the new engineering centre', 16/9/2016.

La Repubblica digital archives. F. De Luca. 'Così rinasce Napoli', 'Thus Naples is reborn', 17/2/1983.

La Repubblica digital archives. *La Repubblica* editorial. 'Napoli nel caos. Una polveriera di

Archival Sources

cassintegrati e senza lavoro', 'Naples in chaos. A powder keg of cassintegrati and without work', *La Repubblica*, 25/8/1993.

La Repubblica digital archives. *La Repubblica* editorial. 'E sul Prg spuntano nuovi ostacoli', 'And new obstacles arise on the PRG', *La Repubblica*, 8/7/2003.

La Repubblica digital archives. *La Repubblica* editorial. 'Si a Napoli Est arriva Fabiani', 'Yes, Fabiani arrives in East Naples', *La Repubblica*, 2/9/1997.

La Repubblica digital archives. P. Russo. 'Aziende in fuga da Napoli Est', 'Companies fleeing East Naples', 29/7/2000.

La Repubblica digital archives. S. Tropea. 'Dal laboratorio di Napoli Est un miracolo chiamato lavoro', 'From the laboratory of East Naples a miracle called work', 13/7/1998.

l'Unità digital archives. N. Daniele. 'In preparazione un convegno del PCI sulla zona orientale', 'A PCI conference on the eastern area is in preparation', 15/1/1977.

l'Unità digital archives. N. Daniele. 'Pensare al "progetto"? Adesso è possibile, ma anche grazie a noi', 'Thinking about the "project"? Now it is possible, but also thanks to us', 10/11/1979.

l'Unità digital archives. F. De Arcangelis. 'Alla SME dicono che San Giovanni è divenuto stretto per la Cirio', 'At SME they say that San Giovanni has become too narrow for Cirio', 25/2/1979.

l'Unità digital archives. F. De Arcangelis. 'Cirio e agroindustria: occorre cambiare strada', 'Cirio and agro-industry: we need to change direction', 9/11/1978.

l'Unità digital archives. F. De Arcangelis. 'Comunicazione giudiziaria al medico provinciale per le colture di mitili autorizzate nel Golfo', 'Judicial communication to the provincial doctor for the authorised mussel cultivation in the Gulf', 17/9/1973.

l'Unità digital archives. F. De Arcangelis. 'Contro la smobilitazione protesta ieri alla Cirio', 'Protest against demobilization yesterday at Cirio', 25/10/1978.

l'Unità digital archives. F. De Arcangelis. 'Il sindaco ha chiesto alla SME: illustrateci il programma Cirio', 'The mayor has asked SME to illustrate the Cirio programme', 9/3/1979.

l'Unità digital archives. F. De Arcangelis. 'Mare in gabbia a Napoli: e accessibile soltanto a chi paga prezzi salatissimi', 'Sea in a cage in Naples: accessible only to those who pay very high prices', 5/7/1973.

l'Unità digital archives. V. Faenza. 'Raffineria e depositi di gas. Disinneschiamo la "bomba" che minaccia Napoli', 'Refinery and gas deposits. Let's defuse the "bomb" that threatens Naples', 14/1/1993.

l'Unità digital archives. V. Faenza. 'Tre operai schiacciati a Napoli', 'Three workers crushed in Naples', 22/12/1990.

l'Unità digital archives. G. Format. 'Napoli: grave colpo all'economia la chiusura delle MCM', 'Naples: serious blow to the economy, the MCM closure', 2/7/1972.

l'Unità digital archives. Editorial. 'L'accordo Cirio assicura sviluppo all'agroindustria', 'The Cirio agreement ensures development for agro-industry', 21/4/1979.

l'Unità digital archives. Editorial. 'La "mortalità industriale" in cifre', 'The "industrial mortality" in figures', 26/10/1979.

l'Unità digital archives. Editorial. 'Lavoratori Cirio domani alla Regione', 'Cirio workers tomorrow at the Region', 18/7/1978.

Valerio Caruso

l'Unità digital archives. Editorial. 'Manifestazione di protesta antinquinamento a Napoli', 'Anti-pollution protest demonstration in Naples', 2/6/1972.

l'Unità digital archives. Editorial. 'Per la Cirio 50 miliardi e difesa dell'occupazione', 'For Cirio 50 billion and defence of the occupation', 14/4/1979.

l'Unità digital archives. Editorial. 'SNIA: oggi assemblea contro la smobilitazione', 'SNIA: today meeting against demobilisation', 18/3/1980.

l'Unità digital archives. Editorial. 'Stamane assemblea alla Cirio. Domani si fermano gli edili', 'This morning the Cirio assembly. Tomorrow the construction workers stop', 7/4/1976.

l'Unità digital archives. Editorial. 'Sulle fibre i ministri litigano mentre avanzano i licenziamenti', 'Ministers quarrel over fibres as layoffs advance', 6/12/1979.

l'Unità digital archives. Editorial. 'La "Vetromeccanica" riprenderà la produzione dopo undici mesi', '"Vetromeccanica" will resume production after eleven months', 16/12/1977.

l'Unità digital archives. E. Puntillo. 'Proposta comunista per superare la crisi di Napoli', 'Communist proposal to overcome the Naples crisis', 30/10/1973.

l'Unità digital archives. E. Puntillo. 'La carenza sanitaria (oltre alle cozze) causa dell'infezione', 'Poor health (in addition to mussels) causing the infection', 4/9/1973.

l'Unità digital archives. M. Riccio. 'Napoli, scoppia la rivolta dell'acqua', 'Naples, the water revolt breaks out', 1/6/1990.

l'Unità digital archives. L. Vicinanza. 'Parte a Napoli il risanamento dei quartieri della periferia', 'The rehabilitation of suburban neighbourhoods starts in Naples', 18/4/1980.

Napolipiù digital archives. G. Manzo. 'Bomba ecologica sotto la Manifattura', 'Ecological bomb under the Manufacture', 20/2/2008.

UrbArc, IanCo, 12/a. 'Lettera del prof. Giulio De Luca al direttore de La Voce Regionale', 'Letter from prof. Giulio De Luca to the director of the newspaper La Voce Regionale', 1967.

UrbArc, IanCo, 39/b. 'Lettera del Comitato Regionale per la Programmazione Economica della Campania a Ministero dell'Industria, del Commercio e dell'Artigianato', 'Letter from the Regional Committee for the Economic Development of the Campania region to the Ministry of Industry, Trade and Craftmanship', 4/12/1968.

UrbArc, IanCo, 45/b. 'Lettera dei consigli di fabbrica dei lavoratori MobilOil alla MobilOil, alla Regione Campania e al Comune di Napoli', 'Letter from MobilOil Works Councils to MobilOil management, to the regional administration and to the Municipality of Naples', 31/10/1975.

UrbArc, IanCo, 45/b. *l'Unità* editorial board. 'Comunicazioni giudiziarie per casi di inquinamento', 'Judicial communications for pollution cases', *l'Unità*, 10/10/1975.

UrbArc, IanCo, 91/g. G. Bruzzano. 'Fiamme in un deposito di gas liquido. Poteva saltare in aria tutta la città', 'Flames in a liquid gas depot. The whole city could have blown up', *il Roma*, 8/8/1977.

UrbArc, IanCo, 91/g. *il Roma* editorial. 'I primi a fuggire gli operai della fabbrica', 'Factory workers the first to flee', *il Roma*, 8/8/1977.

UrbArc, IanCo, 91/h. 'Dattiloscritto di Antonio Iannello sullo spostamento delle raffinerie Mobil', 'Typescript by Antonio Iannello on the Mobil refineries' delocalisation', 11/1/1972.

UrbArc, IanCo 91/h. 'Lettera di Maurizio de Tilla ad Antonio Iannello per conto del Wwf',

Archival Sources

'Letter from Maurizio de Tilla, on behalf of the WWF, to Antonio Iannello', 4/8/1977.

UrbArc, IanCo, 99/b. 'Lettera del Prof. G.C. Carrada della Stazione Zoologica di Napoli al Consiglio Superiore dei Lavori Pubblici', 'Letter from Prof. Carrada, director of the Zoological Station of Naples, to the Superintendency for the Public Works', 17/4/1971.

UrbArc, IanCo 99/b. 'Lettera MobilOil Italiana a Ministero dell'Industria e Commercio, Ministero della marina mercantile e Ministero delle Finanze', 'Letter from MobilOil Italy to the Ministries of Industry and Trade, Merchant Navy and Finances', 28/7/1969.

UrbArc, IanCo, 99/b. 'Parere del Consiglio Superiore dei Lavori Pubblici sulla delocalizzazione della raffineria petrolifera di Napoli', 'Note by the High Council for Public Works concerning the relocation of the refinery of Naples', 17/7/1973.

UrbArc, IanCo, 99/c. 'Appunto del Provveditorato Regionale alle Opere Pubbliche della Campania al Ministero dei Lavori Pubblici', 'Note from the Regional Superintendency for the Public Works to the Ministry of Public Works', 23/12/1970.

UrbArc, IanCo, 99/c. 'Fonogramma del Ministero dell'industria e del Commercio al Ministero dei Lavori Pubblici', 'Phonogram by the Ministry of Industry and Trade to the Ministry for Public Works', 14/6/1971.

UrbArc, IanCo, 99/c. 'Lettera della Direzione Generale Urbanistica al Ministero del Bilancio e della Programmazione', 'Letter from the Urban Planning Board to the Ministry of Budget and Planning', 24/7/1971.

UrbArc, IanCo, 99/c. 'Verbale dell'adunanza straordinaria del Consiglio Superiore dei Lavori Pubblici', 'High Council for Public Works extraordinary meeting report', 10/5/1971.

UrbArc, IanCo, 99/d. 'Comunicato stampa di Italia Nostra', 'Italia Nostra press release', 18/7/1971.

UrbArc, IanCo, 99/e. 'Dattiloscritto firmato da Antonio Iannello in merito all'esplosione dei serbatoi AGIP', 'Typescript by Antonio Iannello concerning the 1985 Agip oil tanks fire', 21/12/1985.

UrbArc, IanCo, 99/g. A. Baglivo. 'Un'altra ipotesi: contrabbandieri di benzina', 'Another hypothesis: petrol smugglers', *Corriere della Sera*, 24/12/1985.

UrbArc, IanCo, 99/g. A. Cederna. 'Come si distrugge il Bel Paese', 'How the Bel Paese is being destroyed', *La Repubblica*, 23/12/1985.

UrbArc, IanCo, 99/g. E. Corsi. 'Tutte quelle raffinerie sono bombe nella città', 'All those refineries are bombs in the city', *La Repubblica*, 23/12/1985.

UrbArc, IanCo, 99/g. M. De Tilla. 'Sempre più nebulosa la vicenda della Mobil', 'The Mobil affair is increasingly nebulous', *il Roma*, 19/10/1975.

UrbArc, IanCo, 99/g. *l'Unità* editorial. 'Dopo il boato crollavano i muri', 'After the roar the walls collapsed', *l'Unità*, 22/12/1985.

UrbArc, IanCo, 99/g. F. Foresta Martin. 'Napoli avvolta da un vulcano di fuoco', 'Naples enveloped by a volcano of fire', *Corriere della Sera*, 22/12/1985.

UrbArc, IanCo, 99/g. L. Grasso. 'Sì all'impianto della Mobil', 'Yes to the Mobil facility', *il Mattino*, 2/11/1975.

UrbArc, IanCo, 99/g. *La Voce di Napoli* editorial board. 'Il ricatto della Mobil', 'The blackmail of Mobil', *La Voce di Napoli*, 24/10/1975.

UrbArc, IanCo, 99/g. *l'Unità* editorial. 'Il rogo è stato domato ma per 2,300 sfollati comincia l'emergenza', 'The fire was tamed but the emergency begins for 2,300 displaced persons', *l'Unità*, 27/12/1985

UrbArc, IanCo, 99/g. *il Mattino* editorial. 'I progetti Mobil: perché si oppone il Fondo Mondiale per la Natura', 'Mobil projects: why the World Fund for Nature is against them', *il Mattino*, 26/4/1977.

UrbArc, IanCo, 99/g. *La Stampa* editorial. 'La città dei senzatetto', 'The city of the homeless', *La Stampa*, 24/12/1985.

UrbArc, IanCo, 99/g. S. Romano. 'Un delitto urbanistico', 'An urban planning crime', *il Mattino*, 24/12/1985

UrbArc, IanCo, 99/g. *Il Giorno* editorial. 'Sconfitto il serbatoio 16, torna la calma', 'Tank 16 extinguished, calm returns', *Il Giorno*, 27/12/1985.

UrbArc, IanCo, 99/g. S. Troise. 'Approvato l'ammodernamento Mobil, aumentato il capitale dell'ex Merrell', 'Mobil modernisation approved, capital of former Merrell increased', *l'Unità*, 5/7/1977.

UrbArc, IanCo, 99/g. *Corriere della Sera* editorial board. 'Un operaio: "ho visto due compagni sparire tra le fiamme"', 'A worker: "I saw two comrades disappear in the flames"', *Corriere della Sera*, 22/12/1985.

UrbArc, IanCo, 119/s. 'Comunicato stampa della sezione di Napoli di Italia Nostra', 'Press release of the Naples section of Italia Nostra', 16/11/1973.

UrbArc, IanCo, 125/o. Antonio Iannello. 'Il Centro Direzionale della città di Napoli ed il nuovo Palazzo di Giustizia', 'The Business Center of the City of Naples and the new Palace of Justice', 1974.

UrbArc, IanCo, 145/f. 'Alla giunta la scelta del centro direzionale', 'The council has to decide about the business center', *La Cronaca di Napoli*, 21/7/1967.

UrbArc, IanCo, 169/e. 'Appunto n°2 per il Dir. Martuscelli sul C.D. di Napoli', 'Note n.2 on the Business Center, addressed to Director Martuscelli', signed by Antonio Iannello, n.d.

UrbArc, IanCo, 225/a. Alberto Servidio. 'Deliberazione di proposta sulla ubicazione del nuovo Palazzo di Giustizia e per una variante di piano regolatore concernente la complessiva zona interessata con la relazione illustrativa dell'Assessore avv. Alberto Servidio', 'Deliberation by the Municipal Council on the location of the new Palace of Justice and for a modification of the General Urban Plan, concerning the entire area, with an illustrated report by Councillor law. Alberto Servidio', 1967.

SITOGRAPHY

cid-torviscosa.it
comunedinapoli.it
google.com/intl/it/earth
museopietrarsa.it
napolicapitaleuropea.wordpress.com
napoli.repubblica.it
teatrosancarlo.it
treccani.it.
wikimedia.org

INDEX

A

activist, activism 40, 48, 60, 76, 78, 125, 137
Adorno, Salvatore 22, 33,
Aerfer 61
Afan De Rivera, Carlo 15
AGIP – Azienda Generale Italiana Petroli 27, 98
    fire, explosion 81, 96–100, 104, 121, 126, 145, 160–62, 166, 167, 172, 178, 183
Agoch, Jorit 94
agriculture 7, 15, 16, 83
agro-industry 19, 30, 48, 114
Altena, Bert 42
Arpac – Agenzia Regionale per la Protezione dell'Ambiente Campania 115
artisan, artisanal 6, 49, 106, 111, 155, 157, 170
ASI – Area di Sviluppo Industriale 34–35, 104
Autonomous Authority of the Port 24

B

Bagnoli 20, 66, 181
Barbagallo, Francesco 91
Barra 5, 6, 13, 14, 24, 25, 27, 31, 50, 54, 69, 71, 75, 87, 88, 89, 94, 95, 116, 137, 169, 170, 174, 180, 189, 190
Bassolino, Antonio 103, 104, 168
Belli, Attilio 62, 64, 81
Bevilacqua, Piero 91, 92
Bini, Elisabetta 8
Bluestone, Barry 40, 42
'Bronx' 93, 94, 189, 190
brownfield 50, 106, 111, 113, 153, 177, 193, 194
Buonomo, Bruno 123
Business Centre 53, 56, 58, 60–62, 64, 78, 83, 105, 120, 179, 181, 192

C

Camorra 92, 125, 134, 149, 150, 172, 174–76
Campania 33, 47, 48, 69, 74, 108, 115, 143, 170, 179
cannery; canning 5, 6, 19, 25, 29, 30, 47, 48, 114
carabinieri 147, 150
Casa del Popolo (People's House) 67
Casellato, Alessandro 123
Casmez – Cassa per il Mezzogiorno 34–35
Cederna, Antonio 92, 93, 100, 142
Cenzato, Giuseppe 28, 49
Censis – Centro Studi Investimenti Sociali (Centre for Social Investment Studies) 45, 50
Cesan – Centro Studi Aziendali 'Giuseppe Cenzato' (Business Studies Centre 'Giuseppe Cenzato') 49, 50, 63
Chamber of Deputies 46, 63, 116, 117
Chamber of Labour 134
chaos; chaotic 5, 6, 7, 10, 18, 22, 44, 50, 52, 55, 71, 83, 85, 111, 122, 130, 131
cholera 18, 70, 80, 82, 92, 119, 121, 165
CIPE – Comitato Interministeriale Programmazione Economica (Interministerial Economic Planning Committee) 46
Cirio 5, 19, 21, 25, 26, 29, 30, 32, 37, 45–49, 106, 108, 114, 115, 125, 130, 132, 138, 149, 171, 176, 193, 194, 195
civic committee 115, 124
Civil Protection 96, 98
closure (of factory) 29, 39, 41, 46, 78
coast; coastal 6, 10–13, 14, 15, 18, 19, 21, 23–26, 29, 30, 35, 53, 54, 55, 66, 72, 89, 105–09, 111, 113, 125, 126, 139, 147, 151, 153, 160, 161, 179, 180–82, 191, 193–94, 195, 196
communist; communism *see also* PCI 44, 48,

51, 61, 67, 69, 70, 82–85, 94, 100, 102, 124–26, 131, 133, 135–37, 139, 141, 144, 145, 178
competition; competitiveness (in market) 39, 40, 46, 47, 50–52, 69, 95, 103, 105, 110, 115, 119, 122, 155–56
congestion; congested 30, 33, 47, 49, 59, 61, 63, 71, 72, 75, 78, 106, 177
Corona, Gabriella 8, 36, 40, 43, 44, 52, 62, 65, 67, 69, 82–83, 86, 87, 89, 91–92, 99, 102, 103, 123, 126
Corradini 6, 19, 21, 23, 29, 30, 106–08, 113, 117, 158, 193–95
Cosenza, Luigi 33
councillor 45, 124, 126, 132, 166–69
crime; criminal *see also* illegal activities 99, 125, 131, 134, 148–50, 158, 174, 175–76
crisis (economic; industrial) 19, 25, 39–40, 43–46, 49–50, 52, 63, 69, 77–78, 80, 102, 103, 110, 111, 115, 144–45, 155, 165, 166, 177

D

D'Amato, Carlo 100
Daniele, Gaetano (Nino) 9, 45, 69, 93, 126, 169–78
DC – Democrazia Cristiana 2, 55, 84
decision-making 45, 49, 52, 121, 145
  acephaly 36, 37, 46
degradation, urban 5, 7, 8, 23, 69, 70, 81, 82–84, 87, 93, 104, 110, 117–19, 121, 122, 139, 140, 164, 167, 173, 174, 176, 177, 184
deindustrialisation 7, 8, 22, 38, 39–43, 52, 64, 80, 81, 99, 103, 110, 111, 118, 121–24, 126, 139, 150, 171, 172, 174, 177, 182
Deindustrialisation Studies 8, 40–43
delocalisation 47, 56, 74, 77, 105, 110, 126, 146, 153, 172
De Luca, Giulio 60–62, 89, 90
De Lucia, Vezio 30–31, 80, 90, 95, 102, 168, 186
De Tilla, Maurizio 76, 78–79
development *see also* redevelopment 15, 17, 21, 22–24, 27, 32–35, 38, 48, 52,
54, 55, 58–60, 66, 71, 82, 87, 95, 104, 110, 112, 114, 115, 118, 119, 122, 126, 150, 155, 177, 180, 186, 187
Development Plan
  General *see* GDP
  Town 30, 35, 101, 108
disaster 5, 72, 81, 86, 96, 98, 102, 103, 140, 164
discharge (of effluent) *see also* pollution 66–67, 69, 72, 76, 116, 155, 158, 165, 195
Dispoto, Giovanni 9, 24, 52, 56, 90, 94, 104, 113, 126, 178–97
Duca Carafa di Noja 13
Dudley, Kathryn Marie 41

E

earthquake 5, 81–82, 85–86, 91, 94–96, 99, 104, 121, 126, 128, 142–43, 145, 152, 159, 161–62, 165, 166, 172, 178, 183, 185, 187, 189
East Naples 5–8, 10–11, 13–18, 20, 21, 23–25, 27–34, 36–38, 44–46, 49, 50, 51, 53–56, 58, 61, 63–64, 66–67, 69, 70, 71, 74–80, 82–83, 85, 88, 90–91, 95, 99–101, 103, 104–12, 115, 117–22, 124–26, 155, 169, 173–74, 177–81, 183, 188, 191–92, 194–96
EAV – Ente Autonomo Volturno (Volturno Autonomous Authority) 141, 167–68
ecology; ecological 7, 8, 52, 64, 69, 70, 72, 73, 76, 77, 80, 105, 117, 119, 120, 127, 174
  awareness 66, 80, 102, 119, 121
  history 52, 70
  problems 52, 65, 69, 82, 118, 119, 121, 125
  risks 8, 50, 80, 102, 113, 117, 193
ecosystem 7, 65, 110, 113, 121
economy; economic 7, 8, 11, 14, 15, 16, 20, 24, 28, 31, 33, 36, 37, 39–45, 48, 50, 53, 55, 58, 61–63, 64, 65, 69, 70, 71, 73, 74, 79, 80, 83, 93, 95, 105, 106, 109, 110, 111, 118, 120,

Index

121, 122, 126, 143–45, 172, 177, 194, 195
crisis 42, 43, 52, 63, 80, 103, 165–66
decline; recession 7, 44, 50–52, 81, 82, 99, 110, 118, 119, 121
development; growth 23, 35, 59, 95, 119, 126
resurgence; revival 20–22, 104
emergency 78, 80, 86, 87, 92, 94–95, 99, 102, 115, 120, 121, 163, 164, 185, 188
'blackmail of the' 30, 80
emissions *see also* pollution 61, 65, 67
engineer; engineering 15, 20, 28, 29, 45, 48, 53, 55, 61, 72, 78, 114, 163
Enel – Ente nazionale per l'energia elettrica 107, 108, 109, 149, 160
environment; environmental *see also* sustainability 7, 8, 22, 23, 28, 37, 44, 48, 49, 51, 52, 56, 65, 66, 70, 74, 81, 82, 92, 95, 100, 102, 104, 105, 107, 109, 120, 121, 124, 125, 144, 179, 182, 183, 191, 197
    awareness *see* ecological awareness
    damage; degradation; disorder; dysfunction 7, 32, 41, 49, 50, 51, 52, 98, 110, 118, 121, 122, 139, 140, 161, 174
    history *see* ecological history
    issues 7, 66, 69
    problems *see* ecological problems
    risks *see* ecological risks
environmentalism; environmentalist 60, 65, 74, 76, 77, 100, 102–03, 155, 180
equipment 69, 70, 72, 76, 83, 85, 95, 104, 108, 117, 151, 152, 189
epidemic *see* cholera
Erbani, Francesco 58, 60–62, 92
expansion
    industrial 21, 22, 23, 31, 36, 46, 47, 63, 71–72, 74, 75, 78, 113, 141, 161, 179, 182, 194
    urban 7, 15, 17–20, 22, 24, 30, 31, 50, 52–54, 59, 64, 65, 67, 103, 108, 181, 184, 191
explosion *see also* AGIP 5, 79, 81, 96–98, 100, 101, 104, 121, 126, 145, 160, 161, 162, 163, 167, 178, 183
external investments

F

factory 5, 6, 13, 14, 16–23, 25–26, 29–30, 32, 34, 36, 39, 41–49, 51, 55, 56, 63, 66–70, 76, 79, 103, 105–08, 112, 113, 115–17, 122, 124–26, 128–33, 137–38, 141, 149–54, 156–57, 159, 162, 165, 170, 174–75, 182, 193, 195
farmland; farm *see also* agriculture; horticulture 11, 13, 53
Ferrante, Elena 22
fire Brigade 79, 96, 163
First World War 23
Fondacaro, Antonio 9, 47, 124, 125, 127–50
Frascani, Paolo 39, 43
free zone 21, 24–25, 28
Funel, Carlo 72, 78

G

Galasso, Giuseppe 102
Garden City Movement 92, 103
Garruccio, Roberta 9, 40, 41, 43, 123
Gava, Silvio 74
GDP – General Development Plan; Town Development Plan 21, 30, 35, 54–57, 59–62, 70, 72, 79, 101, 104, 108, 126, 146, 178, 181–82, 184, 191, 194
Giannì, Roberto 89, 186
Gianturco 5, 27, 32, 50, 71, 95, 115, 151, 153, 192
glassworks 19, 47, 48, 114
green belt 63, 105
green space 73, 79, 83, 89, 91, 92, 106, 186
Grippo, Ugo 55, 74

H

Harrison, Bennett 40
health *see* public health; *see also* hygiene
heavy industry 27, 55–56, 104, 106
High Commissioner for the city and the province of Naples 24–25, 27

High Council for Public Works *see also* Ministry of Public Works 18, 60, 62, 73, 75, 146, 179
High, Steven 123
hinterland 35, 45, 48, 69, 99, 105, 130 146, 153, 157, 163
Hirsch, Etienne 32
historical sedimentation 7, 8, 55, 105, 111, 118, 122
horticulture 6, 10, 11, 106, 190
hydrocarbon 28, 66, 72, 115, 165
hygiene; hygienist 17–18, 20, 22–24, 66–67, 74, 119

I
Iannello, Antonio 59–62, 74–75, 100, 101, 109, 119
Ignis 36, 130
illegal activities *see also* crime 36, 60, 67, 83, 89, 91, 116, 120, 121, 132–34, 144, 155, 161, 184, 189
Il Mattino 78, 99
Il Roma 76, 79
industrial area *see also* Industrial Zone 5, 16, 20–22, 28–30, 44–45, 48, 55, 57, 70, 74, 106, 109, 111, 119, 138–40, 148, 169, 192, 195
industrialisation *see also* deindustrialisation 7, 8, 16, 19, 20, 22, 31, 33–34, 42, 105, 118, 140, 144, 172
industrial mortality 44, 49
Industrial Zone *see also* industrial area 21, 24, 25, 29, 31, 32, 50, 56, 63, 66, 75
Infrastructure 12, 15–17, 20–22, 27, 29, 34–36, 45, 55–56, 63, 67, 71, 75, 104–05, 173, 180, 193
Institute of Hygiene of the University of Naples 66
IRI – Istituto per la Ricostruzione Industriale (Institute for Industrial Reconstruction) 33, 37, 45, 73
Istat – Istituto Nazionale di Statistica (National Institute of Statistics) 42, 47, 50
Italian economic miracle 31, 43–44
Italia Nostra 60, 65, 74–76

K
Kuwait Petroleum, Q8 101, 107, 109–10, 116, 147, 195

L
labour *see also* worker 36, 39, 42, 44, 69, 70, 133, 134, 144, 174
land consumption, land use 52, 59, 81, 108, 121, 180–81
La Repubblica 101, 104, 109, 132, 142
Large industry 20, 52, 111
Lauro, Achille 30–31, 34–35
Leone, Ugo 109
Lucarella, Cristoforo 11, 19
L'Unità 44–48, 62, 66–67, 69–70, 76, 96, 98, 100, 176

M
Maestri di Strada ONLUS 9
mafia *see also* Camorra 133, 174–75
Manifattura Tabacchi 5, 32, 115
manufacturing 6, 14–15, 18, 20, 35, 39–41, 43–44, 50, 56, 61–63, 67–69, 103, 170
Martuscelli, Michele 60, 72
master plan *see also* GDP 116, 178–80, 195
MCM – Manifatture Cotoniere Meridionali 23–24, 32, 61
Mecfond 61, 115, 153, 195
Mededil SpA 59–61
Meridiana, Rivista di Storia e Scienze Sociali 43
metalworking 16, 29, 61, 67–68, 74, 113
militancy 67, 137–38, 143, 166, 169
Ministry of Industry 71, 73–75
Ministry of State Participations 37
Ministry of the Environment 65, 102, 112–13, 116
Ministry of Public Works *see also* High Council for Public Works 71, 109
Mobil; MobilOil; MobilOil Italiana 27, 29, 32, 36, 44, 70–80, 96, 100–01, 109, 130
Moliterno, Giovanni 9, 69, 125, 150–69
Morreale, Vincenzo 9, 19, 29, 36–37, 75, 124, 127–31, 136–68
Municipality of Naples 18, 25, 30, 31, 48,

Index

50, 53–54, 56, 59, 63, 83, 85, 87, 93, 103–08, 113, 126, 159, 164, 168, 169, 187, 194, 195
municipal council 18, 59, 60, 145, 169
Muto, Giovanni 10, 11

N
neighbourhood 5, 6, 25, 41, 54, 61, 67, 70, 86, 91, 94, 113, 115, 120, 135, 137, 139, 141–43, 145, 148, 149, 165–67, 169, 174, 176, 187
Neri Serneri, Simone 23
Noja, Duke of 13, 19, 140
Nuova Villa 88–89, 156

O
oil *see also* petrochemical; petroleum
    activities 70–74, 77, 79, 81, 95, 100, 101, 110, 191
    area 5, 54, 56, 74, 79, 81, 100, 105–06, 109–10, 116, 120, 141, 146–47, 161, 195
    crisis 39, 44, 77
    depot 36, 96, 98, 99, 105, 107–09, 147, 160–61, 177, 181–83, 191, 195
    industry 27, 33, 71, 73, 182, 191
    pipeline 55, 70–73, 105, 116, 160, 163, 180, 182, 191, 193, 195
    refinery 27, 70–75, 77–79, 95, 96, 100–01, 105–07, 116, 130, 145–47, 163, 182–83, 195
outskirts *see also* suburb 15, 83, 91, 95, 181–82, 186
overcrowding 18, 28, 50, 51, 67

P
Pacichelli, Piazza (San Giovanni a Teduccio) 86, 127, 136, 143, 150
Palace of Justice 62
Parisi, Roberto 9, 14–18, 20–21, 24–25, 27–28, 30, 32–36, 54, 99, 111, 145, 191
Parliamentary Commission of Inquiry 186
parule 7, 10, 160, 162
Pazzigno 13, 19, 51, 54, 88–89, 128, 161–63, 165, 167, 180, 190

PCI – Partito Comunista Italiano *see also* communist 67, 82, 130–31, 135–36, 141, 145, 149, 159, 169–70
periphery; peripheral 52, 54, 55, 69, 70, 82–84, 90, 95, 172–73, 180, 183–84, 187–88, 191
petrochemical *see also* oil 27, 32, 36, 70, 71, 79, 145, 182
petroleum 27, 36, 75, 101, 105, 106, 109, 110, 116, 164
Piccinato, Luigi 28, 191
Pietrarsa 6, 16, 24, 25, 113, 140, 194
Poggioreale 5, 14, 17, 18, 24, 28, 31, 50, 53, 59, 59, 61, 87, 163, 164, 167, 180, 182, 192
Pollena 85, 98, 158, 164
pollution *see also* emissions 18, 28, 45, 55, 56, 60–63, 65–70, 72, 76–78, 104, 106, 109, 112, 117, 121, 125, 126, 143, 151, 156, 158, 170, 171, 181-83, 188, 193
pons paludis 10, 13, 16, 18, 106
Ponticelli 5, 6, 13, 24, 25, 31, 36, 44, 50, 53, 54, 64, 71, 78, 89–91, 95, 137, 147, 152, 155, 156, 169, 170, 180, 183, 185, 187, 190, 192
port 11, 18–19, 56, 58, 70, 72, 75, 106–08, 113, 116, 141, 146, 163–65, 177–80, 183, 191, 193–97
Portici 6, 11, 28, 140, 174
post-war 25, 30, 32, 33, 65, 80, 87, 159, 170, 179
power plant 6, 21, 25, 29, 34, 70, 107, 109, 114, 132, 141, 146, 160, 194
PRI – Partito Repubblicano Italiano 60
printing 36, 37, 127–30
production; productivity 6, 7, 1, 11, 14–23, 25, 27, 29, 30, 32, 34, 35, 36, 39–41, 43–50, 52, 55, 56, 61, 63–66, 69–7, 73, 75, 81, 82, 92, 95, 99, 101, 103–07, 109–12, 114, 118, 132, 144, 146, 147, 170–72, 176–77, 180, 187, 195
progress 22, 119
PSER – Piano Straordinario di Edilizia Residenziale 88–93, 95, 103, 183, 186–89

public administration *see also* Municipality of Naples; municipal council 56, 108, 177, 187, 189
public health 17–18, 20, 23, 67
public housing 5, 6, 22, 52, 106, 167
public works *see also* High Council of Public Works; Ministry of PublicWorks 24, 34

Q
Q8 *see* Kuwait Petroleum

R
railway 5, 6, 15–17, 19, 21, 28, 51, 55, 56, 78, 86, 98, 104, 133, 138, 140, 180, 181, 191–92, 195, 196
reconstruction 11, 28–31, 87, 91–92, 95, 121, 126, 142–43, 159, 172, 174, 183, 187–89, 194, 197
redevelopment 6, 62, 82–84, 88–89, 92, 103, 105–10, 112–18, 121, 126–27, 132, 142, 147, 161, 181, 183, 187, 189, 190, 194, 195
refinery *see* oil
region; regional administration 31, 33–35, 39, 40, 48, 53, 56, 70–75, 101, 108, 110, 114, 126, 169, 179, 182, 185, 188
Regional Commission for Industrial Reconstruction 29
Regional Committee for Atmospheric Pollution 76
Regional Superintendency for the Public Works 71–72
relocation
    of industry 18, 23, 28, 39, 40, 43–45, 48–50, 55-56, 61, 70, 72–77, 79, 95, 100, 104–08, 120, 138, 144, 155, 157, 165, 194
    of people 84–86, 98, 99, 178
residence; residential 5, 6, 7, 11, 13, 17, 18, 21–25, 27–32, 35, 53–56, 63, 71, 78, 83, 85, 88, 91, 92, 94, 101, 103, 105, 109, 113, 115, 118, 162, 167, 189–90, 193
risk 8, 50, 52, 62, 67, 73, 79–81, 98–102, 108–09, 112–13, 116–17, 120–21, 146, 150, 162, 163, 164, 183, 184, 185, 193, 196

S
Sagraf 36–37, 75, 129, 130, 145
San Carlo Theatre 6, 114
San Giorgio a Cremano 54, 140, 174
San Giovanni a Teduccio 5, 6, 8, 9, 13, 14, 19, 21, 23–27, 29–31, 36, 37, 45–48, 50–51, 54–55, 66, 68, 69, 71, 79, 83–89, 92–96, 113–14, 116, 124–32, 135–37, 140–41, 145, 149–51, 156, 158, 159, 164–71, 174, 180, 189–90, 192–96
sanitation *see also* hygiene 67, 83
Sant'Arpino 163, 166–67, 173, 178
saturation, urban 28, 32, 47, 48, 51, 54, 59, 76, 105, 177
Sebeto 10, 11, 14, 105, 110, 180, 82
secondary industry 7, 31, 41, 50, 56, 103, 110–11
Second World War 28, 39, 148
Segreto, Luciano 42
Sereni, Emilio 11
Simonetti, Lucia 10, 13–14, 16–17, 20–22, 25, 28–29, 31–32, 34–36, 49–50, 96, 111–13, 115
SIN – Sito di Interesse Nazionale 111, 183
SME – Società Meridionale Elettricità (Southern Electricity Society) 25, 28, 37, 45, 47–48
Snia Viscosa 25, 27, 29, 32, 44–46, 49, 76, 106, 115, 171
SoconyMobil *see also* Mobil 27, 32
special law 20, 22, 32, 34, 35, 105, 108
stagnation 40, 41, 50, 63, 103, 111, 120
Strangleman, Tim 123
strike 47, 125, 134
suburb *see also* outskirts 6–8, 20, 22, 24, 28, 54, 56, 63, 79, 82–85, 87, 92, 105, 106, 111, 142, 179, 182–84, 188, 191, 193
Suburban Plan 82–83, 85, 87–89, 103, 126, 161, 173, 183–85, 188
Superior Council of Public Works *see* High Council for Public Works
sustainability *see also* unsustainability 8, 52,

Index

56, 64, 101, 103, 107, 110, 112, 114, 121, 189
Svimez – Associazione per lo Sviluppo dell'Industria nel Mezzogiorno 32–35
synthetic fibres *see also* Snia Viscosa 25, 44, 45
swamp 7, 10, 14, 51, 54, 63, 111, 122, 139, 140, 160

T

tank farm 70, 122
tannery; tanning 6, 17, 21, 67–69, 114, 125–26, 151–58, 170
Taverna del Ferro 89, 91–94, 114, 149, 187, 189, 190
tertiary industry 43, 45, 52–53, 56, 58–59, 64, 103, 105–06, 110, 176–77
thermoelectric plant *see* power plant
Town Development Plan *see* GDP
Trigilia, Carlo 35

U

unemployment 32, 39, 40, 42, 44, 45, 50, 111, 150, 176, 188
unsustainability *see also* sustainability 7, 64, 65, 118, 119, 122
UrbaNa – Naples Archives of Urban Planning 9, 57, 64, 68, 87–88, 90, 107
urban disorder 23, 27, 32, 35, 51–52, 71, 83, 113, 118–19, 122, 180, 182, 184, 193
urban environment 52, 82, 92, 119, 122
urbanisation 6–8, 16, 17, 23, 65, 81, 88, 105, 118, 180, 181, 188, 193
urban plan; urban planner; urban planning *see also* GDP 27, 58–60, 120, 127, 177, 193

V

Valenzi, Maurizio 69, 102, 136, 139, 159, 167, 169, 179, 183
Van der Linden, Marcel 42
Vergallo, Luigi 39, 41–43
Vesuvian Villas 6, 13, 83
Vesuvius 5, 10, 15, 58, 180–83
Vigliena 5, 21, 24–25, 27, 29, 34, 107, 109, 113, 114, 132, 138, 141, 153, 158, 194, 196
volcano 96, 102, 182
Volturno 75
    Autonomous Authority 21
    river 74

W

worker; workforce *see also* labour 16, 18–21, 23, 24, 27, 28, 32, 36, 39, 41, 44, 45–47, 48, 50, 61, 63, 67–70, 75–77, 79, 96, 98, 100, 110, 111, 124, 125, 129, 130–31, 136–39, 141, 145, 149, 150, 152–53, 157, 163, 165, 174–76, 188
World Wildlife Fund

Z

Zazzara, Gilda 13
Zona Industriale *see* Industrial Zone
Zoological Station of Naples 66, 72–73

www.ingramcontent.com/pod-product-compliance
Lightning Source LLC
Chambersburg PA
CBHW020410230426
43664CB00009B/1247